Wilson, Major L.

E
338
.W684

Space, time, and
freedom

DATE DUE

JUN 1 6 2009			

SPACE, TIME, AND FREEDOM

RECENT TITLES IN CONTRIBUTIONS IN AMERICAN HISTORY

Series Editor: Jon L. Wakelyn

SPACE
TIME
and
FREEDOM

The Quest for Nationality
and the Irrepressible Conflict
1815 - 1861

Major L. Wilson

Contributions in American History, Number 35

GREENWOOD PRESS
Westport, Connecticut • London, England

Library of Congress Cataloging in Publication Data

Wilson, Major L
  Space, time, and freedom.

  (Contributions in American history, no. 35)
  Includes bibliographical references.
  1. United States—Politics and government—1815-
1861. 2. Nationalism—United States. I.Title.
E338.W684   320.9'73'05   74-287
ISBN 0-8371-7373-6

Library of Congress Catalog Card Number: 74-287
ISBN: 0-8371-7373-6

First published in 1974

Greenwood Press, a division of Williamhouse-Regency Inc.
51 Riverside Avenue, Westport, Connecticut 06880

Manufactured in the United States of America

Contents

Preface

As a venture in intellectual history, the present study will hopefully find its place among a growing number of works dealing with the subject of American nationalism. It reflects the effort to analyze in a systematic fashion the rhetoric of political debate in the national arena and, with special focus upon the moments of greatest crisis and controversy, to formulate more clearly and fully what held Americans together in the years after 1815 and what drove them at last to civil conflict by 1861. For this purpose the work of Hans Kohn, *American Nationalism: An Interpretative Essay* (New York: Macmillan, 1957), provided a good starting point. The essence of American nationalism, according to Kohn, lay in an idea—the idea of freedom. As a complex rather than a simple idea, it blended the English heritage of liberty with the tendency in French Enlightenment thought to conceive of freedom as a natural or universal right. The birthright of Englishmen thus fused with the birthright of all mankind to produce a peculiarly American concept of freedom. The nation of freemen was at once the product of history and of nature, that is, a nation shaped by past experience yet also defined by its conformity to an idea, which was presumed to be universally valid and therefore timeless. The historical element spared Americans the dangers of radical utopianism to be seen in the French Revolution; while the universal element tended to generate the belief that the nation had already achieved essential perfection.

In two closely related ways, however, Kohn's work invites further analysis. First of all, he did not deal with the pattern of tensions within the complex idea of freedom or suggest which of its elements was the more vital one during the National Period. A major task of the present study will be to trace the advance of the universal or natural element. Stated in other terms, the National Period was characterized by the growth of "larger liberty" as Americans, confronting an uncertain future on a continent of vast and unsettled spaces, had to grope for an order to the common life relatively free from the institutional guidelines of the past. Secondly, there is a need to examine the dialectical nature of the process. At any point along the way the substantive content of the national idea of freedom can be fully understood only by a close look at what it then opposed. Through its successive manifestations in Jacksonian Democracy and Free-Soil Republicanism, the advance of larger liberty came at last to define, by its opposition to expansion-minded slaveholders, an irrepressible conflict within the nation.

Great insight into these matters came from a number of studies on the literature, religion, and other aspects of culture in the nineteenth century. Among the more perceptive and helpful are the works of Henry Nash Smith, Perry Miller, Sidney E. Mead, Louis Hartz, Daniel J. Boorstin, Marvin Meyers, John William Ward, and David W. Noble. All draw attention in one way or another to the quality of timelessness in the outlook of many Americans, an outlook gaining substance from the unsettled spaces of the country and indicating by its growth the progressive triumph of larger liberty. In a more immediate way the effort of the present study to trace the dialectic of this development was influenced greatly by the approach suggested in R. W. B. Lewis, *The American Adam: Innocence, Tragedy, and Tradition in the Nineteenth Century* (Chicago: University of Chicago

Press, 1955). "Intellectual history, properly conducted, exposes not only the dominant ideas of a period, or of a nation," he argued, "but more important, the dominant clashes over ideas." (2). The quest for identity in a vital and maturing culture, he supposed, could only be pursued through the means of an unfolding dialogue. Thus the contending ideas of freedom can be seen as a central manifestation, in the political sphere, of this quest for nationality. To be American meant to be free, and in the contours of the national debate Americans searched for the meaning of their freedom.

The records left by leading spokesmen in the national dialogue are necessarily the basic sources for this study. I have relied primarily on the congressional debates and presidential messages, with printed correspondence and memoirs, newspapers, and a limited amount of manuscript material as a valuable supplement. In the use of these materials I have dismissed as overdrawn the sharp distinction some pragmatic-minded historians make between "rhetoric" and "reality." Modes of political argument and persuasion are themselves a part of reality and something more than handy tools for rationalizing the particular interests or enterprises of the moment. They have a life of their own, in a sense, and can best be seen as "world views" or "ideologies," that is, as shareable ways for people in society to perceive and act upon the realities of the common life. A careful analysis of these perceptions, it is therefore believed, can throw added light upon the actual course of events.

The present study was initially suggested by Professor Clifford S. Griffin at the University of Kansas, and a good deal of credit for whatever is good in the work is due to him. Welcome support along the way came from sympathetic editors who made their journals accessible for articles, thus enabling me to explore one or another aspect of the larger subject at a critical point. Special acknowledgment should be made for permission to incorporate all or parts of articles which first appeared in the *Tennessee Historical Quarterly, Journal of Southern History, American Quarterly, and Civil War History*. Some financial assistance from Memphis State University and the American Philosophical Society speeded up the process of research and writing. Finally, I owe the greatest debt to my wife, Donna, for she has made all of the work possible.

SPACE, TIME, AND FREEDOM

1
Liberty and Union

"Liberty *and* Union, now and forever, one and insepara-ble!" With this formula, fashioned in his reply to Senator Robert Y. Hayne in 1830, Daniel Webster met the challenge of the South Carolina nullifiers, and in prospect the seces-sionists as well, that liberty and the Union were separable and liberty more dear. President Andrew Jackson readily agreed, and in the decades to follow, Stephen A. Douglas, Abraham Lincoln, and William Henry Seward, among other leaders, gave equally strong support to this position. All rejected the notion that the Union was only a means for the ends of freemen, an entity easily dissolvable. In one sense, they tended to regard the Union as an absolute, an end in itself, for the growth of economic, social, and politi-cal relations since the Revolution had forged seemingly irreversible bonds of national unity.[1] In another sense, however, they took the Union to be an absolute precisely because it was an invaluable means, a framework of order within which freemen could pursue happiness in their sev-eral ways. Controversy during the National Period, as a consequence, focused less upon the issue of liberty versus the Union than upon the kind of freedom that gave mean-ing to the Union. It involved at last a profound debate over the true nature of the national idea of freedom—and with it, more fatefully, the proper relation of slavery to a Union of freemen.[2]

The course of the political debate in the national arena during the years from 1815 to the outbreak of the Civil War proceeded through three stages. Up to the nullification crisis a corporate concept of freedom shaped the debate. Conscious of their common bond with both ancestors and posterity, adherents of the corporate outlook took time far more seriously than did their opponents and successors. They welcomed the institutions and elements of order coming from the past. Champions of the old religious establishments accordingly sought with some success to harness the energies of religious revivalism to their purposes, while others embraced the enterprise of reform as a mode of social control. The growing influence of the legal profession and the survival of the common law in the face of initially strong popular hostility likewise assured other forms of discipline from the past.[3] Looking to the future, the advocates of corporate freedom would use the instrument of government in a positive way to achieve through time the goods of increasing order and improvement. Confronted with the claims of larger liberty, they espoused what was later called a "doctrine of institutions," for they sought to objectify and institutionalize in some degree the subjective sense of national unity which came out of the War of 1812. The varied policies of the American System—a national bank, internal improvements, the protective tariff, and a land policy for moderating the rate of westward settlement—would hopefully forge new bonds of mutual dependence and reciprocal advantage. The elements of order to be achieved by the resulting diversity of economic pursuits, a relatively stable and compacted population, and a more homogeneous "national character" also pointed to progressive improvement. Because the pursuit of happiness was assumed to be cumulative and ongoing in nature, there was the long-run goal of enriching the conditions of the common life as the nation moved through time up the scale of civilization.[4]

In other terms this corporate outlook evinced what Guido de Ruggiero called the positive aspect or phase of the liberal mind. Liberation from the evil prescriptions of the past thus presented a golden opportunity for social man to add a cubit to his stature. Qualitative progress would mark the movement of the nation through time and, as Ruggiero would phrase it in more formal terms, there would be more freedom at the end than at the beginning of the historical process.[5] The predilection of the advocates of the American System for a loose interpretation of the Constitution clearly manifested this point of view. They demanded the right to bend the literal wording of the national charter to the reason, the needs, and the peculiar opportunities of each successive generation. They also accepted the accumulating corpus of legislative precedents and judicial decisions as useful guidelines for directing the common course. In this context the Union under the Constitution was reckoned to be the kind of entity that grew through time.

An ambivalent attitude with regard to slavery reflected the dual emphasis of order and improvement to be found in the corporate concept of freedom. With a greater concern for the peculiar pedigree of American liberty, Daniel Webster tolerated slavery as one of the historical elements within the developing order of the Union. By contrast, John Quincy Adams, because of his interest in qualitative improvement, grew more certain by the time of the nullification controversy that slavery constituted a very real and permanent obstacle to his hopes for national progress. As the alternative to secession and a separate union composed exclusively of free states, Adams and others of like mind were to be tempted in the following decades to join the crusade against slavery. They would argue that such a crusade was necessary as the precondition for resuming the task of enriching the quality of national life.

Under the banner of federative freedom the opponents of the American System of policies gained their victory during the nullification controversy and provided the basic structure to the national debate until the end of the 1840s. Central in this outlook was the demand for freedom from the efforts of the federal government to direct or control in any substantial way the nation's course through time. A larger liberty for individuals, the sovereignty of each generation, essential autonomy for local communities and states—however contradictory these goods would prove to be—all bore common witness by 1830 against the institutional imperatives of the corporate outlook and its premise of directed, qualitative change through time.[6] In other aspects, all exhibited one form of what Ruggiero called the negative moment or phase of the liberal mind. By supposing freedom established in its entirety at the beginning, the advocates of federative freedom were therefore led to believe that the passage of time tended only to derogate from, because it could never improve upon the quality of freedom. Their penchant for strict interpretation expressed this position well; for if the Constitution had defined at the outset a perfect order of freedom, then loose construction and the consolidation of the nation that came in its train were bound to subvert the true nature of the Union of freemen.

By the formula of nullification and secession, John C. Calhoun gave a truly radical reading to federative freedom, and President Jackson therefore turned to Webster and others for aid in securing the integrity of the Union. But beyond the simple use of force against the nullifiers, which Webster was prepared to do, Jackson looked to another and more peaceful way to save the Union. Since the nation was ultimately held together by a belief in the idea of freedom from essential control, the only certain way to preserve the nation in time of crisis was to restore its original principle. He rejected the claim of Calhoun that liberty and the Union were separable goods, because he held the Union to be a grand order of freedom for individuals and states. To him the Union was less a coercive institutional presence than the sustaining will for a common and glorious destiny that rose up from the hearts of men grateful for their freedom. By a vigorous use of the executive veto Jackson would dismantle the policies of the American System that sought to commit the nation in time. In the rhetoric of the "Jacksonian Persuasion," as one student has perceptively observed, Jackson set out to remove the evils that had grown up through time and to restore the nation to the pure and simple design of the Early Republic.[7]

A further analysis, drawn from a wealth of recent studies on various aspects of American culture, will serve to illuminate more fully this quality of timelessness in the national idea of the Jacksonians. Central in the thought of most Americans by the nineteenth century, according to these studies, has been the belief that the nation constituted an essentially perfect order of freedom. This evinced what Daniel J. Boorstin has termed the "preformation theory," that is, the belief of successive generations that the nation began its existence with a design perfect and entire. Wesley Frank Craven has likewise noted "the common inclination of the American people to look back to the origins of their country for an explanation of its essential character." Since 1830, David W. Noble similarly argues, leading historians in America assumed the nation of freemen to be in timeless harmony with nature and therefore immune from the vicissitudes of history.[8]

Progress for the nation, therefore, was to come automatically, as freemen pursued happiness in their several and

separate ways. The good that came through time reflected
the natural fruits of fidelity to the perfect order of freedom,
and the future would bring more of the same. In other
terms the future was to be a continuation of the present,
world without end, and to be marked by a quantitative
spread of good rather than any qualitative change in the
order of freedom itself. As has been remarked, Americans
not only believed they were progressing: they held even
more profoundly with the view that America *was* progress.
Whatever evils might creep in through time were to be
reckoned a divergence from the true order of things. Progress in this context thus tended to take on the more immediate and paradoxical meaning of a return to the beginning, for it involved the task of eliminating the temporal
elements of degeneration and of restoring the primitive
principles of the nation. In the same way that Jeffersonians
regarded the "revolution of 1800" as a return to the "spirit
of '76," Jackson also looked to a regeneration of the national idea.[9]

On its negative side, this appeal to primitive principle
provided Americans with a means of dealing with what
Mircea Eliade called the "terror of history." For a people cut
off from much of a usable past and caught up in the swirl of
rapid change, the experience of the "evils of time" must
have often become acute. Hence such a periodic movement
as that of Jacksonian Democracy to make an "eternal return" to the original design of the fathers took on an immense ritualistic no less than political significance, for it was
a way to regain and strengthen the sense of a common
meaning or identity in the national life. In his study of the
matter Arthur P. Dudden also discovered in the ideological
conservatism of most Americans a "covert" sense of nostalgia to match their optimistic and "overtly" expressed belief
in the future. Others have professed to see in the pattern
the inadequacies of the developing democratic order and

evidence of the "burden of freedom." In essentially Burk-
ean terms, Rowland Berthoff has characterized the period
after 1815 as one of increasing "social disorder," an era in
which individualism and uncontrolled economic enterprise
dissolved older elements of a corporate, hierarchical, and
functional social order. Fred Somkin has similarly noted
the "unquiet eagle" of American freedom, made restive as
material "desire" overbalanced the "memory" of communal
and traditional values. A profound sense of "anxiety and
despair" accompanied the progressive triumph of larger
liberty, according to Page Smith, and constituted a revealing measure of the high price Americans were beginning to
pay for their freedom. The declining sense of a corporate
and institutional dimension to the common life therefore
tended to generate an absolutist spirit or temper which, in
the thought of Stanley M. Elkins, would ill-prepare the
nation to deal peacefully with the fateful issue of slavery.[10]

But if freedom was a burden to be borne, it was also, in
the ambiguous nature of things, a good to be embraced.
And here on its more positive side the political faith of
Jacksonian Democracy surely reflected that pattern of affirmation by negation to be found in the rhythms of Protestant revivalism. According to H. Richard Niebuhr, witness
against the institutions, liturgies, and creedal formulations
which arise through time has usually been secondary in
recurring Protestant movements to the fact of revival itself.
The effort to purge false and mediocre definitions of the
true faith necessarily accompanied a quickening urge to
regain that direct communion the primitive Church held
with God. The issue had seldom been, as critics claimed,
one between order on one side and the sinful pride of
individualism on the other. Dynamic Protestantism manifested instead a recurring need to appeal from the corporate and historical order of existing authority to the true
order of spiritual freedom. With special opportunities in a

country so spacious, as Sidney Mead has shown, Americans believed they could remove the evils of time and restore the primitive faith to its "true and ancient foundations." Such were the pitfalls of time, however, that Protestant revivalists seldom regarded the spread of the faith as a regular or unbroken linear advance. Ernest Lee Tuveson has described this progress rather as a spiral pattern, marked by a succession of triumphs over enemies who would reduce the true faith to a temporal and institutional idol.[11]

In spite of conservative critics, however, this ahistorical and anti-institutional tendency in American Protestantism did not point to disorder and chaos. In a paradoxical way the anti-establishment spirit of revivalism itself became the "established" means for sustaining unity and order. Clearly the revivalists rejected the older concept of the Church as a historical carrier of truth, or as an institution which possessed coercive power over the successive generations to be nurtured and saved. For them the true Church was a fellowship of the faithful, a timeless communion to be realized, indeed recreated, in each successive age. As a visible presence the Church rose up from below, and its unchanging essence remained throughout the bond of faith shared by regenerated individuals. "Thus," William G. McLoughlin concluded, "revivalism replaced the establishment as the American method of maintaining moral order without (it was thought) abandoning moral freedom." The pluralism of sects and the fragmented appearance of religious organization bespoke vitality and not disorder, giving form to the common life of a people moving rapidly across unsettled spaces.[12]

And it was a form that contributed most to the shape of the political order in democratic America of the nineteenth century. As he saw the matter in perspective, Perry Miller found no influence more seminal than the pervasive categories of the revival experience. While Puritan New

England once rekindled its sense of identity by a communal "owning of the covenant," Americans in the National Period also hit upon another means more consonant with their social mobility, geographical diffusion, and democratic leveling. In the revival, Miller claimed, the salvation of the individual soul involved both a profound affirmation of community and "a vote for the Federal Union." Revivalists at the time "were not preaching nationalism," he noted, "they were enacting it." Though individual Americans were sinners still, they were "sinners in the hands of a benevolent God," and the regeneration of their virtue was the voucher for a happy and unchanging order to the common life.[13] The Union, in this view, was to be taken less as an institutional presence than as a communion of men faithful to the timeless national idea of freedom.

The triumph of Jacksonian Democracy can hence be regarded as a species of political revivalism. In the terms of its own rhetoric the Union was to be saved and purified by a regeneration of the essential national idea of freedom. Since specific content for the idea in the political arena came in the dialectic of opposition to those with a more corporate outlook, it was, in addition, a faith that could in a very real and practical way hold all parts of the country together. Martin Van Buren of New York, who did so much to create the Jacksonian party, called it an alliance of "planters and plain republicans." For plain republicans the dismantling of the American System of policies and the war on the national bank served to unfetter the energies of a fiercely expansive enterprise in the North and West. With a facile belief that the good of the whole would automatically arise, freemen were now invited to pursue unchecked their interests in the present. Meanwhile, the disavowal of power at the center to shape the future course of the nation tended to allay the anxieties southern planters felt for the security of their slaves.[14]

As it pertained to the political course of the nation, finally, there was an emphasis in the Jacksonian concept of federative freedom that pointed rather clearly toward a "manifest destiny" of expansion. While opposing a tariff and other policies which would commit the nation in time, Jackson's call for liberal land laws and the removal of the Indians presaged new territorial acquisitions in the 1840s and a bolder foreign policy. Central to the process of westward movement was the spectacle of freemen moving out to unformed space without direction from the center to settle the earth and create society anew. At a later point in time freemen would then constitute themselves into a new state and enter upon a basis of full equality into a federative Union uniquely suited to comprehend what it did not control. While the corporate outlook, held by most Whig opponents, contemplated a national destiny of qualitative improvement, the Jacksonians here entertained the alternative of quantitative progress for freedom across the unsettled spaces. Jackson himself gave classic expression to this concept of the nation's future with the phrase, "extending the area of freedom."[15]

To a growing number of Northerners by the end of the 1840s, however, the policy of national expansion seemed far more likely to extend the area of slavery than of freedom. At the very time the Jacksonian protegé, President James K. Polk, was preparing to surrender claims to the Oregon territory north of the 49th parallel, he accepted the annexation of Texas as a slave state, and on terms that would allow even more slave states to be carved out of it later on. The outbreak of the Mexican War on the heels of the annexation of Texas likewise opened the prospect of further acquisitions of territory suited to the purposes of slavery, and the spirit of filibustering began to range more widely over Central America and the Caribbean. It was at this juncture that Representative David Wilmot of Pennsylvania introduced his fateful proviso. As an amendment to a money bill which contemplated the possibility of acquiring new territory from Mexico, it provided that any such territory would be absolutely closed to the spread of slavery. The controversy sparked by the proviso brought rapidly to a close the old debate between those who had wanted the nation to develop in a more disciplined way through time and the Jacksonians who looked to a speedier movement across the unsettled spaces. Beyond the issue of expansion for the nation the new debate now focused upon which element within the nation had a right to expand. As expressed in the proviso and then more fully refined, the Free-Soil claim of a monopoly for non-slaveholding freemen gave basic form to the national debate from the Mexican War to the outbreak of civil strife in 1861.[16]

The Free Soilers firmly believed that what held the nation together was the idea of individual freedom, an idea at once more universal and more exclusive than that of democracy in its first reading under Jackson. The equalitarian passion behind the demand for excluding slavery from the unsettled territories of the nation appealed to the natural birthright of all mankind found in the Declaration of Independence. But in political terms the dialectical presence of an aristocratic slaveholding class informed the Free-Soil idea of freedom with the practicable meaning of equality of opportunity for non-slaveholding, free white men.[17] Application of the idea in the political arena of a nation spreading rapidly across space thus had the effect of denationalizing the slaveholders. With an emphasis on freedom from control shaped by their opposition to the corporate idea of freedom, Jacksonians had fashioned a consensus wide enough to incorporate both the planters of the South and the plain republicans of the North. By contrast the Free-

Soil movement represented a growing consensus among plain republicans and their erstwhile political foes along clearly drawn sectional lines.

One revealing manifestation of this developing sectional consensus is found in the final form and rationale the Free-Soil spokesmen gave to the idea of the federal government as a broker state for freemen. The contrast of the preceding debate over the proper role of the government will make this clear. Those with a corporate outlook had wanted the government to act in a positive way to exercise some degree of history-making power in directing the nation's course. They sought, with such measures as the tariff and a land policy for moderating the speed of westward settlement, to build up the country. By contrast, the Jacksonian ideal of freedom from control was matched by the inclination to spread out across space. Advocates of this position supposed that positive action by the government could only lead to bad consequences and that, if the government did not assume a history-making role, the good of the whole would somehow automatically arise.

But the Free-Soil party at the end of the 1840s and the new Republican party in the following decade confounded the terms of this old debate. By placing a tariff plank on the same platform with the homestead provision for free lands they indicated no serious or consistent concern with the task of building up or spreading out the nation. The government belonged to the people, as Representative Wilmot put it in 1850, for whatever they might want. "They have a right to mould it to their pleasure, to determine its policy, to direct it to the advancement of their happiness and prosperity." Preoccupation with the overriding issue of expanding slavery blurred the earlier distinctions and made freedom a term as broad and inclusive as middle-class America.[18] The chief concern was to root out the aristocratic influence of the slave power in order for the government to become responsive to the present will of freemen. Free Soilers here believed in strict construction as a barrier against the evil purposes of slavery and in loose construction for the present goods of freedom. Government aid, but not direction, to free enterprise, they thought, would promote happiness for individuals and the welfare of society as a whole. The government was to exercise no sustaining, history-making role, either for the good, as some had hoped, or for the bad, as Jacksonians had feared. As a giver of good things in the present, in effect, the broker state of the Free Soilers reflected a peculiar species of negative liberalism that pointed to what Vernon Parrington called the "Great Barbecue."[19]

Far more significant than the effect of the new consensus on economic affairs, however, was the fact that the moral imperatives of the Free-Soil movement served to define the terms of irrepressible conflict. Here was to be seen, in a form much more intense than during the Jacksonian Era, the force of political revivalism and the urgency to make an "eternal return" to the original and perfect design of the fathers. According to the Free-Soil spokesmen, the Founding Fathers had created the nation on the timeless principle of individual freedom. To be sure, they tolerated slavery in the original localities of the Union where it had existed since colonial days, but they simultaneously placed a ban on the spread of slavery into new and unsettled areas. The fathers supposed, moreover, that slavery would soon die out in the old part of the Union when it ceased to grow into the new part. In this fashion the inevitable demise of slavery in the course of time would bring about in fact a Union in perfect harmony with its national idea. The terms of "freedom national" and "slavery local" thus summarized the Free Soilers' perception of slavery's expansion.

In these terms, the actual spread of slavery since the beginning of the nation represented a subversion of its

original design. While Free Soilers often disagreed about
many of the details of the process of subversion, most of
them felt by the 1840s that aggression upon the national
idea had become open, bold, and menacing. The image of a
slave power conspiracy was used to explain the process, and
the warning went out that a small slaveholding class was
using the power of the federal government to extend and
perpetuate slavery. The spectacle was presented of a nation
founded in freedom about to be irretrievably lost to the evil
of slavery. There was hence the need to revive the national
faith in the hearts of freemen and to use it in the political
arena for stopping absolutely the farther spread of evil. In
this way the nation might remove the wearing evils of time
and resume the timeless tenor of its way.[20]

To match the Free-Soil formula of "freedom national,"
John C. Calhoun developed a position by the end of the
1840s which struck most Northerners as one of "slavery
national." In substance he invited his fellows in the South to
move beyond the shelter provided by the federative concept of freedom and to demand from the central government the positive protection of expanding slavery. Central
to his argument, however robed in the old garments of
states' rights, was the assumption that the Constitution, of
its own inherent force, automatically extended the shield of
its protection over slavery in all national territories.
Calhoun's position thus anticipated the Dred Scott decision
in 1857 and the demand southern Democrats made three
years later for Congress to pass a slave code of federal
protection for the territories.[21] Meanwhile, a growing
number of southern spokesmen began to confront the
broker-state individualism of the Free Soilers with an inflexible posture of laissez-faire. It was in these terms of
irrepressible conflict that the nation approached a profound crisis by 1849 over the disposition of the fruits of
manifest destiny plucked from Mexico.

Compromise the following year enabled the nation to pass the crisis in a peaceful way; yet the circumstances of the compromise showed it to be an enforced peace and not a genuine resolution of the conflict. Invoking the good of the corporate order of the Union, Webster and Henry Clay lent their influence to the proposals for sectional reconciliation. A much greater force for compromise, however, came from the Democrats under the leadership of Senator Stephen A. Douglas of Illinois. By the principle of popular sovereignty they also adduced what appeared to be a more solid basis for the compromise. The principle actually reflected an *ad hoc* application of the concept of federative freedom to the issue of slavery's expansion. Rejecting alike the positions of "freedom national" and "slavery national," which had polarized the Jacksonian consensus of planters and plain republicans, Douglas would take the power to decide the issue away from the central government and place it in the hands of the people living in the territory. Under this doctrine, California came into the Union as a free state, while New Mexico and Utah received territorial organization without a Free-Soil ban on slavery. Many moderate Southerners could approve this solution because slavery was at least allowed to enter the new territories during the initial stage of settlement. Much northern support, at the same time, reflected the secret assurance that the superior energy of freedom would outdistance slavery in any open race for the territories. Most of all, as Douglas argued, the principle would take bitter debate out of the halls of Congress, thereby removing the chief internal obstacle to the realization of a further manifest destiny for the nation.[22]

If the principle of popular sovereignty brought peace in 1850, however, its doctrinaire application to the Kansas-Nebraska Bill four years later "let slip the dogs of war." Repeal of the Missouri Compromise ban on slavery north of

36°30', its advocates claimed, cleared the way for organizing the new territories upon the true basis of federative
freedom. But to spokesmen of the new Republican party
that arose out of the furious northern reaction to the measure, repeal appeared, not as a triumphant assertion of
federative freedom, but an opening wedge for consummat-
ing the designs of an aggressive slave power. The Dred
Scott decision thus appeared to be a logical progression
from the Kansas-Nebraska Bill, while the efforts of the
administration of President James Buchanan to make Kansas a slave state under the Lecompton Constitution manifested a bold resolve to commit the nation irreversibly to
the temporal evil of slavery. In the developing dialectic of
controversy, the debate as the Free Soilers thus perceived it
ceased to be one between two kinds of freedom—individual
versus federative—and became instead a life and death
contest between the national idea of freedom on the one
hand and the alien element of an expansionist slave power
on the other.

It was in this context that Lincoln gave classic expression
to the Free-Soil position with his formula of the "house
divided." With the alternative of dissolution ruled out, he
supposed that the Union would become either a monism of
slavery or a monism of freedom. Moreover, he professed to
believe that the nation was rapidly approaching the critical
point of no return. If slavery were allowed the right to
shape the new part of the Union, then the whole would be
reshaped in its image. On the other hand, a monopoly for
freedom in the territories, prescribed, he felt, by the Constitution, would place slavery "in the course of ultimate
extinction." The unsettled spaces that lay before him in
time provided an opportunity to create the new Union after
the archetype of timeless freedom. By inflexible opposition
to the further spread of slavery, Lincoln would purge the
evil accretions of time and restore the Union to the true

faith of the fathers. With a spirit of moral absolutism that anticipated his refusal as President-elect to compromise the issue of slavery's extension, he concluded the Cooper Union speech on February 27, 1860, with the call for the nation to stand firmly on its pristine principle and leave the consequences to God.[23]

Civil War was the consequence; and however the orderings of Providence may ultimately account for the conflict, the immediate cause surely lay in the failure of compromise. Little was to be expected from the idea of popular sovereignty, of course, for as a compromise formula in 1850 it had been effectively discredited by Free-Soil rhetoric in the aftermath of the Kansas-Nebraska Bill. But Senator Douglas and other Jacksonians still identified with the concept of federative freedom did lend their support to the one serious compromise effort set forth by Senator John J. Crittenden of Kentucky. The central feature in his proposal would revive and extend the line of 36°30' to the Pacific and, by casting it in the form of a constitutional amendment, he hoped permanently to settle the issue of slavery expansion in all territories then existing or to be acquired. Quite clearly the plan reposed on the old corporate idea of freedom, for it supposed that power lay indifferently in the federal government to extend or to restrict the spread of slavery. In this view the exercise of government power would be a matter of political expediency and not of moral principle. In actual practice a balance of slave and free states had been maintained as the nation grew across space, and Crittenden now reckoned this relative balance a matter of the highest political expediency in securing the historic order of the Union.[24]

By his rejection of the Crittenden proposal, however, President-elect Lincoln dashed whatever remaining hopes there were that Congress might effect a compromise settlement. In ideological terms the plan was totally inadmissi-

ble to him. The spread of slavery into territory south of any
line, however narrowly drawn, would directly contravene
the imperatives of "freedom national" that individual freedom alone should give form to the new and unsettled part
of the Union—and ultimately to the Union as a whole. Six
other states of the Lower South thereupon followed South
Carolina out of the Union, setting the stage for the Sumter
crisis and the outbreak of military hostilities.

Corporate, federative, and individual freedom—in turn
each of these formulations of the national idea gave shape
to the course of the political debate from 1815 to the outbreak of the Civil War. The effort after the War of 1812 to
consolidate national life by a measure of direction from the
center gave way to the idea that the true destiny of the
nation would be realized if individuals and local communities remained essentially free from control. Finally,
the emphasis on rapid expansion involved in this vision of
the nation's destiny generated the fateful conflict between
freedom and slavery over which element should be allowed
to expand across the unsettled spaces of the nation.

In a rather revealing way, the statecraft of William Henry
Seward during the final crisis constitutes a summary of the
entire process. Though only circumstantial, the evidence
strongly suggests that he was inclined to support the Crittenden compromise.[25] His Whiggish lineage and the fundamental corporate elements in his vision of the nation's
destiny lend further substance to this view. When the failure of compromise brought the nation to the eve of the
Sumter crisis, Seward then advised President Lincoln to
avert the crisis and reunite the sundered nation with a bold
foreign stroke. War with France and Spain seemed clearly
indicated by his advice. Success in such a venture would
have established the nation's hegemony in the Western
Hemisphere, a goal of "manifest destiny" which Seward
had sought to realize since the 1840s in a more peaceful and

certain way through careful direction and encouragement to economic development. He would, in other terms, graft the American System of policies onto the Jacksonian impulse for expansion. Only after the fall of Sumter did he accept the irrepressible conflict as defined in the Free-Soil outlook of Lincoln. To be sure, Seward had actually fashioned the phrase, "irrepressible conflict," but his reading of the conflict between freedom and slavery was far more economic than moral in nature. He had, in effect, assimilated the struggle between freedom and slavery into his corporate vision of empire, and by the end of the 1850s he seemed ready to award the palm of victory to the superior energies of freemen. In a foreshortened fashion, the corporate, federative, and individual elements fused in the outlook of Seward thus served to recapitulate the American quest for meaning in the National Period. The failure of his statesmanship in the crisis at the end of the period constitutes, by the pattern it evinces, a good way to chart the triumph of larger liberty through the course of the entire period.

2

The Missouri
Controversy

If the statesmanship of William Henry Seward sum-
marizes the course of the political debate during the National Period, the controversy over Missouri is a preview of
it. The controversy erupted in 1819 when James Tallmadge, Jr., of New York offered an amendment to the
House bill for bringing Missouri into the Union as a slave
state. He proposed that the federal government place an
absolute ban upon the further entry of slaves into Missouri
and into the remaining territory of the Louisiana Purchase
out of which the new state was formed. Additionally,
Tallmadge's amendment would set free, at the age of
twenty-five, all children thereafter born of slaves. Having
begun its existence in the Union with slavery, Missouri
would thus be gradually transformed into a free state.[1]

The debate precipitated by the Tallmadge amendment
soon grew bitter, as the protagonists professed to see far
more at stake than the status of Missouri alone. The admission of Missouri would immediately affect the existing balance of political power in the Union between slave and free
states. More importantly, the principle of its admission
would cast the fate of numerous other states ultimately to be
carved from the vast territory west of the Mississippi River.
"Freedom and slavery are the parties which stand this day

before the senate," Rufus King of New York solemnly declared.[2] Victory for the one, he supposed, necessarily brought permanent dominion over the other. Sectional self-consciousness rose to a new level, and threats of disunion and war were uttered, according to Representative John Tyler of Virginia, "with perfect nonchalance and indifference." "Like a fire-bell in the night," the controversy awakened the aging Thomas Jefferson; and John Quincy Adams deemed it "a title-page to a great tragic volume."[3] The controversy was at last a debate about the very nature and destiny of the Union of freemen.

Ideologically, the debate was defined by the concepts of corporate and federative freedom. In these terms it actually represented. a continuation of the old dialogue between Federalists and Republicans. While admitting that a loose construction of the Constitution gave the nation equal power either to extend or to stop the spread of slavery, restrictionists in the Federalist tradition deemed a ban highly expedient for promoting the general welfare. Spokesmen for the slaveholding section countered with equally familiar canons drawn from Jeffersonian thought of strict construction and states' rights. Since no power to touch the existence of slavery had been delegated to the federal government, efforts to stop its extension were likened to the consolidating tendencies of such measures as a national bank, the protective tariff, and internal improvements. All were calculated, in the view of the old Republican orthodoxy, to subvert the federative nature of the Union as the fathers had fashioned it.

But a second mode of Free-Soil thought began to emerge during the Missouri controversy which transcended the terms of the old debate between Federalists and Republicans. Giving voice to this position were many northern Republicans in the Jeffersonian tradition. They insisted that the expansion of slavery was not a matter of political expediency, as the Federalists assumed, but ultimately one of moral obligation. The natural right of individual freedom, clearly expressed in the Declaration of Independence and incorporated into the Constitution, simply allowed no legitimate power at all to extend slavery into a new area. Fidelity to this national idea of freedom required a strict construction of the Constitution; and, in direct contrast to the view of southern Jeffersonians, strict construction here required an absolute ban on slavery. The issue at stake was not one between two kinds of freedom, corporate and federative, but between freedom and slavery. Not until the 1840s would this mode of Free-Soil thought become the dominant one, but its presence in the Missouri controversy served to complicate the debates and to influence the terms of the final compromise settlement.[4]

A full analysis of the debates will make this clear. First of all, the Federalists had a keen sense of the Union in temporal and historical terms, of its relation to the past and the future, to the old states and the new. By the power that flowed out of the "reservoir" of the pre-existing states, as Senator Harrison Gray Otis of Massachusetts put it, the Union came into existence at a particular point in space and time. Though only the creature of the "old thirteen" at the time, however, the Union immediately assumed the status of a sovereign being with a will and purposes of its own. This meant, in turn, that the Union possessed the power to create new states that came after it in time. The Union was a "fountain," to quote Otis again, from whence issued the animating force to call new areas into being.[5] In the very nature of things, as a consequence, the Union would undergo change through time as it moved out to fill the void of the unsettled spaces.

Federalists wanted to impose some degree of direction and control over the process of national growth. Because the new "colonies" of the nation would be incorporated into the body politic as states, Representative John Sergeant of Pennsylvania hoped to see them "properly formed." The "quality and character" of their nurture was so crucial, Lemuel Shaw added, precisely because the creation of new states had the substantial political effect of recreating the Union itself. Daniel Webster stated the same idea in constitutional terms. Since Congress enjoyed wide discretion in fixing the terms of compact by which a new state entered the Union, these terms actually amounted to an amendment of the constitutional compact made by the original states.[6] In short, the Federalist spokesmen saw the Union in a process of continuous reconstruction, and they hoped to achieve the goal of qualitative improvement as it developed through time.

The distinction Federalists drew between the old and the new states was of great importance in relation to the expansion of slavery. The provisos of the Constitution bearing upon slavery—the three-fifths ratio of representation, the fugitive slave clause, and the toleration of the foreign slave trade until 1808—pertained only, as Senator Prentiss Mellen of Massachusetts phrased it, to "the high contracting parties," the original states. As the terms of the original compact, these carefully contrived provisions reflected the peculiar configuration of relations which obtained at that particular moment between the slave and free states. And even here, Senator James Burrill of Rhode Island added, they comprised less a grant than a "limitation on the otherwise unlimited power of Congress" to deal with slavery. Territories belonging to the original states were included in the compact, to be sure, and it was for this reason that a number of slave states from the Old Southwest had entered the corporate Union without a contest.[7]

But in the area beyond the "ancient limits" of the Union, Rufus King insisted that an entirely different condition obtained. There the constitutional sanctions and plighted faith of the nation did not apply, Webster agreed, and the power of Congress over slavery was therefore "complete and universal." The duty of making "needful rules" for the territories included the right to determine what was needful. The provision that Congress "may" admit new states implied a wide discretion in fixing the terms of the compact for admission. The clause regarding the "migration" of persons also provided another basis for the restriction of slavery. In sum, Sergeant looked to the unsettled spaces beyond the original Union as the sphere for "new political creation." The Constitution's provisions regarding slavery did not automatically extend beyond the boundaries enjoyed by the Union in 1789.[8] Congress therefore possessed corporate freedom, in the view of the Federalists, to shape in crucial ways the new part of the Union. They strongly opposed the admission of Missouri as a slave state without the Tallmadge amendment, and they wanted absolutely to prevent any further entry of slaves into the territory west of the Mississippi.

In the exercise of this sovereign power over the new areas of the Union, it should be stressed again, the Federalists supposed for the government a position of moral neutrality. That is, the power to prohibit the further spread of slavery could also be exercised to promote the expansion of slavery, a decision, in either case, "political," not "moral." Disdaining to consider the issue of slavery expansion in moral terms, Rufus King rather laid down the following goals for government action: "the common defence, the general welfare, and that wise administration of government which as far as possible may produce the impartial distribution of benefits and burdens throughout the Union."[9]

For a number of reasons, King thought, the fulfillment of these goals required a policy of restricting slavery. The standing danger of insurrection made slavery an element of

military weakness within, and this threat to security would
be aggravated as the system moved out to the frontiers. By
excluding or degrading free labor, preventing the diversification of pursuits, and leaving plundered or undeveloped resources in its wake, slavery also retarded
economic progress. Socially, the slave system generated a
feudal pattern of relationships and values, while its inherent tendency to geographical diffusion precluded a density
of population great enough for a high civilization.

Nor was the general welfare in the newly settled parts of
the Union the only thing at stake. Indeed, the Federalists
deplored the spread of slavery most of all because of its
adverse effects upon the older part of the Union. Specifically, they charged that the three-fifths ratio of representation in the House and an equal voice in the Senate made the
new and sparsely settled slave states nothing more than
rotten boroughs of the South. With this added power the
slaveholding section might forever control the destinies of
the nation, thereby enjoying a permanent veto over measures needed to promote the diverse interests of northern
freemen. King illustrated the injustice of the system by
showing that a northern member of the House represented
35,000 freemen, whereas only 25,559 were required in the
state of Virginia to earn a House seat. This violated "an
original radical principle" of the Union, Senator Burrill
added, by which a majority of citizens or their agents were
to direct the corporate concerns of the nation. While reaffirming the sanctity of the three-fifths ratio for the old
states, he bitterly opposed its extension.[10]

A final argument in behalf of restricting slavery emphasized the need for the nation to take a necessary first
step toward the eventual emancipation of slaves. No claim
was made, of course, for the direct use of federal power to
abolish slavery where it then existed under the protection
of slave states. This goal might rather be accomplished

peacefully and indirectly through a Free-Soil policy for the territories. Without the safety valve of unsettled lands to ameliorate the evils of slavery in the more densely settled parts of the South, so the reasoning went, the slave states would soon be compelled to deal with these increasing evils and work out a plan of emancipation. The further diffusion of slaves over the territories, Senator Mellen thus warned, would serve only "to postpone the evil day." In a similar vein, Otis expressed the fear that the spread of slavery over too vast an area might make the evil "absolutely remediless."[11]

All of the plans suggested by the Federalists for the eventual emancipation of slaves bluntly assumed the inferiority of the Negro and looked, not to his well-being, but to the corporate welfare of existing freemen. Many would use federal funds to subsidize state schemes for freeing the slaves and colonizing them in Africa, the Caribbean, or in some remote region of the western territory. Many others, however, doubtless shared the view of Daniel Raymond that any plan for wholesale colonization was "utterly chimerical," and that the end of slavery would entail the need for the coexistence of the races. Supposing coexistence tolerable only where the Negroes comprised a permanent minority, Raymond invoked certain "laws of population" to show that the process of emancipation itself could alone produce this desirable social result. Free Negroes multiplied far more slowly than the whites in the old part of the Union, according to these laws, while Negro slaves increased far more rapidly than whites in new areas of settlement. The obvious solution, then, was to keep slaves out of the new part of the Union and to set in motion a plan for freeing them in the old. Though the fate of the freedmen remained incidental to his purpose, Raymond believed that many might, within the limits of second-class citizenship, make some improvement in their condition. Along the same line, King made the suggestion that the free Negroes could be bound to the soil and allowed to share in the fruits of their labor somewhat on the order of "ancient villeinage."[12]

Federalist thought about the fate of slavery thus reflected their larger corporate vision of the Union. All expressed the need for the nation to exert some degree of purposive direction over its course through time. John Sergeant therefore rejected the southern plea "to leave the matter to Providence." God had bestowed on man the faculty of reason, he protested, and enjoined each generation to contribute its share in the ongoing and cumulative pursuit of happiness. The final removal of slavery might take a long time, Raymond admitted, but to a nation that hoped for immortality a century was but a day. The important thing was to make a commitment to the right direction. In this perspective, Robert Walsh placed the corporate right of control far above the right of local self-government invoked by the people of Missouri. From the temporary opinions and selfish interests of the few then living in the new state, he appealed to the collective wisdom of the past, the present will of the entire nation, and the fate of "unborn millions." The true welfare of the nation contemplated "the interests of the whole empire in their most enlarged sense."[13] In sum, the Federalist outlook here involved a temporal concept of progress. The nation was to experience qualitative improvement through time as it moved across the unsettled spaces of the continent.

To meet the challenge of the Federalist Free Soilers, southern spokesmen for the old Republican orthodoxy adduced a distinctly different concept of liberty and Union. At the heart of this outlook was the idea of the Union as a timeless and unchanging entity, created by the states and imbued with the essence of federative freedom. Though the Constitution had been fashioned at a particular mo-

ment in time, that moment was normative and thus the
Union was forever immune from substantive change. The
Constitution was, in this view, "the holy ark of the covenant"
to be carried by the nation across unsettled spaces and
through all ages to come. Representative Philip P. Barbour
of Virginia thus rejected the Federalist claim of any congressional power to reconstitute the Union as it proceeded
through time. "We are the creatures of the Constitution,
not its creators," he said, "we are called here to execute, [the
Constitution] not to make one."[14] In contrast to the notion
of a corporate enterprise exerting purposive direction and
control to national life, he conceived of the Union as a
partnership of essentially self-governing communities extending across space, reproducing in its unchanged and
unchanging form the good of federative freedom.

With this view southern Republicans condemned the
"colonial policy" involved in the distinction Federalists
made between the old and the new states. Such a policy was
"contrary to the whole genius of our constitution," the
Richmond *Enquirer* noted, indeed, the very cause of the
American Revolution. Whereas the Federalists thought
that only the old states had created the Union, spokesmen
for the slaveholding section insisted that the Union was the
creature of all the states, of the new as well as the old. This
miracle of federative freedom, according to Representative
John Tyler, grew out of the existence of unsettled space.
Freemen moved out from the older parts of the Union
carrying with them the principles of a free government and
a stock of intelligence comparable to that of the people left
behind. At a later point in time, as settlement progressed,
the people would organize into a body politic and assume a
sovereign power equal to that of the original states. In
substance if not in precise form, so the reasoning went, this
power was not devolved upon the new state by Congress,
but rose up from below where it had been held in abeyance

during the territorial stage. Each new state could therefore bring to the "common stock" of the Union, Representative Benjamin Hardin of Kentucky rejoiced, the "same capital" of power that the old states had originally deposited. The Jeffersonian ideal of an eternally present freedom would, in this way, be fully realized. Since the earth belonged to the living, each new community in space no less than each new generation in time might claim a freedom equal to its predecessors.[15]

It was this principle of the equality of states which provided the chief basis for opposing the Federalist policy of slavery restriction.[16] The old Union, defined once and for all by the Constitution, was thought to be one of severely limited powers. Since no power touching the existence of slavery had been delegated to the central government, sovereignty over the matter remained exclusively with the states. Because the new states differed from the old ones "only in the circumstance of age," Representative Barbour added, absolutely no distinction could be drawn between them. Senator William Pinkney of Maryland agreed that the Union of states was one of equals, *"inter pares,"* and that new states were to be admitted into "this Union" and none other. If denied the sovereign right of the old states to make its own decision with regard to slavery, he went on, Missouri would be "shorn of its beams" and the Union of equals totally subverted. In like spirit Senator Richard M. Johnson of Kentucky condemned the Federalist Free Soilers as "constitution makers." They disregarded the unchanging terms of the Union defined by the fathers in the Constitution, he charged, and sought to fix entirely different terms in the compact for admitting a new state.[17]

So long as the Federalist Free Soilers remained the chief adversary, the argument of strict construction and states' rights continued to have a strong appeal. The federative Union thus defined allowed for the spread of slavery, yet the southern spokesmen were able to make the good of freedom from control overshadow the goal of gaining security for their slaves. Specifically, a doctrine of strict construction seemed to divest them of selfish motives and states' rights to make them champions of freedom. If slavery continued to spread out across space, in this view, it was not because they wanted the central government to promote slavery but simply because no power at all over the subject had been given. The decision in all cases lay with freemen migrating from the old parts of the Union and with the new state at the end of the territorial stage. Conversely, the Federalist effort at restriction could, by its indulgence of loose construction, be made to appear a gross usurpation of power by the central government. It was akin to other such measures as the national bank, internal improvements, and a tariff of protection, John Taylor of Caroline warned, for all were designed to swallow up the liberties of the nation in "the gulph of consolidation." Great Britain had made the same mistake, Senator Nathaniel Macon of North Carolina added, "by attempting to govern too much, and to introduce new principles of government."[18]

In two other ways this outlook could command wide popular support. First of all, it provided the basis for a policy of "manifest destiny." The "admirable expanding principle" in the federative Union made possible an indefinite extension of the nation across space, Representative Charles Pinckney of South Carolina noted, and the further expansion of the nation served in turn to strengthen the federative principle against the forces of consolidation. Senator Johnson of Kentucky pointed to "the beautiful fabric of this Western empire" in order to refute the Federalist claim that the people were incapable of self-government. It exploded "the doctrine of saving the people from their worst enemy, themselves," Senator Freeman

Walker of Georgia readily agreed. But for ill-advised efforts at consolidation or disunion, John Tyler rejoiced that nothing could impede "our onward march" or "set limits to our glory." The Federalists contemplated a destiny of qualitative improvement through time, but the southern Republicans offered the alternative of quantitative development across space. Freedom allowed for expansion and expansion brought greater security to freedom. The Union's unchanging essence of federative freedom would, in the process, be most fully achieved. To use Jackson's famous phrase again, the Union would realize itself best in "extending the area of freedom."[19]

In the second place, the concept of the Union as an unchanging entity played an important mythological function. It supplied specific content to the popular belief in the perfection of the nation and its mission to the world.[20] The "home-bred" system of limited power, written constitutions, and divided sovereignty represented, in the view of John Taylor, a totally new departure in human affairs. In contrast to the European system, according to another observer, it was "the best plan ever formed for the security and happiness of man." Fidelity to its essential principle would assure success for the "experiment" in the United States, Senator Macon believed, and enable the young nation to serve as the model for the ultimate regeneration of the world.[21] Whereas Federalists tended to think of political truth as the kind of good that accumulated through time, the Republicans here evinced a concept of progress in which truth had been embraced in its entirety all at once. The highest task of the statesman was not to direct the nation's course through time but rather to guard its unchanging essence from subversion or decay. Thus, in the "iron age" of consolidation, climaxed by the effort to restrict slavery in Missouri, the Richmond *Enquirer* called upon the nation to regenerate "the holy principles of the

revolution." Jefferson compared this enterprise of reaffir-
mation to the "first revolution" against Great Britain and
the "second revolution" consummated by the election of
1800.[22]

While the old Republican concept of freedom possessed
undoubted appeal, the fact still remained that it helped to
justify the spread of slavery. As a function of space, it
provided in effect the basis for a moratorium on substantial
change. This served, in turn, to secure slavery as their
hostage to time. Two basic arguments for diffusion reveal
the pattern very clearly. The first one actually claimed
emancipation as a final goal. Diffuse slavery across space
and into the hands of a great number of owners, it was
contended, and the closer relations of master and slaves
would quicken human sympathies and lead to voluntary
manumission. Yet in the very same context, Jefferson admitted that widespread emancipation was unthinkable unless accompanied by colonization. Because of the problem
of race, to use his words, the South had the "wolf by the
ears."[23]

The leading feature of the second argument for diffusion was the professed desire to ameliorate the condition of
the slaves. In Malthusian terms, it was claimed, the dense
population in the older areas pressed the limited resources
and lowered the level of subsistence. The unsettled lands of
the West, by contrast, offered the opportunity for raising
the level of subsistence. Behind this humanitarian plea,
however, lay anxieties about the alternative to expansion. If
restricted to the old areas, Representative George Tucker
of Virginia argued, the value of labor would decline to such
a point that, out of sheer economic necessity, the master
would be compelled to free his slaves. Or, before that day
arrived, the beleaguered slaves might rise up to claim their
freedom in violence and blood. Whites would then face the
choice of abandoning the graves of their sires or of remain-

ing to prosecute a war of the races.[24] The spread of slavery
across space was, in this light, a means of avoiding the evils
of slavery that accumulated through time in the old part of
the Union. Thus in a general sense the federative Union
was less a means for extending the good of freedom across
space than of using space as a safety valve for securing the
evils of slavery.

It was precisely in this context that a second basis for
opposing the extension of slavery arose. As formulated by
many northern Jeffersonians at the time, it held the Union
to be a means for promoting the good of individual freedom and not for spreading the evil of slavery. Though not
unmindful of the "political" aspect and the Federalist concern for the general welfare, these Republican Free Soilers
focused in the first instance upon the "moral" aspect of the
problem. In doing so they went beyond the terms of the old
debate between corporate and federative freedom to make
the issue a stark confrontation between freedom on one
side and slavery on the other. Their appeal to the Declaration of Independence's concept of the freedom of the individual stood in absolute opposition to slavery. The "foundation stone" of that document, as one put it, was "equal
rights, not of states, but of men."[25]

To be sure, this moral emphasis was "used" by many
during the Missouri debates as distinctly ancillary to their
political argument for slavery restriction. Appeal to the
Declaration of Independence, a recent student has noted,
obviously brought great emotional and rhetorical force to
bear upon their case after the purely constitutional arguments had been exhausted. Rufus King provides a clear
example of this practice. It was only "after giving & sustaining as well as I could the true construction of the Constitution on the subject" that he "referred the decision of the
Restriction in Missouri to the broad principles of the law of
Nature." He hoped by this "bold position" to influence the

votes of many northern Republicans of the House who had
come to the Senate gallery to hear him speak.[26] Senator Otis
in like fashion wanted to gain wide popular support across
the North in behalf of slavery restriction. While personally
disposed to view the matter "entirely as a question of policy," he perceived the strong effect which the moral argument might produce. Otis was especially anxious to tone
down the Federalist press and to encourage the "Democratic papers" to become "higher spiced." This use of popular
rhetoric in a political cause revealed the pattern, which a
recent student of latter-day Federalists has discovered, of "a
silent elite in the midst of a speaking multitude."[27]

To use the phrase later insisted upon by proslavery
spokesmen, the moral argument represented the appeal to
a "higher law" than the Constitution. John Quincy Adams,
who followed the debates very closely from his vantage
point in the cabinet of President James Monroe, perceived
the matter in this light. He ruefully admitted that a clear
distinction must be made between the timeless principle of
freedom found in the Declaration of Independence and
the actual makeup of the Union formed at a particular
point in time. "The fault is in the Constitution of the United
States," he said, "which has sanctioned a dishonorable compromise with slavery." The bargain it made between freedom and slavery was "morally and politically vicious," he
further explained, and "inconsistent with the principles
upon which alone our Revolution can be justified." For this
reason Adams supported the compromise proposals in
1820 as the best freemen had reason to expect, yet he
privately dreamed of a bolder course. An adamant stand
against concessions to the South might have brought a
dissolution of the Union, he supposed, and with it the
opportunity for the free states to fashion a new Union
based unequivocally on the principle of freedom.[28]

It would be wrong, however, to assume that the moral

argument remained at this point during the Missouri controversy. Many others moved beyond Adams to give a fairly rounded interpretation of the Union in moral terms. They dismissed the need to create the Union anew on the basis of freedom, because the old Union already reposed upon that principle. The "higher law" of individual freedom was not a higher law at all, in this view, but the principle of the existing Union under the Constitution. Put another way, "the laws of nature and of Nature's God" referred not to a state of nature before the organization of society but to a substantive moral principle already "established" in the free society of the United States. In sum, these Free Soilers in 1820 clearly anticipated the Republican party platform of 1860 which maintained that "the principles promulgated in the Declaration of Independence" had been "embodied in the Federal Constitution."[29]

The concept of the Union developed by the northern Jeffersonians was at once more democratic, absolute, and nationalistic than that of the Federalists. Individual freedom, as the national idea, marked a wide departure from the elitist tendencies to be found in the corporate idea of freedom. At the same time, the compact of Union was far more absolute because it claimed sanctions of far greater solemnity than the mere obligation of man-made agreements. "The covenant of our fathers," Senator Jonathan Roberts of Pennsylvania explained, had been made with "the Supreme Judge of the world." For this reason, Representative Daniel Cook of Illinois added, "our conduct as a nation is passing in hourly review before Him who sits aloft."[30]

That which made the view of the Republican Free Soilers so nationalistic, finally, was the fact that they moved the timing of the compact backward from the Constitution to the Declaration of Independence. The Constitution served merely as an instrument, Charles Rich of Vermont ex-

plained in the House, to distribute between the federal and
the state governments the "legitimate attributes" of
sovereignty found in the "national covenant" of the Declaration. In taking this view he advanced toward the position,
later made fully explicit by President Abraham Lincoln,
that the Union was older than the states and, indeed, the
creator of all the states.[31] Here was a mystique of freedom
equal, though exactly opposite in its consequences, to the
southern view that the Union remained throughout all time
the creature of all the states. The intensity of its nationalism
can be measured, moreover, by the degree to which it went
beyond the historical thought of the Federalist Free Soilers.
The latter only claimed for the Union the power to create
new states, for they supposed the old states had enjoyed an
independent existence before they formed the Union.

With specific regard to slavery, it was true, the Republican Free Soilers did retain the distinction between the old
and the new states. But the distinction was practical, not
substantive, they insisted, because the principle of individual freedom underlay the entire Union, the old as well as
the new part. The fathers founded the Union on this "predominant principle," Representative Timothy Fuller of
Massachusetts said, and constituted it from the beginning a
monism of freedom. They made an "exception" to the
slavery existing at the time, but in two ways it was thought
slavery represented only a temporary negation of the timeless national idea. In the first place, Representative James
Tallmadge of New York noted that the fathers had not
commited the "original sin" of creating slavery. Entailed
rather by the old British empire, it had become so inter-
twined in the society of many states that efforts at immediate abolition would have brought even greater evils.
The old states thus enjoyed, Joseph Hemphill of Pennsylvania told the House members, "a certain kind of rights
which have grown up out of original wrongs." But the

fathers had no intention, Representative William Plumer, Jr., of New Hampshire noted in the second place, of making the exception a permanent one. Instead, they looked to certain measures—an end to the foreign slave trade, the prohibition of slavery in the Old Northwest, cooperation with the states in plans of colonization—as "leading gradually to the abolition of slavery in the old States." For this reason as well, the word "slave" had been omitted from the Constitution: in time to come there would be no reminder that the evil of slavery had ever existed in the land of the free.[32]

Even in the old part of the Union, then, the Republican Free Soilers maintained a concept of monistic freedom. Slavery existed there by "local" rather than "federal" right, Representative William Darlington of Pennsylvania said, and therefore derogated in no way from the essential national principle of individual freedom. In the new part of the Union, meanwhile, absolutely nothing stood in the way of immediate realization of this principle. Here, memorialists from Connecticut affirmed, "the original principle" which had been avowed in the Declaration of Independence revived in all "its primitive force." The phrasing of the idea foreshadowed the Republican party's claim in 1860 that "the normal condition of all the territory of the United States is that of freedom." The Constitution was essentially antislavery, in this view, and automatically carried freedom across all the unsettled spaces of the nation. As "the sacred ark of your liberties," Senator David Morrill of New Hampshire compared it to a cloud by day and a pillar of fire by night "to cheer the desert of your western country" and extend the area of freedom from the Atlantic to the Pacific. Since the Constitution gave no inherent power to establish slavery in a new area, the actual task of Congress in restricting it was a negative one. It needed only to guarantee a republican form of government to a new state, according to

Representative John Taylor of New York, and to keep the
evil seeds of slavery from being planted in the "uncorrupt
soil" of the territory.[33]

In many obvious ways the style and approach of the
Republican Free Soilers differed from that of the
Federalists. On the assumption of moral neutrality, the
latter admitted that the sovereign power in Congress to stop
the spread of slavery might equally be used to extend it.
Because he regarded the Constitution as distinctly antislavery and not morally neutral, Representative Plumer invoked the rule of strict construction to combat the "new and
alarming doctrines" of slavery expansionists. Federalists
professed to act in a positive fashion for promoting the
general welfare, and they justified the need to override the
will of the people of Missouri on these grounds. Representative Taylor merely wanted to "forbid them to practice
wrongs," supposing the general welfare would arise in the
absence of evil.[34] In a more comprehensive sense, the
Federalists claimed a corporate freedom to build up and
change the Union as it moved across the territories beyond
the Mississippi. The Republicans, on the other hand, took
the Union to be an unchanging entity defined by the principle of individual freedom. Its destiny was to realize this
principle more fully as it went across the unsettled spaces.
Finally, an important difference obtained with regard to
the integrity of the Union. Many Federalists were vulnerable to the charge of being disunionists, whereas Republicans spoke out strongly and unequivocally in behalf of the
Union as indissoluble.[35]

Much of this difference between the Free Soilers can be
summarized in their contrasting concepts of progress. The
Federalists, as indicated earlier, thought of political good as
the kind of thing that accumulated through time. But the
Republicans held to a view similar in its general form to that
of the southern Jeffersonians. They, too, thought of truth

as having been established once and for all. Specifically, Representative Darlington noted that the nation had embraced "the sublime doctrines of the rights of man" at the very outset of its existence. Progress for the nation necessarily meant the quantitative spread of this principle, for its initial perfection ruled out the possibility of qualitative improvement through time. Happiness for the nation came in the "course of nature," William Plumer, Sr., thought, by fidelity to its "immutable laws." In a vital sense the Union was to be regarded as an emanation of nature and not the product of history. Because it violated the immutable principles of the Union, the expansion of slavery represented an absolute threat to progress. It constituted sad proof that "the maxims of tyrants have imperceptibly crept into the Constitution," Representative Clifton Claggett of New Hampshire warned, and pointed to the task of purging these maxims "root and branch" in order that the true faith of the fathers might be restored. A regeneration of fundamental principles was the need at such a crisis, Representative Rich agreed, a faithful return "to the covenant we have made with the Judge of the Universe."[36]

The very terms in which it contrasted with Federalist thought underscored, as well, the profound challenge which Republican Free Soilers presented to the slaveholding section. That which made the conflict so potentially irrepressible was the fact that, as negative liberals, each arrived at exactly opposite conclusions within a common frame of perceiving political reality. Southern spokesmen during the Missouri controversy thought of the Union as the creature of all the states, new as well as old, for it was formed and sustained by the archetype of federative freedom. The Republican Free Soilers, by contrast, deemed the Union to be the creator of all the states, fashioned on the model of timeless individual freedom. Yet both equally held to a view of the Union as in essence an unchanging entity. In rejecting the Federalist notion that the compact of the Constitution applied only to the original states, moreover, both supposed it to be the ark of the covenant for guiding the nation in all time to come across its unsettled spaces. Progress in either case was to be measured by the spread of the initially perfect design of the nation, and a crisis would come at the point in time when the enemies of true freedom sought to subvert the design. Within their own terms, finally, each commanded popular appeal; for each clearly differed from what John Taylor of Caroline called the "substantially European" mode of Federalist thought.[37]

So long as northern and southern Jeffersonians remained in the dialectical presence of Federalism, they would be able to manage the inner tensions generated by the dual emphasis on personal and states' rights. But, in the absence of the old foil of freedom, conflict might easily mature and, in the temper of negative liberalism, become irrepressible. The disposition of Republican Free Soilers to regard individual freedom as the essence of the Union served, in effect, to denationalize slavery by placing it under "the ban of the Constitution."[38] When they succeeded in making the ban effective, many southern spokesmen would then feel compelled to make the protection of slavery, and not the good of federative freedom within the Union, their ultimate task. For them, to state the matter another way, liberty and the Union were to be considered separable goods and liberty far more dear.

Certain of the southern responses during the Missouri controversy clearly revealed the challenge of the Republican Free Soilers and an inclination to accept the irrepressible conflict thus defined. Senator Macon considered the moral principles of the Declaration of Independence as comprising a "higher law" which had absolutely no relevance to the Union formed by the fathers under the Con-

stitution. Nor was the higher law any more relevant to the
new part of the Union than the old. Senator James Barbour
of Virginia thus explicitly repudiated the double standard
in the Free-Soil ethic, "inoperative on the left" but "om-
nipotent on the right bank" of the Mississippi River. While
most southern leaders in 1820 still admitted slavery to be a
political evil, Senator William Smith of South Carolina gave
a preview of the later arguments for slavery as a positive
good. In like spirit the Richmond *Enquirer* advised congressmen to oppose the compromise to the last hazard. The
admission of Missouri without restriction came at too high a
price, it was urged, because the ban on slavery north of
36°30′ involved the fateful concession that power resided
somewhere outside the sovereign states to touch the existence of slavery. Here was an avowal that the security of
slavery, in or out of the Union, constituted the highest
political good. "The Union is a *means*," Senator Pinkney
solemnly declared, "not an *end*."[39]

But it was not until the resumption of the controversy
over the issue of slavery expansion at the end of the 1840s
that the irrepressible conflict became fully defined. The
Missouri Compromise served, in this perspective, to postpone the split in the ranks of the Jeffersonians. By its
provisions Missouri entered the Union as a slave state without the Tallmadge amendment, and the political equilibrium was maintained by admitting Maine as a free state.
The line of 36°30′ was then drawn to settle in advance all
questions about the expansion of slavery into the remaining
territories of the Louisiana Purchase.

The compromise was basically a southern measure, and
the terms of support for it reflected in different ways the
equivocal basis of the settlement. Some spokesmen from
the slaveholding section made the positive claim, it was true,
that the compromise actually represented a victory for the
concept of federative freedom. Because the debates had

dealt almost exclusively with the status of slavery in Missouri, and not in the unsettled territories, its admission without the Tallmadge amendment seemed to vindicate the principle of perfect equality among all of the states, new as well as old. It demonstrated the fact, clearly in contrast to the Federalist ideas, that the slavery provisions in the original Constitution had indeed moved out in unchanged form across new space. Nor did advocates of this position regard the ban on slavery north of 36°30′ a defeat, and certainly not a total one. It was held to be an ordinary act of legislation that could be repealed by a later Congress.[40] Since the territory in question had not been opened to settlement, moreover, the restriction was prospective in nature, abridging the present right of no freemen in the South.[41] Finally, they supposed that the restriction, if not repealed beforehand, would cease absolutely to operate at the end of the territorial stage. At that time the people would be entitled to organize into a state and claim the fullness of sovereign power enjoyed by the old states.[42]

In practical terms, as well, these southern proponents of compromise argued that it gained time for the slaveholding section to strengthen its power within the Union. Representative Pinckney of South Carolina deemed it, in this light, a substantial victory. Since no effort had been made to remove the Indian titles to the territory north of 36°30′, he supposed it would be a long time before settlement there could increase the number of free states. Meanwhile, he savored the prospect that Arkansas, most likely Florida, and possibly a number of states from the Spanish province of Texas would follow Missouri into the Union as slave states. Pinckney thought the added power of these new states assured the safety of slavery in the Union for the foreseeable future, while it strengthened the possibility of repealing the compromise line. Some substance for the southern claim of victory can be seen in the fact that Rufus

King used an almost identical language in judging the compromise a profound defeat. At a crucial moment in its
development, he feared, the nation had forfeited the opportunity to give purpose and direction to its course. Talk
of dissolving the Union was generally confined to private
correspondence, yet it doubtless expressed the feeling of
many Federalists at the time.[43]

Others in the South, a majority in the view of leading
scholars, supported compromise in a more negative way.[44]
Representative Hugh Nelson of Virginia expressed this
attitude very well: "I have taken it because I thought it
better to make some sacrifice to form, than lose the substance." In like fashion Senator Montfort Stokes of North
Carolina admitted that the only hope for gaining enough
northern votes to bring Missouri in as a slave state depended upon the southern concession of the right of Congress to prohibit slavery in the unsettled territory. Both
thus regarded the compromise less a victory over the
Federalists than a way of avoiding total defeat at the hands
of northern Republicans. Stated in a converse fashion,
southern leaders could urge concessions as a means for
restoring their alliance with the "plain republicans" of the
North, for they perceived this alliance to be the political
basis of their security within the Union.[45]

It is only in this context that the idea of the Missouri
controversy as a "Federalist plot" has full meaning. Under
"the auspices of morality," Jefferson charged, the
Federalists played upon "the honest feelings" of the northern Republicans "to seduce them from their kindred
spirits" in the South. Similarly aware of this effort "to de-
lude and mislead our northern brethren," another close
observer came out in favor of the compromise line precisely
at that point when Senator King reinforced his "political"
argument for slavery restriction with his "moral" appeal to
the laws of nature. Andrew Jackson likewise condemned as

a "wicked design" the attempt of Federalist "demagogues" to divide northern and southern Republicans on the issue of slavery and thereby form a purely sectional party in the North.[46] Historians have failed to discover any systematic Federalist conspiracy to recoup their declining political fortunes in this way; but they have found an apparently widespread belief that such a plot did exist.[47] The belief, in any case, proved very useful to southern leaders. By pointing anew to the menacing presence of the old Federalist enemy of freedom, they might hope in time to restore the essentials of the old Republican consensus.

The conditions on which some northern Republicans supported the compromise, however, could not have been very reassuring to the South. They invoked the principle of states' rights, to be sure, in justifying their crucial votes for admitting Missouri as a slave state without the Tallmadge amendment. Yet they reaffirmed the belief that freedom from the corporate control Federalists would exert over the nation meant an enlargement of personal freedom no less than of states' rights. In this view they had no doubt that Congress possessed the power, in advance of settlement, to prohibit the spread of slavery into a new territory. The ban on slavery north of 36°30′ could thus be explained to their constituents as a great prospective triumph for individual freedom.[48] Should any future conflict over the extension of slavery focus exclusively on the status of a territory and not a state, as in the Missouri controversy, then the old terms of consensus between northern and southern Jeffersonians would be put to a new and severer test. This was, as it turned out, precisely what happened in the wake of the Mexican War.

Even less assuring for the future was the fact that northern Republicans linked their support for compromise to the idea of an indissoluble Union. One revealing manifestation of this was the way they placed upon the charge of a

Federalist plot a far different emphasis than that given to it by southern spokesmen. The greater danger in the Federalist effort to form a sectional party, as they saw it, lay in failure more than in success. They argued, in a specific way, that the failure to gain political power in the Union to shape its destinies might embolden the Federalists to attempt a dissolution of the Union and the formation of a separate northern confederacy. Here was to be seen a new incarnation of that unhallowed disunionist spirit of rule or ruin which had characterized Federalism in the days of the Hartford Convention. It obviously did great violence to the popular sentiment for the Union which had come out of the War of 1812, making a mockery, as well, of the sacred principle of majority rule. In this setting the northern compromisers found the appeal to the integrity of the Union a strong argument against the Federalist Free Soilers.[49] Whereas most southern Jeffersonians thought of secession as an ultimate way to preserve their freedom and the practice of slavery, their northern fellows here supposed liberty and the Union to be one and inseparable. The one professed to see in Federalism a threat to freedom in the Union, while the other deemed the chief menace to be the Union of freemen itself.

In this equivocal way the Missouri controversy came to an end. For a majority of the people at the time it brought welcome relief and the chance to turn their attention to other affairs. For the historian of ideas, the controversy serves as a synopsis of the National Period. The basic terms of the debate between Federalist and Republican involved alternative views of the destiny of the nation in space and time which would, when applied to matters other than slavery, essentially define the dialogue until the end of the 1840s between the champions of the American System and Jacksonian Democracy. The ideological shape of the remaining years before the Civil War was also foreshadowed in the Missouri controversy by the emergence of the Republican mode of Free-Soil thought. With a strong moral resolve and a focus upon individual freedom as the essence of the national idea, this outlook would transcend the debate between corporate and federative freedom and define an irrepressible conflict between freedom and slavery. "The seeds of the Declaration of Independence are yet maturing," John Quincy Adams noted in his diary at the time. "The harvest will be what West, the painter, calls the terrible and sublime."[50]

3
Time and the American System

For a decade and a half after the War of 1812, the so-called American System of policies formed and dominated political debate. The corporate concept of freedom lay at the heart of the arguments for such policies. Keenly aware of the social nature of man and of the nation's involvement in time, they expressed special concern for some degree of self-conscious direction and control to the common life. Political defeat came in the election of 1828 as a coalition of dissident elements rallied under Andrew Jackson's banner with the call for restoring the old Jeffersonian idea of federative freedom. In the sequel, marked by the dismantling of the American System of policies, President Jackson invited the nation of freemen to move forward to a glorious destiny without essential direction from the federal government.

The testimony of many contemporaries and later historians suggests that the events of the early National Period do not fall quite so easily into such a neat ideological pattern. To them the American System was hardly American and certainly not very systematic at all. Foes of a protective tariff, internal improvements, or a more cautious disposition of the western lands professed to find in the combination of these measures a European pattern of corruption and consolidation tending to undermine freedom. Even the proponents did not always agree about the proper emphasis which the system ought to place on one or another of the measures. John Quincy Adams deemed most important the relation of internal improvements and the land; Richard Rush, land and the tariff; Henry Clay, the tariff and internal improvements. This range of differences doubtless reflected personal and sectional biases toward national affairs, pointing as well to the practical political task of combining diverse interests. In the case of Clay, moreover, preoccupation with the task often seemed to obscure any larger vision of the nation's destiny.[1] The government, in this view, was more of a broker of present interests than a positive instrument for defining and pursuing long-run national goals.

Many works dealing with the decade of the 1820s focus on this idea. According to Frederick Jackson Turner, the "spirit of nationalism and consolidation" which came out of the War of 1812 gave way in the Panic of 1819 to the greater influence of sectional forces. Political leaders then found it necessary to deal in the first instance with the interests of their particular section and to seek combinations with other interests. By the attention he gave to the personal and factional nature of politics, Shaw Livermore, Jr., has likewise discovered a strongly pragmatic and anti-ideological outlook in the period. When, at the end of the War of 1812, President James Madison and fellow Republicans adopted such nationalistic measures of their old political adversary as the bank and a stronger military establishment, any reason for a real and meaningful dialogue ceased to exist. Some of the old Federalist leaders doubtless yearned for a comeback after the disasters of the Hartford Convention, but a greater number indulged their hunger for political office more realistically by participating in the factional politics of the Republican party. By 1828 erstwhile

Federalists had, in roughly equal numbers, identified with the new alignments under John Quincy Adams and Andrew Jackson. Without considering what the new alignments stood for, Livermore rejected the traditional view that they represented a mere reincarnation of the old debate between Federalists and Republicans.[2]

Any study of the period must reckon with these findings; yet a need exists to redress the balance of the account. A close reading of the debates indicates rather that behind the rough and tumble of sectional and factional politics lay an earnest desire to find some unifying national principle. As they entered a new era many thoughtful spokesmen turned their attention to the challenges facing a young and vigorous people on a relatively unsettled continent. In 1817 John C. Calhoun gave voice to much of this concern: "We are great, and rapidly—he was about to say fearfully —growing." It was thus imperative for the nation to "conquer space." The presence of vast unsettled spaces invited profound consideration about the very nature and course of the national venture in time.[3]

One of the many merits of George Dangerfield's work is the recognition of the general outlines of this debate. As he sees it, the Panic of 1819 transformed the Era of Good Feelings into an Era of Introspection, wherein the advocates of economic nationalism faced the rising tide of democratic nationalism. The former, whose view of the Union was one of corporate "realism," sought with the American System of policies to give some degree of direction and control to the development of the nation. Democratic nationalism, born in the panic of a restless frontier spirit and the impulses for unfettered enterprise, expressed a "nominalist" view of the Union, that is, the notion of the Union as a non-corporate entity made up of the individual, the particular, the discrete. While ruling out any system or plan for national development, the democrats might allow some forms of government aid to individual pursuits. In the Tariff of Abominations in 1828 Dangerfield found a true manifestation of this nominalist spirit. As fashioned by Martin Van Buren for the political purpose of drawing together the Middle States and the West by higher duties on raw materials, the tariff violated any rational design for promoting national industry. Yet the absence of system occasioned no difficulty, for Van Buren and his supporters seemed to assume that the destiny of the nation would be a happy one without any basic direction or control.[4]

In two important ways, however, this interpretation needs qualification. First of all, it pays too little attention to the slaveholding element within the ranks that triumphed under Jackson in 1828. The coalition Van Buren had fashioned, after all, was fundamentally one between the "planters" of the South and the "plain republicans" of the North.[5] It was only after this foundation had been laid that he sought, with the Tariff of Abominations, to broaden its base in the non-slaveholding area. If the "nominalism" of the plain republicans required freedom from future control as individuals pursued their separate interests, the planters opposed the controls involved in the American System on an additional and far different ground. Theirs was, at last, an anxiety about the security of slavery which the presence of a powerful central government might threaten. In opposing the consolidating tendency of an internal improvement measure in 1824, John Randolph bluntly voiced this apprehension on the House floor: "If Congress possesses the power to do what is proposed by this bill . . . they may emancipate every slave in the United States—and with stronger color of reason than they can exercise the power now contended for."[6]

By deeming it "moribund," most of all, Dangerfield fails to appreciate the ideological role played by the American

System in providing "system" to the rising force of democratic nationalism. As of 1828 Jacksonians ranged under
the vague banner of restoring the purity and simplicity of
the old Republican orthodoxy. Great diversity if not inconsistency characterized their stance on specific issues. Western spokesmen in favor of roads and canals found themselves at odds with Van Buren and the New Yorkers; while
both groups faced the rising hostility of the South to higher
tariff duties. In effect, the Jacksonians of 1828 were without a coherent policy, simply Jeffersonian idealists in search
of common ideas. Only during the course of the nullification controversy which followed would the new revival of
the old Republican faith assume a more distinct form. The
dialectic of the American system supplied much of that
form. Had no adversary to freedom existed, it is tempting
to say, there would have been the need to invent one.
During the crusade to dismantle the American System of
policies, in any event, President Jackson hit upon a principle of unity which managed to accommodate new facts of
national development while it reaffirmed fidelity to the
pristine purity of the Early Republic.[7]

In this context the American System constituted, as it
were, the "thesis" for the period from the War of 1812 to
the nullification crisis. Building upon the nationalist spirit
of the post-war years, its proponents sought to exercise
some control over the growth and development of the
country in the following decade. They wanted to encourage
manufacturing, effect a balance of economic pursuits, and
achieve a greater degree of national self-sufficiency. Involved for many in the fulfillment of these economic goals
was also the good of a more solid social and political order.
By stress upon cultural homogeneity, political consolidation, and the values of continuity they thus evinced, in the
terms used by Fred Somkin, a strong impulse to "memory"
as well as to "desire."[8] On the basis of greater order, finally,

they looked to the progressive enrichment in the quality of
the common life as the nation moved through time.

Here was to be found a mixture of elitism and democratic
optimism, a blend of Hamiltonian elements with what
Dangerfield called Jeffersonian "realism." By the desire to
promote manufactures, the advocates of the American System obviously ran counter to the commercial predilections
and salt water orientation of most old Federalists; yet a
kinship obtained with regard to the emphasis on order,
measured progress, and a creative role for the government.
A keen awareness of the nation within the process of time,
at once a product and a producer of change, was central to
this outlook. So, John Quincy Adams invited his generation
to build upon the work of the past in the ongoing and
cumulative pursuit of happiness for the sake of both the
present and the future. The government thus exercised a
distinct history-making power, for social man was deemed
able to define and fulfill many beneficent purposes. As
positive liberals, in the formal language of Guido de Ruggiero, Adams and his fellows reflected the belief that there
would be more freedom at the end than at the beginning of
the historical process.[9]

A good point at which to commence a fuller analysis of
the thought in the American System is with the positive
concept of the "good of the whole." As explicitly used by
some and generally assumed by others, it contained two
emphases which struck opponents as perversely metaphysical and un-American in nature. First of all, the general
interest was deemed to be an entity in its own right, something other than the mere aggregate of separate and particular interests. Secondly, it was the sort of good which
took time to mature. In Aristotelian terms, the general
good constituted a final cause. It was the kind of thing
capable of being discerned by present statesmen and prescribed for in such a way that its potentiality could be more

fully actualized through time. Spokesmen for the American System did not always agree about specific policies or goals, but in one fashion or another they resisted the notion that the good of the whole automatically arose out of the interplay of separate interests.

When applied to practical political affairs, the positive concept of the good of the whole provided a clear justification for the sacrifice of what were deemed to be the present interests of individuals and groups. In his most "nationalist" phase after the War of 1812, Calhoun argued that the "common good" to be achieved by a tariff and improvements "may apparently be opposed to the interest of particular sections." He also defended the additional taxes for building a stronger military establishment on the ground that the future "security of the country" far outweighed the "love of present ease." In like fashion, Richard Rush, Secretary of the Treasury under President Adams, scorned the "calculations of the existing hour" which stood in the way of "solid and durable" good to be achieved by economic self-sufficiency for the nation.[10] Because he was more sensitive to the political art of combining diverse elements into a workable majority, Clay invoked the spirit of "mutual concession" to equalize as much as possible the benefits and burdens which the policy of tariff protection placed on present interests. But this species of "log rolling" was to be disciplined by a clear view of the "general interest" to be realized through time. "Present temporary inconvenience may be well submitted to," he explained, "for the sake of future permanent benefit."[11]

Another consequence of this teleological way of thinking was the distinct tendency toward a consensus view of politics, that is, the position which ruled out the idea of a permanent two-party system. Since time was needed to achieve any larger good, the organized opportunity for a present minority to gain power and then undo the policy commitments of the majority threatened to weaken, if not entirely destroy, the vital links in what Senator Benjamin Ruggles of Ohio called "the great chain of policy that is to elevate the power and wealth of this nation." The "true" interest of the minority would rather be fulfilled, in this view of things, by being incorporated more fully into the national interest as the beneficent consequences of present policies began to unfold. "Keep firmly to your purposes," Representative Charles Kinsey of New Jersey noted, "and the voice of the Republic will sanction your act." As a leader who professed to be the "Man of the Whole People," President John Quincy Adams exemplified most clearly this holistic and organic predilection in the American System. By condemning the "baneful weed of party strife," indeed, he seemed to reject the very notion of a plural society no less than the solution to the problem of minorities therein offered by the two-party system.[12]

Underlying this tactic of political consensus was a corporate concept of liberty and the Union. The belief that the apparent conflict of interests in the present would issue into a greater harmony and good through time meant that the Union was the kind of grand and ongoing enterprise which reposed upon the collective will of all generations. Political freedom was thus to be considered a function of time: each generation participated in the blessings of liberty bestowed by the past and worked to enlarge the good for its successors. Among the publicists for the American System, Daniel Raymond dealt fully and explicitly with the corporate concept, but tt found its most concise expression in the formula of Adams that "liberty is power." Having attained its freedom, Adams wanted the nation to use and enjoy it in a constructive way.[13]

One clear manifestation of the corporate outlook can be seen in the thought many gave to the nature of representation in Congress. Henry C. Martindale of New York advised his fellows in the House that they gave voice to far more than the present interests of their particular constituents. "We are, then, each one of us the representative of every interest, and, of course, of the whole," he declared. "Let us be Americans, sir, and feel and act as Americans." In like fashion the nationalist Calhoun dismissed the doctrine of instructions on the ground that Congressmen received their power from the corporate will of the Constitution and not from the people who elected them. The elitist assumption here that the people were perversely present-minded in outlook found even blunter expression in the advice President Adams gave. He called on Congress to act in behalf of the national interest and not be "palsied by the will of our constituents." But Hezekiah Niles among the Jeffersonian realists rejected this assumption, for in his view it necessarily entailed a return to priestcraft and kings. He affirmed instead that the majority of the people could be trusted to perceive the "general good" in its corporate dimensions and to give the American System of policies consistent support.[14]

With regard to the Constitution, supporters of the American System inclined decidedly to a liberal construction. The charter of freedom was to be viewed, not with the eye of "an ingenious advocate," Clay protested, but with the eye of a far-seeing statesman concerned for the "great destinies" of the nation yet to be realized. More danger lay in the atrophy of federal powers than in their abuse. Each generation, Representative John P. Cushman of New York agreed, must assume a considerable latitude of freedom in meeting the "national exigencies" and in seizing the unique opportunities as they arose. By the same token each was to be bound by these interpretations of the past which provided the basis for sustaining the policy commitments of the nation. Representative George Holcombe of New Jersey considered these precedents to be the fruits of national

experience and in some sense as amendments to the Constitution, for he supposed the Constitution was the kind of
thing that could grow through time. In any case he condemned the tendency of strict constructionists to regard the
Constitution as an absolute and unchanging entity, an idol
to be worshipped. He called on freemen to enter its precinct
in the upright posture of rational creatures and not as
cringing slaves before the throne of an oriental prince.
With freemen rather lay the god-like power to define and
promote the "public good."[15]

In terms of the specific goods to be achieved, the basis of
the American System in the 1820s was laid in the post-war
years of the preceding decade. With memories still fresh of
the financial and military embarrassments experienced in
the second contest with Great Britain, many in Congress
rallied behind President Madison in building a stronger
peacetime defense establishment and in seeking once more
with a national bank to stabilize the currency. To comple-
ment these measures for greater national security, the President also called for higher tariff duties to protect and
promote the manufacture of items needed in time of war.
By his special interest in those domestic manufactures
which used the raw materials produced within the country,
Madison also anticipated the home market emphasis of the
full-blown American System. On constitutional grounds, it
was true, he vetoed the Bonus Bill which had earmarked
the revenues from the bank for building roads and canals;
but his proposal for an amendment indicated his belief in
their importance. Among members of Congress at the time
Calhoun spoke most strongly in their behalf, noting not
only the military needs for interior communication but also
the incidental benefits to be derived for commerce and for
the goal of political consolidation.[16]

With the Panic of 1819, a new demand arose to extend
the scope of governmental action in order to achieve a far

greater degree of economic self-sufficiency for the nation than that contemplated in the preceding years. Considering the collapse of the European market for American staples to be permanent, Representative Henry Baldwin of Pennsylvania invited Congress to meet squarely the challenge of the new era. In retrospect he supposed the entire period since the writing of the Constitution had been shaped by the abnormal condition of war in Europe and that this "ephemeral" basis for the great profits in commerce and agriculture had forever passed away. Clay agreed that the future well-being of the nation required a "systematic" effort by the government to promote manufactures, create a home market for agricultural staples, and effect a close interdependence of domestic pursuits. Only by this truly American System, he argued, could maturity and lasting substance be given to the political independence gained at an earlier time.[17]

A protective tariff constituted the key policy for achieving this prospective good. Such a policy was designed not only to protect existing interests, Representative Martindale explained, but also to create new interests and to rearrange the relationship of them all. The government thus possessed a positive history-making power, Alexander H. Everett agreed, for it served in some degree to divert the employments of capital and labor from old channels dug by self-interest and habit into new channels calculated to promote the long-run interest of the nation. Clay dismissed the charge that high duties amounted to a bounty for the privileged few by showing that protection created a national and not an individual monopoly, a general frame within which real domestic competition might take place. Even in the narrow terms of "present mercantile gain," moreover, Richard Rush argued that domestic competition would eventually make prices lower. Meanwhile, the relative increase in manufacturing and decline in agricultural

pursuits would provide a home market for the productions
of both and new employments for men of commerce once
exclusively engaged in the hazardous channels of foreign
trade. Thus might be laid, Representative Kinsey of New
Jersey rejoiced, "the permanent basis of our future
greatness."[18]

A system of roads and canals was, in this view, to com-
plement the tariff in achieving the goal of greater economic
self-sufficiency. By cutting across state and regional lines
roads and canals would facilitate the exchange of domestic
productions and tend to fix irreversibly the patterns of
internal commerce. New channels of communication illustrated the creative role of the government in other ways, for
they determined in some measure the direction as well as
the speed of national development across the continent.
They would also make new resources available and, in the
process of creating new interests, relate them to all others.
Representative Andrew Stewart of Pennsylvania, awed by
the wealth and diversity of resources bestowed by "divine
Providence," claimed for the nation the manifest destiny of
becoming a world within itself. Nature had left so very little
for the arts of men to do, he added, in realizing this teleological design. And Clay reiterated the view that it was a
corporate task. Capital and some degree of government
planning were needed to supply the deficiencies of individual enterprise; while posterity necessarily became incorporated by helping to retire the debts incurred and by
sharing the benefits that accumulated through time. Here
as elsewhere most supporters of the American System rejected the Jeffersonian ideal that the earth belonged to the
living or that each generation constituted a separate nation
in the pursuit of happiness.[19]

As the goal of greater economic independence became
more clearly defined in the 1820s, spokesmen for the
American System gave clearer consideration to the relation

of the public lands to internal improvements and the tariff. Success in building up manufactures and a home market obviously required some diversion of capital and labor from the task of clearing the wilderness. For this purpose few publicly demanded an increase in the minimum price of $1.25 per acre; and, indeed, President Adams found it politically expedient to approve several special pre-emption measures which allowed squatters to purchase their clearings at that price. Much more politically feasible was the proposal for placing limits upon the amount of public lands offered for sale. By tending to drive up the price of the lands already on the market well above the minimum, restriction would serve to moderate in some degree the westward movement of the people. A similar effect might be achieved as carefully planned roads and canals increased the value of the surrounding lands.[20]

From another angle Richard Rush argued that the liberality of existing land laws fully justified the countervailing force to be gained by the "correlative duties" of tariff protection. And in all cases he and others rejected the rising demand to turn the national domain over to the states in which it was located, or the even more radical claim that the lands belonged, by natural right, to the people and not to the government. Rufus King of New York here voiced the common belief that the lands comprised a corporate trust fund for promoting the welfare of the whole nation. On this basis another proposal sought permanently to distribute land revenues to all of the states for purposes of education and internal improvement.[21]

Involved in the fulfillment of its economic goals, as many identified with the American System supposed, was also the good of increasing social and political order. In a negative way this impulse to order found expression in the undesirable alternatives some saw in a policy of uncontrolled expansion for the nation across space. Josiah Quincy voiced

anew the old Federalist fear that rapid multiplication of
states would eventually make it impossible to harmonize the
plurality of interests. Senator David Barton of Missouri
deplored, at the same time, the "natural propensity" of his
fellows to return to "the free and wild state of nature" in the
unsettled West. In a more general way Representative Silas
Wood of New York warned that, in default of some national
discipline, a Roman spirit of imperialism would develop.
"The spirit of conquest lessens the force of domestic at-
tachments," he explained, "relaxes the ties that bind society
together, and enfeebles the restraints of moral obligation."
The 1820s comprised a prime opportunity for the government to "mould the passions" of the people, Wood concluded, or else the passions of the people would ultimately
control the government.[22]

Many hoped, by contrast, that a policy for building up the
nation through time would bring greater stability and
order. Since emigration to the West weakened the force of
"social compacts," Jared Sparks welcomed the discipline of
the varied social institutions made possible by a denser
population. In a similar way diversity of economic pursuits
and social callings might bind people more closely together
through a keener awareness of the interdependent and
organic nature of the common life. Niles stressed the importance of full employment to be gained by national self-
sufficiency, believing it served far better than traditional
religion in promoting individual virtue and the general
good. Supremely, the spokesmen of the 1820s saw in public
education the one institution which could replace all the old
"establishments" in Europe. Education would enable talent
among the humble to rise and identify with the existing
order, so the reasoning went, while sustaining a larger sense
of shared values, historical memories, and common aspirations. The plan of distributing land revenues for education
thus might create order in a double sense, slowing down the

movement to the wilderness state of nature as it cultivated the "second nature" of the people where they were.[23]

By the widespread call for building a "national character" contemporaries generally summarized the good of order. The subjective spirit of national unity, renewed and deepened by the War of 1812, was now to be objectified and institutionalized. Niles rejoiced in the prospect of transforming the American people beyond the dreams of Ovid. A correspondent of Clay remarked how "momentous" the task while the nation still provided the "plastic" materials. One aspect of the task, as Clay himself saw it, was to fashion a new basis of patriotism. By moderating the movement to the West he hoped to retain the force of instinctive patriotism as one generation succeeded another in the same place. But the realities of great social mobility and the ideal of bettering one's condition required another and more rational kind of patriotism grounded in self-interest. By this process, the development of manufactures and the thickening patterns of internal commerce and improvements would create irreversible ties of Union, bringing new interests into being and relating them in the self-same process to the good of the whole. Indeed, Niles adopted the view that such "a close community of interests" would bind Americans far more strongly than "a daily recollection of their consanguinity." In this way, might the American System conquer space.[24]

As opponents often charged, the desire to build a national character actually involved the creation of a new national community across existing state and regional lines. Edward Everett protested that political reality lay with the states and that the Union was the "metaphysical thing"; yet the impulses existed for realizing more fully the essence of national unity. As Clay put it, there was the need to give economic and social substance to the "merely political" entity created by the fathers in the constitutional compact.[25]

In formal terms the Union was to be thought of as both a means and an end. It was an efficient instrument in the present for setting in motion the forces working through time for a more solid and durable order.

Within the framework of developing national order, finally, many advocates of the American System looked for qualitative progress in the common life of the nation. They wanted the quality of national life to keep pace with its material advancement. In contrast with the relative backwardness of a purely agricultural society, Richard Rush thought the encouragement of industry led in a more general way to progress in knowledge and "refinement in a nation." Since "excellence is of slow growth," however, he warned anew of the need to see the process in its corporate dimensions. In a similar vein, Alexander H. Everett noted how the diversity of economic pursuits and social callings served to elicit the wide range of talents in society and to realize more fully the potential of the national mind. He especially stressed the importance of a highly articulated social organism, for he deemed it the only milieu in which the creative genius of the country could blossom. Beyond its role in creating this milieu for cultural progress, others wanted the government, by its patronage of "establishments like those of Europe," to encourage more directly the arts and sciences.[26] Paradoxically, the national economic means of the American System would lead to the cosmopolitan end of a higher civilization, here defined in essentially European terms.

To be sure, some elements of what Henry Nash Smith called "primitivism" remained. According to Niles, the good society to be realized was one in which a balance of pursuits and the relative decentralization of industry precluded the European vices of density and overcivilization. In like spirit, Clay clung to the Jeffersonian view that an independent yeomanry was still necessary for political virtue and the permanence of the republic. Nevertheless they gave to the future a very optimistic and positive reading. Unsettled space was for them less a safety valve from the evils of civilization than the means for building up the good of civilization over the entire continent. By slowing down the movement to the West Alexander H. Everett believed that the "standard of civilization" would continue to rise in the old part of the Union and that the new part might cherish the hope of a similar elevation. Representative Tristam Burges of Rhode Island summarized the matter well: "Population, settlement, education, and improvement, will hold their united march until your whole territory, cultivated and improved, is filled with a well educated, great, and prosperous people."[27] If the evils of civilization would eventually overtake the nation, this approach at least indefinitely postponed the evil day by a more rational use of the valuable resource of empty space.

Among those identified with the American System John Quincy Adams most fully embraced what Charles A. Beard called the "idea of civilization." Noting the spirit of progress at work across the entire Western world, he reminded fellow Americans that the very end of the social compact was, "in the moral purposes of his Creator," to improve the condition of its members. The agenda of policies in his first annual message contemplated the progressive enrichment of a society in which every man could rise in the scale of being. The young nation would also be able to pay off its debts to the Old World and, by adding to the accumulating store of civilization, promote in a constructive way its mission to the world. A wise management of the national domain constituted the central political means, for he thought its revenues were a corporate fund for the long-run purposes of the nation. Not until near the end of his life did Adams provide a systematic statement of his concept of progress, but it pervaded all his public utterances and dreams. Only the practical failures of his administration could begin to match the grandeur of his vision of progress for a free people on a rich and relatively unsettled continent.[28]

Progress, order, economic self-sufficiency and independence—these were thus the leading goods to be realized for the nation by the American System. Considerable difference did obtain among its proponents about the exact priority of goods or the degree of emphasis to be placed on one or another of its policies. Beneath these variations, however, lay a common mode of perceiving the nation and its destiny within the process of time. It was a teleological way of thinking which focused not only upon the existing state of the Union but also upon what it could and ought to be.

A further understanding of the American System can be gained by considering the opposition which was arising by the end of the 1820s. Ranged under the standard of the old Republican orthodoxy, foes mounted a crusade against the system and more particularly against its incarnation in the administration of Adams. Until his death in 1826 ex-President Thomas Jefferson sounded the alarm, warning that the consolidating tendency of the day represented in a new form the perennial Tory aim of undermining the "primitive principles" of freedom. Younger disciples echoed the theme. Representative James K. Polk of Tennessee yearned for the "original republican simplicity & purity" with which the nation began its existence. Van Buren invoked anew the principle of strict construction and states' rights, while Calhoun hoped that another "revolution of 1800" might put the nation back on the old Republican track.[29]

It was one thing to call for a return to orthodox truth, however, and an entirely different matter to define it with any degree of precision. Closer analysis, indeed, reveals a lack of "system" among the foes of the American System. Instead, two fundamentally different concepts of the nation and its destiny were active. With some room for exceptions, these ideas roughly reflected the differences between the planters of the South and the plain republicans of the North.

Southern spokesmen, first of all, rejected the teleological view that the Union was at once a means and an end, an agency in the present for achieving through time a greater degree of order and nationality. In rejecting "the whole theory and its ideal consequences," Representative Archibald Austin of Virginia claimed that the true essence of the Union was to be found in the past, informed once and for all by the unchanging prescriptions of a written Constitution. Such a view clearly ruled out a liberal interpretation and the doctrine of precedents. Representative Andrew Stevenson of Virginia accordingly warned that "the mighty chain of constructive power" was in process of rearing a "splendid government" to replace the simple one designed by the fathers. Ideally, movement through time was to bring more of the same, Dr. Thomas Cooper of South Carolina agreed, but any fundamental change would present the need either to restore the Union to its original design or to dissolve it. Regarding the Union as a means for freedom and not an end in itself, he thus concluded that his fellows might one day be compelled "to calculate the value of our Union."[30]

Because of its unchanging essence, moreover, opponents of the American System denied that the permanence of the Union depended upon the policies of consolidation. In contrast to the call for the "artificial regulations" of government to fashion through time new objective bonds of Union, Senator Nathaniel Macon of North Carolina stressed the greater value of subjective feelings in linking the people of the various states and sections together.

"They must be bound together by love," he said. One such subjective bond of Union, according to John Randolph, rose up from a more elemental love of family, state, and section. To supplement the power of this instinctive patriotism, Representative John Tyler of Virginia would add the force of self-interest to be enlisted by simply leaving people alone. While "heart burnings" and even greater discontents would arise from the efforts of the government to harmonize irreducibly plural interests, he believed that irreversible bonds of Union could be forged by allowing men to be, as God had made them, essentially free from direction and control. The Union in this sense was not a "thickening" institutional or coercive presence, but rather a fellowship of freemen faithful to the simple charter made by the fathers.[31]

In purely economic terms, as well, southern spokesmen denied that the government played a history-making role for the good. The diversion of capital and labor into channels "dug by yourselves" would rather, Tyler protested, lead to multiplying evils through time. As, in substance, a tax on the export of domestic staples, first of all, a protective tariff wrought immediate injustice upon the agricultural interests and weakened thereby a vital source of national prosperity. By the inducements offered to capital and labor in certain enterprises, furthermore, high duties would drive up the costs of production in all other industries and make domestic productions generally less and less able to meet the challenge of foreign competition. The "land's end" of the American System would arrive when Congress prohibited imports altogether and, by a system of export bounties, made it possible for domestic productions to enter the foreign market. Injustice to the agricultural interests would reach its culmination as direct taxation replaced import duties for financing the central government. In the name of an "ideal good of the whole," Randolph bitterly complained, the happiness, prosperity, and hopes of the nation would be destroyed.[32]

As an alternative to the artificial effort by the government to build up the nation through time, opponents of the American System pointed to a destiny of spreading out across space. The existence of a vast wilderness naturally invited the best investment of capital and labor, Representative George McDuffie of South Carolina argued, for it stimulated most fully the self-interest of freemen seeking to better their condition. Only in this way could the good of the whole be truly achieved, Representative Philip P. Barbour of Virginia agreed, because he took the general interest to be nothing more than the aggregate of separate and individual interests. Expansion would also have the political effect of securing the permanence of that simple design the fathers originally gave to the federative Union. Rapid settlement of the West served to increase the pluralism of interests within the Union and, as Representative Christopher Rankin of Mississippi happily noted, the admission of new states lent added force against the efforts at further consolidation. Freedom from control, taken to be the essential national idea, would thus grow upon itself and help to preserve the Union in its unchanging form.[33]

Moral considerations likewise recommended the course of expansion. A protective tariff and its related policies for slowing down the westward movement would, Representative John Carter of South Carolina warned, superinduce "before their time, all the infirmities of old age." The evils of overcivilization in Europe—crowded cities and multiplying vices, vast inequalities of wealth, a servile laboring class, a moneyed aristocracy and political corruption—would then arise in the New World. Only the saving virtue of a sturdy yeomanry spread out across the continent, he argued, might assure permanence to the nation. With their goal of higher civilization, the proponents of the American

System clearly thought of freedom as a function of time, a corporate good to be more fully realized. But southern critics conceived of freedom rather as a function of space and, as such, a good likely to be subverted in the thickening process of time.[34] That Southerners viewed slavery in its relation to space and time in the same way is very revealing, and it demonstrates in another way how much their contribution to Jacksonian Democracy would be shaped by their peculiar institution.

Finally, Calhoun spelled out by the end of the 1820s that tendency in the thought of southern planters to condemn as pernicious the two-party system. But he approached this position, which many advocates of the American System shared, from an exactly opposite direction. John Quincy Adams among others rejected the need for a party system on the ground that the "good of the whole" to be realized in the future actually included the "true" interests of the present minority. Calhoun, by contrast, looked away from the consensus of the future to a consensus of the past. In writing the Constitution, he argued, the Founding Fathers had delegated very little power to the central government. It was to be a government of minorities, of irreducibly plural interests, and the political arena it defined was far too narrow to invite legitimate party contests for power. The very existence of intense party conflicts, as a consequence, bespoke subversion of this simple design and threatened the tyranny of a numerical majority. In this precise situation, nullification was a means for restoring the consensus of the past or, by compelling others to initiate the amending process, for defining a new consensus acceptable to the plural interests of the present. By the exercise of its veto power, each minority interest—in practicable terms, each state—might thereby preserve its freedom within the Union. Secession remained all the while as the ultimate defense of freedom, whenever it was thought the Union had become subverted beyond the hope of restoration.[35]

It was precisely at this point that the plain republicans of the North, for whom Van Buren spoke, stood most clearly in contrast with the planters of the South. While equally facile in using the Jeffersonian rhetoric of restoration, his chief aim was to restore the integrity of the Republican party itself after the no-party heresy of Presidents Monroe and Adams. Calhoun invoked the consensus of the past and Adams that of the future, but Van Buren here sought a means for organizing the consensus of the present. Faced with a pluralism of interests he sought neither to leave them in a disparate state of nature nor to harmonize them fully into a perfect unity. By a permanent party structure he wanted rather to achieve that degree of consensus which would provide for an orderly mode of permanent competition.[36]

The concept of a two-party system gave Van Buren and his followers a distinctly different means from that of Southerners for opposing the corporate and teleological bias of the American System. Minorities of the present were not to be incorporated into some future good of the whole, but would rather gain security for their freedom in the organized opportunity to replace the majority in power.[37] The frequent changes in party fortunes, in turn, obviously ruled out that degree of continuity and policy commitment which advocates of the American System believed necessary for promoting the general good. Greater focus upon the present thus tended to dispel the notion of a corporate pursuit of happiness sustained by the collective will of all generations.

By the same measure the good of the whole was no longer thought of as a teleological entity to be discerned and promoted in a positive way. It became easier to believe, instead, that the general good arose automatically as separate interests competed in the economic sphere and sought favors in the political arena from a government designed to extend aid, but not direction or control. In this sense the government exercised no history-making role, serving rather as a broker for the interests of the present majority.[38]

It was the "nominalism" in this outlook which Dangerfield took to be the essential spirit of rising democratic nationalism in the 1820s. Among the policy manifestations of this spirit were the Tariff of Abominations, piecemeal and unsystematic appropriations for internal improvements, and a growing demand from the West to turn the public lands over to the states and to individuals. Involved in this spirit as well was a distinct concept of the Union. Many associated with the American System conceived of the Union in formal terms as both a means and an end, while Southerners tended to view it ultimately as a means. Democratic nationalists such as Van Buren, by contrast, inclined to the idea of the Union as an end in itself, as the highest political good. It was valued so highly because it provided a frame of order, within which freemen of each successive generation might separately define and pursue the blessings of liberty. Behind the rhetoric of strict construction and states' rights lay the assumption that a national community already existed and a belief in the absolute rightness of the present majority to rule.[39]

In many obvious ways, then, the planters and plain republicans ranged under the Jackson banner in 1828 did not fully share a common view of the nature and destiny of the Union. Indeed, it was Van Buren's Tariff of Abominations which precipitated the nullification movement in South Carolina and defined the basic problem facing Jackson during his first administration. Only in the course of meeting the crisis of nullification would Jacksonian Democracy assume a clearer and more distinct form, one arrived at by the process of dismantling the policies of the American System.

4
Nullification and the Emergence of Jacksonian Democracy

The part President Andrew Jackson played in the nullification crisis has not been fully appreciated. One important reason for this has been the failure of his contemporaries and of many later historians to perceive the underlying unity in his thought about the nature of the Union and the proper role of the central government. Because of his views, Jackson was actually far more than Henry Clay the great compromiser. While opposing both the nullifiers and the proponents of the American System of policies, he supported with equal facility the dual aspect of compromise—the Force Bill and the new tariff. He agreed with Daniel Webster that liberty and the Union were one and inseparable, but he shared no less with Calhoun the view that the Union, as a means for freemen to pursue happiness, was one of severely limited powers. He would consolidate the power of the federal government in order to defend the Union against the threat of nullification. Yet he was equally prepared to undo the protective tariff and related policies and to devolve power on the states and the people. The "preservation of the rights of the several states and the integrity of the Union," he affirmed on the morrow

of compromise in 1833, constituted two "necessarily connected" goals of his administration.[1]

Many contemporaries of Jackson, however, found
nothing but contradiction between the "Federalist" consolidation of power to save the Union and the "Republicanism" in his states' rights pronouncements. Their comment was especially pointed with regard to the fuller statement of views which Jackson gave in two basic state papers
of the crisis—the Fourth Annual Message on December 4,
1832, and the Proclamation to the people of South Carolina
six days later. "One short week produced the message and
the proclamation," Clay observed, "the former ultra on the
side of State rights, the latter on the side of consolidation."
John Quincy Adams, back in Congress after his term as
President, found it no less difficult to reconcile "the glaring
inconsistencies of principle" lodged in the two documents.
In a lead editorial Hezekiah Niles exulted in the fact that
with the Proclamation Jackson had at least rejected the
"starched theories" of the Virginia school and embraced
the position of loose interpretation of the Constitution.
With opposite emotions, such elders of the old Republican
faith as John Randolph and Nathaniel Macon ruefully
agreed. In like fashion a South Carolina editor damned the
Proclamation as "black cockade Federalism," while another
found some cause for rejoicing in the fact that "we are again
Federalists and Republicans." Martin Van Buren, Vice-
President elect at the time, also thought that "some of the
doctrinal points of the Proclamation" violated the
President's true political faith. Upon further reflection, he
could only suppose that Jackson's lapse from consistency
betrayed the Federalist influences in the cabinet.[2]

Many historians have echoed this contemporary judgment. James Parton wanted to believe that the true Jackson
came out in the Proclamation. "It was such a blending of
argument and feeling," he wrote, "as Alexander Hamilton

would have drawn up for Patrick Henry." But he could find
no way at all to explain why Jackson accepted the new tariff
of 1833. "It would have been more like him to have vetoed
it," Parton helplessly concluded, "and I do not know why he
did not veto it." James Schouler, Hermann von Holst, and
John Bach McMaster also regarded the compromise as a
surrender to the nullifiers. The Force Bill accompanying
the tariff amounted to no real vindication of the absolute
Union, in their judgment, and Jackson's failure to test the
Union in 1833 only served to postpone a showdown.
Claude G. Bowers and Marquis James among later students
of the period have discovered a greater unity in Jackson's
actions and thought, but it was a kind of unity forged
mainly by the coalition of his personal and political
enemies. In a more critical vein Thomas P. Abernethy
could agree, for he supposed that Jackson always reacted to
events on the basis of personal feeling rather than of consistent principle or careful thought. John Spencer Bassett also
found that Jackson's constitutional views were more of sentiment than of close reasoning and that those views had
been nourished in the earlier Republican era. In a contradictory fashion, he thus concluded, Jackson "forsook his
old position, cast aside the formulas of his party, and declared for the Union when it was in danger." One of
Jackson's foremost critics at the present time, Charles M.
Wiltse, has passed severe judgment on this seeming inconsistency: "In four short years Jackson had led his party from
bitter opposition to the 'consolidating' tendencies of John
Quincy Adams to a form of authoritarianism that outdid
even the Alien and Sedition Acts of Adams' father."[3]

But for Jackson there appeared to be no contradiction at
all. In the name of the people—the planters and plain
republicans—the President embraced a view of the Union
which blended the key emphases of each element. Because
they felt the Union to be a true reflection of their will, plain

republicans would preserve it as the highest good. At the same time, planters were equally certain that the blessings of liberty within the Union could only be secured if freemen were left alone. As the spokesman of the people Jackson accordingly isolated two enemies of freedom to be routed.[4] One, the nullifiers, comprised a fretful minority of ambitious demagogues who sought by deluding the people to destroy the blessed Union. Hardly less alien to the true interests of the people was a second group made up of the narrow and selfish interests, the monopolists and promoters, who ever sought special favors from the government. Jackson would use force against the nullifiers and eliminate the need for force by restoring the true policies of the government. By holding in unity elements "Federalist" and "Republican," he stood ready in 1833 to enforce the peace.

On the "Republican" side of his thought Jackson did not get around to a systematic statement on the issues of the day until his Fourth Annual Message on December 4, 1832. The timing of the statement is very revealing; for it came within five months of the Bank veto, shortly after the Presidential contest with Clay, on the very heels of South Carolina's Ordinance of Nullification. Thomas Hart Benton later claimed that the message truly formulated the mandate Jackson had won in the election of 1832 against Clay. Many of Clay's supporters, by contrast, regarded the message as a total surrender to the nullifiers. It was both and more. In proposing to remove the real grievances of the nullifiers by a repeal of the American System, Jackson sought to save the Union in a peaceful way by what the Washington *Globe* took to be "the restoration of the primitive simplicity and purity of our institutions."[5]

In the tone of the message, no less than in its specific provisions, Jackson evinced the desire to dismantle the American System of policies. He wanted on principle to reduce the power of the federal government and to remand the pursuit of happiness more completely to the states and the people. The first of his four basic recommendations called for the government to dispose of all its shares in private improvement corporations. Along with the likelihood of removing the deposits from the Bank of the United States, he hoped that such a policy would reduce the government to "that simple machine" intended by the Founding Fathers for "discharging unfelt" most of its functions. Jackson, in the second place, called for a gradual, but certain, reduction of the tariff to a "revenue standard." By comparison with his earlier statements that protection was in some degree both expedient and just, this represented a new and far more unequivocal position. Equally clear was his attitude lodged in the proposal, for in contrast to earlier nationalist sentiments he now regarded most advocates of protection as self-seeking monopolists. A third part of the message repeated his earlier strictures against a general system of internal improvements. Because the country was so extended and diverse in soils, climate, and pursuits, he argued that only a few projects could be truly national in their nature. The log-rolling "combinations to squander the treasure of the country" thus represented the artificial majorities of the selfish interests. They not only undermined the true will of the people to be left alone, but they also threatened to destroy the popular respect for the sacred principle of majority rule.[6]

A final feature of the message pertained to the public lands. Jackson's official silence on the issue was now broken by the proposal to reduce the price of the public lands for actual settlers to a level barely sufficient to cover the costs of administering them. The speedy settlement of the lands to be achieved by this policy might, he believed, promote the "true interest" of the nation in two ways. It would multiply the number of freemen across space and, by hastening the withdrawal of the national administration from the landed

states, help to restore the proper balance of power among
the different parts of the federative Union.[7] Such a policy,
in any event, clearly rejected the corporate concept, as held
by many in the American System, that the lands were a
common fund for enriching and building up through time
the life of the whole nation.

In two particulars, one of exclusion and one of inclusion,
the Fourth Annual Message obviously reflected, as the
critics claimed, the pressure of the nullifiers. Jackson made
no mention, in the first instance, of his earlier plan for
turning over to the states the surplus revenues of the federal treasury. The plan, fully outlined in the first two years
of his administration, offered a solution to what he considered the chief problem of the day, namely, the mounting
evil of "flagicious logg-rolling" appropriations for internal
improvements. The matter urgently demanded a permanent settlement, he thought, because the impending retirement of the national debt would otherwise make even
greater sums of money available for the legislative
"scramble."[8] But the aspect of the distribution scheme most
relevant to the nullifiers was its bearing upon the tariff, for
they feared that the withdrawal of revenues from the treasury would make it necessary to maintain import duties at a
high level. John C. Calhoun and Robert Y. Hayne thus
stood in bitter opposition, arguing that Jackson's plan assured the permanence of the policy of protection.[9] Against
their protests before 1832 the President had persisted, but
his silence on distribution now indicated an acquiescence in
their views.

By his clear and explicit call for reducing the tariff to a
revenue standard, Jackson responded in a second way to
the demands of the nullifiers. Before the election of 1828
he had actually shared many of Clay's nationalist sentiments about protection. Though his early remarks on the
question as President were more judicious, they still pro-

vided grounds for some degree of protection. The support he gave to the new tariff measure in 1832 betrayed this same point of view, because that measure did retain real elements of protection.[10] By removing the duty on many items not produced in the country, as many nullifiers justly observed, the new tariff fixed the principle all the more. Jackson hailed it as a permanent settlement, however, and expressed the belief that the reduced duty on cotton bagging and coarse woolens among other things would remove the real grievances in the South. The new tariff was not to go into effect until the following year, yet he confidently predicted in 1832 that the nullification movement would soon die down.[11] When the nullifiers in South Carolina belied his prophecy and brought matters to a head in late November, Jackson asked Congress to make new tariff concessions to replace the measure which he had shortly before regarded as a permanent one. There is no certain knowledge about who assisted Jackson in preparing the Fourth Annual Message, but it is hard to escape the conclusion that the call for a revenue tariff clearly represented a bow to the pressure of the nullifiers.[12]

In this way Jackson sought to preserve the Union by peaceful means. He did not, it was true, dictate the specific provisions that made up the tariff part of the compromise in 1833. The Verplanck Bill, under administration auspices, called for a reduction in existing duties by fifty percent within a two-year period. The successful Clay substitute, by contrast, proposed more gradual reductions at two-year intervals until the maximum level of twenty percent had been reached by 1842. A home valuation clause, moreover, and the proviso that the largest reductions be held off until 1842 served to make the measure more protectionist than Jackson desired.[13] But his demand for some kind of tariff concessions did compel Clay to come up with an alternative proposal, since the demand apparently voiced a growing popular sentiment against protection. That such a sail-trimmer on the tariff as Van Buren came out unequivocally for reduction in 1833 attested the pressure. Clay frankly admitted as much in his call for fellow protectionists in the Senate to help salvage something from impending ruin. He wanted, as he later explained, "to protect manufacturers for the present and gain time with its chapter of accidents." In his praise of Clay, manufacturer Abbot Lawrence thus expressed the hope that by 1842 "a great change in public sentiment" would assure the restoration of full protection. Benton wryly concluded that, under Jackson's pressure, the manufacturers who had left home to oppose Clay's bill stayed over in Washington to give it strong support.[14]

In addition to the force he exerted on the tariff matter, Jackson did exercise a determining voice on one substantive part of the compromise. He gave a pocket veto to the bill Clay had pushed through Congress along with the tariff for distributing land revenues to the states. The bill had passed both houses with some southern support and, according to Adams, had been regarded by many as "an equivalent for the tariff." One sympathetic editor, indeed, saw fit to characterize the measure as "at least of equal importance" with the new measure on import duties. For this reason Benton warned in the Senate that success for the distribution scheme might give new life to the entire American System.[15] By his veto, then, Jackson triumphantly asserted his opposition to this form of direction and control over the nation's course.

If the "Republicanism" in Jackson's thought supplied one basis for compromise in 1833, his "Federalism" provided another, for he regarded the Force Bill as an integral part of the settlement. In announcing a new system of policies for freemen, he also insisted on proclaiming that their Union was indissoluble. "I have always thought that Congress should reduce the tariff to the wants of the Government," he remarked after the compromise, "and the passage of such a bill became peculiarly proper after Congress had, by the passage of the 'enforcing' bill, so fully shewn to the world that she would not be deterred by a faction."[16] Jackson actually took certain liberties with the truth here, because the Force Bill did not clear the House until after the passage of the tariff measure. The substantial fact remained, however, that he could sign a new tariff bill because it was accompanied by a vigorous resolve to maintain the integrity of the government. It is otherwise hard to believe that the President would have accepted the one without the other. The reasoning of Representative Charles F. Mercer of Virginia, a former Federalist, clearly reflected this attitude. He justified his vote against the tariff solely on the grounds that it had not been preceded by the Force Bill. The order of their passage, he insisted, "was of material consequence to the character of the nation."[17]

It would, of course, be easy to argue that personal feelings alone inspired Jackson's forceful posture. His privately expressed desire to march in person with an army to arrest Calhoun and other nullifiers, Van Buren admitted, was a feeling that approached "to a passion." When Clay and Calhoun threatened with their tariff substitute to run away with all the glory for bringing peace to the country, Jackson doubtless tended to look on the Force Bill as in some degree a face-saving device. "It is due to the country, it is due to me," he prodded Senator Felix Grundy of Tennessee, that the measure be passed ahead of Clay's tariff bill.[18] But he also regarded the issue in a far larger perspective. While Benton skulked and Van Buren cautiously advised against making the crisis "a season for the settlement or discussion of abstract propositions," Jackson persisted. "The preservation of the Union," he sharply reminded the incoming Vice President, "is the supreme law." He wanted to fix the principle that the Union was indissoluble. He also wanted to make the Force Bill a test of party loyalty no less than of patriotism. "Lay all delicacy aside," he instructed Grundy about the vote in the Senate, "and compel every man's name to appear on the journals that the nullifiers may *all* be distinguished from those who are in support of the laws and the Union." He recognized many close personal friends from the South among the nullifiers, yet he wanted the people back home to know that as "traitors at heart" they could no longer claim his support.[19]

Nor was Jackson's determination to preserve the Union the impulse of the moment or the exclusive product of his counsellors. In 1828, to go no further back, he gave voice to the idea of an absolute Union. "There is nothing I shudder at more," he wrote to a prospective nullifier, "than the idea of a separate Union." His memorable toast at the Jefferson Day dinner in 1830 expressed the same sentiment and found fuller explication in a letter to South Carolina Unionists.[20] In 1831 Jackson bluntly turned down Hayne's nominee for a federal post in Charleston on the grounds that a nullifier could not truly serve the Union. "Note," he said, "I draw a wide difference between State Rights and the advocates of them, and a Nullifier." When he came to issue the famous Proclamation, then, the sentiments were his own. Parton vividly described the feverish speed with which Jackson dashed off the first draft and the persistence with which he clung to its basic ideas. Edward Livingston put it in more formal language, but remained under the critical supervision of the President. Not even Major William Lewis could prevail on him to change certain passages calculated to rankle old line Republicans. "Those are my views," he insisted, "and I will not change them nor strike them out." It was true that in the special message to Congress on January 16, 1833, calling for the Force Bill, he did not include some of the more controversial points. Yet he concluded it with the ringing affirmation that "the Constitution and the laws are supreme and the *Union indissoluble*."[21]

Jackson's forceful resolve also served, no less than his willingness to make tariff concessions, as an efficient instrument for compromise. His appeal in the Proclamation to "the good sense of the people" gave him great power for that purpose, for he claimed that the overwhelming response of the "yeomanry of the country" served as a constitutional referendum for the absolute Union. With such support Jackson was able to bring great pressure to bear on South Carolina and, indeed, dramatic proof of it soon appeared. On January 21, 1833, only five days after the special message of the President to Congress requesting a Force Bill, an unofficial meeting of leaders in Charleston undid, in effect, the solemn decree of the state convention, by putting off, beyond February 1, 1833, the time when nullification was to go into operation. It was this postponement, Clay then argued, which opened the way to compromise on the tariff, for it helped to parry the charge that concessions were being extorted from the government by a faction.[22] Calhoun, meanwhile, faced rather harsh alternatives. His acceptance of the more protectionist measure of Clay rather than the Verplanck bill spared him the humiliation of receiving peace from Jackson's hand. But the choice did compel him to travel posthaste to South Carolina in order to try to convince the reassembled state convention that the compromise tariff represented a victory for nullification.[23]

No one was in a position to claim a total victory. In its dual aspect, however, the compromise settlement in 1833 embodied most positively Jackson's views. Many of the postmortems of the crisis recognized in one way or another that Jackson had taken a truly middle ground. John Quincy Adams on one side damned the President for not being "Federalist" enough. Had the Fourth Annual Message been

in "the spirit of the Proclamation," he contended, and had
the Force Bill stood alone without new tariff concessions,
then Jackson might have become the greatest benefactor to
the country since George Washington. But by "halting between Washington, Federalism, and nullification," Jackson
let the grand opportunity slip away. From the other side
Calhoun condemned the President for not being "Republican" enough. Though Jackson claimed to be a votary of the
old faith, Calhoun called him a "pseudo-Republican" who
acted "on the extreme ultra principles of our old opponents." Calhoun therefore longed for a "contest openly
between the two parties" which would compel Jackson to
give up his middle ground. Niles agreed, for he saw only
confusion in the party lines of the nullification crisis. Others
even supposed that Webster, who had given strong support
to the Force Bill, might become a leading minister in
Jackson's administration. But they failed to perceive that
the President's Federalism, unlike that of Webster, blended
with its erstwhile opposite. Isaac Hill, a New Hampshire
partisan of the President, pointed to the difference very
clearly. "Wait till Jackson gets at the Bank again," he wrote
reassuringly to Van Buren, "and then the scalping knives
will glisten once more."[24]

That the monopolists remained the common enemy of
the people after the rout of the nullifiers no less than before
found new expression in Jackson's own afterthoughts of
the crisis. "Nullification, the corrupting influence of the
Bank, the union of Calhoun and Clay, supported by the
corrupt and wicked of all parties," he wrote to James
Buchanan, "engaged all my attention." Liberty and the
Union were inseparable goods, in his view, and the security
of the one necessarily involved the preservation of the
other. "The liberty of the people," he concluded, "requires
that wicked projects, and evil combinations against the government should be exposed and counteracted."[25]

Jacksonian Democracy thus assumed greater form in the course of routing the enemies of freedom. It represented a synthesis in some sense of the "thesis" of corporate freedom and the "antithesis" of radical federative freedom espoused by the nullifiers. In terms of specific policies, the Babel of voices heard among the Jacksonian hosts in 1828 began to fade away, for some degree of "system" came in the process of dismantling the American System of policies. There is a good deal of justice in the claim, made by a recent biographer, that the old Republican credo of James K. Polk contained the essential tenets of the new party orthodoxy. As formulated in the Fourth Annual Message, the general principle of freedom from direction and control gained specific expression in Jackson's strictures against the protective tariff, internal improvements, central management of the public domain and, as the issue came into focus during his administration, the Second Bank of the United States.[26]

Ideologically, the new synthesis gained the great moral force that came with the claim of its being a true revival of the old Republican faith. As many contemporaries viewed the matter, the impending retirement of the national debt provided a practicable political opportunity for that purpose. Freedom from the encumbrances of the past had placed the nation in "a new latitude," Representative Churchill C. Cambreleng of New York observed, and "substituted for debates about woolens, cottons, iron, and sugar, questions involving not only constitutional powers, but the fundamental distinction between a confederate and a national government." Now that the land at last belonged to the living, in Jefferson's phrase, the specific measures to be adopted would be of seminal importance, resembling less the acts of ordinary legislation than of a constituent assembly. Jackson embraced the occasion to undo the policies which had grown up around the debt in the past and

thereby to prevent the nation from being irreversibly com-
mitted in the future to an unnatural course. "In regard to
most of our great interests," he exulted, "we may consider
ourselves as just starting in our career, and after a salutary
experience about to fix upon a permanent basis the best
policy to promote the happiness of the people and facilitate
their progress toward the most complete enjoyment of civil
liberty." The true task of the statesman was not to exercise a
positive history-making role over the future but, in Mircea
Eliade's terms, to peel away the evil accretions of time and
make an "eternal return" to the unchanging design of the
fathers.[27]

The vigorous use of the executive veto might, from
another point of view, be thought of as exhibiting what H.
Richard Niebuhr took to be the dynamics of Protestant
revivalism, namely, that of affirmation by negation—of
reform accompanied by revival of faith. A New York partisan at the time explicitly rejected the charge that Jackson's
high-handed acts pointed to executive tyranny and the total
consolidation of the government. To the contrary, he argued, the President stood on the ramparts of the Constitution to guard against "legislative encroachments" calculated
to bring in their train the evils of time. Jackson likewise
professed the simple goal of restoring the government to
"that simple machine which the Constitution created." His
course of action amounted, in effect, to a self-liquidating
crusade which would end when truth had been restored.[28]

The response of partisans reflected the moral and emotional dimensions of the crusade. With the veto of the
Maysville Road bill Representative Philip P. Barbour of
Virginia hoped that Jackson had brought to a happy close a
thirty-year cycle of gradual degeneration. He praised the
moral courage of the President for recurring to the "original principles" established in the Revolution and reaf-

firmed by Jefferson in the "revolution of 1800." Representative Polk thought the cycle of declension had been of shorter duration, coming chiefly with the American System after 1815, but he equally rejoiced to see Jackson "restore the Constitution to its original reading." In like fashion the Washington *Globe* reckoned the Bank veto an even sublimer spectacle than the Battle of New Orleans. By routing a moneyed aristocracy and its British cohorts, it turned back that "creeping poison" aimed at the very vitals of the free republic. "His message will be hailed by the true Whigs of this day as a *second Declaration of Independence*," the *Globe* concluded, "which they will support with no less ardor and self devotion than their fathers did the first." Though more restrained, the editor of the Richmond *Enquirer* yet professed to find in Jackson's first administration hopeful signs that the "vessel of State" was at last "coming back to the Republican tack."[29]

For the future, as well, Jackson warned his fellows to be vigilant against further efforts to subvert freedom. He invoked for this purpose the old Republican stricture against the exercise of a doubtful power, and he looked to the presidential veto as a means for compelling others to initiate the amending process. If one more than one-fourth of the states thereupon opposed an explicit grant of new power, then he reasoned that the discontents would "far overbalance" any possible good.[30] By giving in to western demands for a more liberal land policy, southern pressure for a lower tariff, and general discontent with improvements Jackson seemed to regard the role of the government as that of a negative broker—as one disposed to undo existing policies and to forebear the adoption of others likely to produce new "heartburnings." In the same mood, he leaned to the view of party as a temporary movement aimed at restoring the originally narrow arena of the central government and not as a permanently organized system of competition for its ample favors. Party activity was, in effect, a species of Protestant revivalism.

The Union, in this Protestant view of things, was to be regarded less as an institutional presence than as a fellowship of freemen faithful to the unchanging essence of the Constitution. Its ultimate bond was that of subjective feeling, of popular affection sustained by a scrupulous observance of the covenant of freedom. Jackson specifically rejected the corporate impulse in the American System to thicken and objectify the bonds of Union. "In thus attempting to make our General Government strong we make it weak," he argued. "Its true strength consists in leaving individuals and States as much as possible to themselves—in making itself felt, not in its power, but in its beneficence; not in its control, but in its protection; not in binding the States more closely to the center, but leaving each to move unobstructed in its proper orbit." He would, in other terms, "rivet the attachment of our citizens to the Government" by simply leaving them alone.[31] Freedom in an eternal present from the prescriptive force of past policies and of future controls at once defined the nature and assured the permanence of the Union.

But in this Jacksonian scheme of things, the Union to be restored was an absolute. While most southern planters regarded secession as an ultimate safety valve for freedom, the element of plain republicanism in the Jacksonian synthesis held liberty and the Union to be one and inseparable. "With us, therefore, the Union is *sacred*," Amos Kendall said during the campaign of 1832. "Its preservation is the *only* means of preserving our civil liberty. We look upon the enemies of the Union as the enemies of liberty."[32]

Jackson brought to bear upon this position the emotional force of his own experience and perceptions. He could only judge as "madness and folly" the disposition of the plain people in South Carolina to follow the nullifiers to the point of becoming "the destroyers of their own prosperity and liberty." In the order of Providence he supposed the Union was the "only means" for pursuing the blessings of liberty.[33] He made no mention of the "old thirteen" during the nullification crisis as a link in the great chain of being, for the Union served much better in an age of mobility and leveling as a giver of identity and the guarantor of the future. Though he thought it contained too many "Federalist" heresies, Representative Cambreleng yet admitted that the President's Proclamation made the mass of people "think and feel like men." Most of all the reality of national growth across space seemed to shape Jackson's thought about the indissoluble Union. It was very revealing that the "one absurdity out of thousands" he found in the doctrine of the nullifiers pertained to a new and not to an old state. He rejected out of hand the right of Louisiana, carved out of territory acquired since the Revolution, to nullify a federal law or secede from the Union and thereby block the outlet of the Mississippi River.[34] The federative nature of the national existence involved a proper distribution of power within the Union, as Jackson saw the matter, and not a theory of its origins or its possible dissolution.

Jackson's more formal thought about the Union reinforced these feelings. The contradictory statements about its origin provide one example. In the Nullification Proclamation three separate times were given for the beginning of the Union. By calling the Constitution "our social compact," he appeared to favor 1787. Yet if the Union were "coeval with our political existence," as he also stated, then the year 1776 had a better claim. At another point he declared that even "before the declaration of independence we were known in our aggregate character as *the United Colonies of America*." A fourth date was given in his correspondence, for here he supposed the "confederated per-

petual union" had been established by the Articles of
Confederation.[35] Confusion also marked his thought about
the parties who had formed the Union. In the Proclamation
he flirted with the view of Webster that it had been brought
into existence by the people as one national body, but elsewhere he took the Union to be the creature of pre-existing
sovereign states. This uncertainty, if not unconcern, for a
precise theory of the origin of the Union, however, contrasted sharply with his great certainty and concern about
one matter vital to its preservation. He thought of the
constitutional compact, whether formed by the states or the
people, as one of sacred and binding obligation. "Because
the Union was formed by a compact," Jackson said with
Calhoun clearly in mind, "it is said the parties to that compact may, when they feel themselves aggrieved, depart
from it; but it is precisely because it is a compact that they
cannot."[36]

If a concern for the integrity of the Union comprised the
distinctive contribution of plain republicans to the Jacksonian synthesis, it involved as well a pragmatic concept of the
nature of freedom within the Union. This can be clearly
seen by considering what, precisely, Jackson was trying to
restore. He did not seek a literal return to a supposed
unequivocal and unchanging essence in the Constitution, as
many planters professed to do, but rather to "revive that
devoted patriotism and spirit of compromise which distinguished the sages of the Revolution and the fathers of our
Union."[37] Except for the National Bank, it is revealing that
his call for undoing the American System of policies placed
no absolute constitutional ban on any other of its measures.
Protection might still be secured as an incident of raising
revenue by import duties; roads, canals, and harbor improvements judged "national" in scope could be promoted
with federal funds; and his proposal for a more liberal land

policy took issue in no way with the claim that the lands belonged to the government and not to the people.

It was true that Jackson advised Congress not to exercise any doubtful constitutional power. His vetoes often assumed, at the same time, a Rousseau-like concept of the general will of the people to be left alone, which stood in contrast to a particular will of the majority fashioned by log-rolling combinations in Congress. But at last Jackson would make the will of the present majority the final arbiter of constitutional meaning. Against the claims of the numerical majority, Calhoun had adduced the right of the concurrent majority, for he believed the veto power of the state could alone preserve freedom in the federative Union. Jackson at this point could only plead anew for the redeeming virtue of the people: "they will always in the end bring about the repeal of any obnoxious laws which violate the Constitution."[38]

In the context of the nullification crisis, this pragmatic democratic temper did provide a solid basis of compromise. Because the Union comprised the "only means" for pursuing the blessings of liberty, the Washington *Globe* proclaimed its preservation "a thousand times more important" than any specific measure freemen in the present might consider. Representative Cambreleng, in like spirit, deplored the "fire and brimstone" with which Webster supported the Force Bill and opposed tariff concessions. The people would not, Senator Silas Wright agreed, "balance this happy government against ten cents upon a pound of wool."[39] Throughout the crisis Van Buren also breathed the spirit of "mutual concession and compromise." His efforts to counter the "Federalist" influences around the President betrayed an anxiety to maintain the political allegiance of Virginia, and the South generally, to the party he had forged of planters and plain republicans.

By its tendency to organize and sustain conflicts along national rather than sectional lines, a vital two-party system might thus serve as an efficient instrument in preserving the Union of freemen.[40]

When the existence of the Union no longer hung in the balance, however, the democratic compromisers were more disposed than the planters to make the government an active means in the pursuit of happiness. Thus Wright and others might ask once more for ten cents on wool and argue that the duties would serve merely to protect existing interests and not, as advocates of the American System hoped, to create new interests and rearrange the whole. On a piecemeal and unsystematic basis, moreover, appropriations for roads and canals during Jackson's administration greatly increased in volume after his veto of the Maysville Road bill. The government was to play no history-making role, yet it was assumed that the destiny of the nation would be a happy one as freemen pursued their interests with the aid, but not control, of their government.[41] Jackson had acted as a negative broker during the nullification crisis to undo the policies which caused discontent, but his embrace of majority rule made it possible for the government to become a positive broker of present interests. While seeking by the dismemberment of the American System to make the government leave the people alone he provided no absolute rule, as the nullifiers rightly saw, to make the people leave the government alone.

The makeup of Jacksonian Democracy by the end of the nullification crisis was thus characterized by ambiguity and paradox. Its predilection for the simplicity and virtue of the Early Republic, as Marvin Meyers has well remarked, stood in striking contrast to the passion for unfettered enterprise in a new age of democratic capitalism. The view of the government as a negative broker for dismantling past controls jostled, however uneasily, with the concept of the government as a positive broker for abetting enterprise in an unplanned future. The urge to remove the evils of time and restore the narrow political consensus of the past found voice in an effectively organized political party. The appeal to the old social order and stability of the past, meanwhile, betrayed the reality of great mobility and change in the age of equalitarianism. In these and other ways students within the entrepreneurial school have sought, with a good deal of success, to explain the nature of Jacksonian Democracy.[42]

By neglecting the slaveholding element, however, and by focusing chiefly upon the central role of the Bank war they have overlooked one important aspect of the paradox. The present chapter, rather, contends that Jacksonian Democracy took on much of its form in the process of meeting the nullification crisis.[43] The common presence of what were reckoned to be two enemies of freedom—the American System and the nullifiers—provided content to the revival of the old Republican faith, which had been promised by the end of the 1820s. On the equivocal grounds of federative freedom from control, many planters and plain republicans could remain together; and it was this outlook which would give predominant shape to the political dialogue of the nation from the nullification crisis to the end of the following decade.

5
Manifest Destiny

From the nullification controversy to the outbreak of the Mexican War the initiative and shape to the national debate came from the ideology of Jacksonian Democracy. By the end of the 1830s the newly established *Democratic Review* gave systematic expression to this position. Taking as its motto, "The world is governed too much," the review pleaded for a larger freedom from the force of past prescriptions and from the coercion of present institutions. Through the workings of the "voluntary principle," it rather supposed, individual "floating atoms" would naturally create and sustain an order "far more perfect and harmonious" than any the "fostering hand" of a paternalistic government might ever devise. In his war on the Second Bank of the United States, President Jackson manifested this idea of larger liberty and generated, as well, a more pervasive spirit of hostility to all forms of government monopoly and privilege. Equality of opportunity for freemen to pursue their several interests in the present, it was claimed, would automatically promote the good of the whole nation and make more manifest its glorious destiny. Of special interest here was the impulse in the Jacksonian outlook to rapid expansion and, with it, the tendency in its spokesmen to make more explicit the idea of freedom as a function of open and unsettled spaces. The floor of the growing empire of freemen, the *Democratic Review* thus exulted, would be "a hemisphere," and its roof would be "the firmament of the star-studded heavens."[1] At last a happy and progressive nation would vindicate the universal truth of its idea of freedom from control.

Fuller analysis of three points will serve to illuminate the course of the national debate from the nullification crisis in the early 1830s to the end of the following decade. A close look will first be given to the way Daniel Webster and John Quincy Adams defended the American System in the crisis against what they reckoned to be the iconoclasm of President Jackson. Secondly, it will be shown how, in a dialectical fashion, many Jacksonians argued for manifest destiny as the true alternative to the American System. Finally, consideration will be given to the clear, but ineffectual, opposition posed by Whig spokesmen in the 1840s to the imperatives of national expansion.

The response of Webster and Adams to the dismantling of the American System during the nullification crisis reveals a good deal about the thrust of Jacksonian Democracy. By their support of the Force Bill, both affirmed the integrity of the Union against the threat of the nullifiers. But they equally opposed the President's other compromise tactic, namely, that of lowering the tariff and undoing with his veto its related policies. While agreeing with Jackson that liberty and the Union were not so easily separated, they conceived of freedom within the Union in a far different way. Both remained identified with a corporate view of social man within the process of time. By its dual emphasis on the good of order from the past and on improvement to be realized through some degree of planning for the future, this corporate concept served to place in sharper relief the Jacksonian impulse to a larger liberty for individuals in the present and a manifest destiny of expansion for the nation.[2]

Throughout the nullification controversy, to consider

Webster first of all, the Massachusetts Senator stressed the order of Union as the highest good. It was an "absolute and vital necessity to our welfare," he told the Senate in reply to Robert Y. Hayne. Later public addresses developed more fully the theme of its "transcendent value," while the speech against Calhoun on the Force Bill brought into fullest form his legal argument for the Union as an end in itself.[3]

In its highest function Webster conceived of the Union under the Constitution as essentially religious in character. It gave stable form to liberty, as he had observed earlier, and thus enabled each generation of freemen to relate itself meaningfully in "the great chain of being." Primal chaos, in such a view, was the only alternative. The emotional appeal and choice of symbols in his reply to Hayne made this very clear. By using a chain, a temple, or a constellation as a symbol Webster dramatized the awful possibility that the snapping of any link, the collapse of a single column, or the bolting of any one star would involve the whole in ruin. Nullification led to secession, he warned, and secession from the "happy constellation" of Union could not stop until all had descended, "star after star, into obscurity and night."[4] The practical import of Hayne's position, as he changed the figure, brought the nation to "the precipice of disunion" and threatened a fatal plunge to "the depths of the abyss below." Repelled by the very thought of disunion, he chose "not to penetrate the veil" to see what might lie hidden in "the dark recess behind."[5]

Less emotion marked Webster's later speeches after the confrontation with Hayne, for popular approval assured him that the Union was safe. But the attribute of order remained central in his thought about the destiny of the Union and the ways freemen pursued happiness within it. In regard to economic policies, as a consequence, he defended the status quo against Jackson's efforts to dismantle the American System. Many at the time hailed the end of the debt as a propitious opportunity for putting the country on a new course. Webster, alarmed rather by the "morbid sort of fervor" on the subject in some quarters, wanted to cling to the existing policies. "The duty of the Government, at the present moment," he said with reference to the tariff, "would seem to be to preserve, not to destroy; to maintain the position which it has assumed. . . ." As a spokesman for the earlier free trade interests in New England, he had long opposed government aid to industry. With considerable capital in his section now diverted into manufacturing, he argued for protection as the "settled course of public policy."[6]

Personal and sectional interests also helped to inspire his protest against Jackson's veto of the bill for rechartering the Second Bank of the United States. "This message," he declared ominously, "calls us to the contemplation of a future, which little resembles the past." In answer to the constitutional scruples of the President he cited the authority of usage and precedent, of the nation's acquiescence in a national bank for forty years. He deplored as well the dislocation which the end of the bank would cause in an economy adapted to its powerful and benign influences. But the greatest alarm was produced by the iconoclastic spirit of the day, he confessed, by the "unaccountable disposition to destroy the most useful and most approved institutions of the Government."[7]

As he looked to the future, then, Webster adduced no new system of policies to shape the destinies of the country. He wanted its course to unfold in a more organic fashion under the steady direction of past policies. Whatever changes were to be made, he supposed, should reflect the new and imperious needs of the time. His votes for western improvements and for special pre-emption laws provided a case in point and illustrated as well his ability to transcend narrow sectional interests. The government was less a

planner of the future, in his way of thinking, than an agency
to comprehend new interests and to harmonize them all.
"The interests of all must be consulted, and reconciled, and
provided for, so far as possible," he explained, "that all may
perceive the benefits of a united government." His earlier
reluctance to place the great interests of the country under
the patronage of government had arisen from the professed belief that harmony could come only where all were
left alone. Now Webster accepted the statesman's task as a
more positive and creative one. His earlier fears that freedom for most people would be doomed in an industrial age
likewise gave way to the hope that laborers under the protection of the government might also acquire "a stake in the
welfare of that community."[8]

A recent student, taking note of the conversion by 1828
from a negative to a more active concept of government,
has concluded that Webster was essentially a player of
roles.[9] The Massachusetts Senator sought, in any case, to
conserve what he took to be the realities of developing
national unity. While the tariff and related policies already
reflected the facts of interdependence, he rejoiced that one
effect of those policies would be to create even stronger ties
of mutual interest. Retrospectively, indeed, he imputed
that same purpose to the Founding Fathers. Consolidation
had been, he affirmed, "the very end of the constitution."
As the bonds of Union grew stronger, he believed that a
fuller "national character" would continue to emerge out of
the disparate elements. Nor did this process rule out moderate growth for the Union across territory already in its
possession. He would "bring the interests of these new
States into the Union," he told a New York audience in
1831, "and incorporate them more closely in the family
compact."[10] But Webster did anticipate here his later opposition to new territorial acquisitions, for he assumed that

there were geographical limits to the development of a homogeneous nation. The destiny of the Union thus involved in large measure the realization of the existing elements of solidarity.

Freedom for each generation caught up in this process had about it a distinctly historical quality. Webster made this clear in the way he vindicated the right of the numerical majority to rule. The will of the numerical majority truly expressed the will of the nation as a whole, he explained, but only when it operated within the framework of the Constitution, the prescriptions of the past, and ultimately the interpretations of the courts. Without the judiciary, Webster ever argued, the Union would cease to exist. In contrast to Jackson's predilection for "mere majorities," he thought the Union of freemen rested on the collected will of all generations. In larger perspective, he deemed freedom in America to be in the family line of English liberties gained and disciplined through the centuries. The American Revolution, in this light, represented a supremely conservative act. Freedom was hence to be regarded less a universal impulse in man than a social product of time, with a history and a pedigree of its own. It was, he explained, "our established, dear-bought, peculiar American liberty."[11]

In two aspects of his formal thought about the Union Webster managed, by taking liberties with the contract theory, to conserve the new national order. He professed to believe, it was true, that the Union was "artificial and founded on agreement." By the way he thought of the parties to the agreement and of the time when it was made, however, he apparently took new ground.[12] Accepting as a literal fact the preamble phrase, "We the people," he insisted that the Constitution had been formed by the people as a whole and not by several peoples separately organized

in state communities. This position involved the further
notion that the people as a whole had organized before
1787, that the Union was older than the Constitution. With
the First Continental Congress in 1774, Webster rather
noted at one point, the people constituted themselves "in
some measure, and to some national purposes," a body
politic. But the agreement in this case could not have been a
very conscious one, for none could possibly have realized
the full consequences of the act. In effect, he read back into
the period before 1787 that sense of nationality which had
subsequently developed. It was, in any case, good patriotic
pedagogy, if not good history. In praise of Webster for
teaching "the citizens in general what their relation to the
Federal government is," an admirer could only express
surprise that no one had thought of it sooner.[13]

In the way he conceived of the nature of the constitutional agreement, Webster diverged even more from the
contract school. He deemed the Constitution to be, not a
continuing agreement among freemen, but an executed
contract. In the same sense that a law "is not the agreement,
but something created by the agreement," he said the Constitution was not itself a compact "but its result." Ratifica-
tion by the people terminated agreement and gave to the
document the force of a supreme law. "The compact is
executed, and the end designed by it attained. Henceforth,
the fruit of the agreement exists, but the agreement itself is
merged in its own accomplishment," he concluded.[14] Webster had earlier argued before the Supreme Court that the
Dartmouth College charter was of this nature. As an irreversible grant it had brought a private corporation into
existence and stamped it with perpetuity. The Constitution
in like fashion had created the corporate Union with "a will
of its own" and the "powers and faculties to execute its own
purposes."[15]

This view of the constitutional agreement as a self-liquidating one did provoke considerable criticism, yet it served Webster's purpose well. It gave legal form to his view of the Union as a grand instrument of order comprehending all generations. It savored as well the historical sentiment of love for the "constitution as it is" and the "union as it is."[16] With the paradoxical stance of a conservative, Webster deemed the Union very firm in its own self-defense, yet fragile in the face of experimentation or radical change. No matter how grand its future prospects, he never forgot that the Union was a unique product of human hands and ever required the solicitude of the statesman. He would thus be disposed to resist any substantial reform, even with regard to what many reckoned the unequal provision for the three-fifths representation of slaves. The Union of freemen was an absolute in the first instance, not because it was strong enough to stand any shock, but because the shock of its dissolution would reduce the life of the nation to nothing. As the advance of larger liberty deepened the rift in the corporate outlook, Webster's position pointed at last to what one student of the 1850s called the "doctrine of institutions." Much of this can be seen in his summary definition of the Union:

The Union is not a temporary partnership of States. It is the association of the people, under a constitution of Government, uniting their power, joining together their highest interests, cementing their present enjoyments, and blending, in one indivisible mass, all their hopes for the future. Whatsoever is steadfast in just political principles, whatsoever is permanent in the structure of human society, whatsoever there is which can derive an enduring character from being founded on deep laid principles of constitutional liberty, and on

the broad foundations of the public will—all these
unite to entitle this instrument to be regarded as a
permanent constitution of Government.[17]

While Webster revered the order from the past, John
Quincy Adams valued most highly the prospect of qualitative progress for the nation in the future. "The Constitution
itself," he said in 1833, "is but one great organized engine of
improvement—physical, moral, political." Assuming that
freedom in America had already been attained and or-
dered, he looked to the fruitful consequences of its full
sway. Liberty here meant the power of men, freed from the
irrational trammels of the past, to work out their own
destinies. "It is the purpose for which intellectual power was
given to man by his Maker," he exclaimed. Hopefully, the
dominion of mind and the arts of peace were in process of
replacing the reign of prejudice, exploitation, and war.[18]
By taking thought, he believed, men could truly advance
toward a higher stage of civilization. While holding progress to be a law of man's nature, he did not suppose it to be a
self-fulfilling one. It rather prescribed the joint and sustained effort of freemen.

Basic in Adams' thinking was the assumption that happiness for the individual necessarily required the improvement of the whole community. The pursuit of happiness
was a collective and cumulative enterprise, in the very nature of things, for social progress created ever-widening
opportunities for self-realization. In its social and economic
aspects, the ideal community possessed a relatively stable
and compacted population, a balance of rural and urban
elements, and great variety in its occupations. Such a milieu
gave scope to the diversity of talents and interests in men,
thus conducing "to their own elevation in the scale of
being." Against the agrarian rhetoric and rampant individualism of the day Adams pleaded for a more collective

mastery over the forces of nature. The task would also require time and the cooperation of oncoming generations. Freemen in any one age would find fulfillment through their participation in the long-range goal of building a better common life. Freedom here involved far more than the mere absence of social or political constraint. It was less a quantitative function of open space than a qualitative function of time. The Union in this sense was at once a positive means for progressive improvement and a teleological ideal to be more fully realized. It was in its grand prospective dimensions "an union of all classes, conditions, and occupations of men; an union coextensive with our territorial dominions; an union for successive ages, without limitation of time."[19]

Because the full measure of the Union's grandeur lay in the future, Adams professed to see the impending retirement of the national debt as a truly rare opportunity. It was given to his age, he supposed, to become the greatest link in the chain of the corporate Union. In a very significant figure he compared the American people to the children of Israel. After a similar travail of forty years, his own nation could at last "survey from the top of Pisgah the happy and promised land" reserved by Providence for its reward and use. By retiring the old debt his generation participated with the Founding Fathers in the glory of gaining freedom. By diverting more of the unencumbered resources of the country to the improvement of the nation's estate, his age might thereby incorporate future generations more fully in the grand pursuit of happiness.[20] Webster lamented the end of the debt as another bond of Union and order set loose, and Jackson welcomed it as an opportunity to gain freedom from the policy determinations of the past. Adams hailed it as the occasion for doing something positive and constructive with the freedom it allowed.

The policies to be adopted or retained at such a moment

were thus of unusual importance. Adams appreciated, no
less than Webster, the role of the government in harmoniz-
ing the interests of the country. But he brought to the
defense of the American System of policies against the
iconoclasm of Jackson a much greater spirit of system. He
wanted the government to direct in an active and self-
conscious way the course of the country. He saw in the
protective tariff a way to continue the diversification of
pursuits and in the National Bank a salutary means to
stimulate yet control the development of the country. Much
of his opposition to the policy of Indian removal arose from
the fear that too rapid a settlement of the West would create
imbalance in the national community. In part for the same
reason he resisted the numerous proposals for the speedy
disposal of the public lands. With the continued revenues
from these lands, moreover, Adams wanted to finance the
key feature in his system, namely, a vastly expanded program of internal improvements. Carefully planned roads
and canals would give direction to the development of
industry and trade within the country. They would also
serve to enhance the value of public lands and hence the
amount of revenue available to the government for promoting the arts and sciences.[21] Though favoring for these
purposes direct appropriations by the central government,
Adams also supported the plan of Henry Clay for distributing land revenues to the states. In either case, orderly
progress and enrichment of the nation through time remained the goal.

It is in this context that the distinctive response Adams
made to the nullification crisis can be most clearly seen.
With a predilection for order, Webster expended the
greatest effort in supporting the Force Bill. Because Adams
looked to the progressive improvement of the nation, he
spent a greater part of his energy in opposing Jackson's
second tactic of compromise, that of dismembering the

American System.[22] The Fourth Annual Message of the President, he bitterly noted, displayed a "speculative aversion to control" which would reduce to a "simple machine" the corporate instrument of government at the disposal of freemen. "It is the adoption for the future of a system of policy directly opposite to that with which the administration of Washington laid the foundations of the social existence of the great community—our National and Federal Union." Since much of the Union's true meaning lay in what it might in time become, the destruction of policies for that purpose would "untie the ligaments of the Union." Adams especially deplored the President's disposition to throw away the treasure of western lands. "The American Union as a moral person in the family of nations," he later observed, "is to live from hand to mouth, to cast away, instead of using for the improvement of its own condition, the bounties of Providence, and to raise to the summit of power a succession of Presidents the consummation of whose glory will be to growl and snarl with impotent fury against a money broker's shop, to rivet into perpetuity the clanking chain of the Slave, and to waste in boundless bribery to the West the invaluable inheritance of the Public Lands."[23]

Adams attributed the downfall of the American System to planters and plain republicans, or, in cruder polemical terms, to "the nullifiers of the South and the land-robbers of the West." He supposed that the "Sable Genius" of the South had been chiefly responsible.[24] As he looked to the future, moreover, it seemed to present a permanent obstacle to his hopes for the progressive improvement of the nation. Consequently in the bitterness of the moment, he defined the political force of the evil genius in terms which gained wider currency later on as that of the slave power. Because of the added weight of three-fifths representation and the sectional solidarity that the peculiar institu-

tion forged, a small and declining minority of slaveholders were able to suborn plain republicans in the
North and effectively rule the destinies of the nation. In the
same spirit Adams felt compelled to surrender the optimistic premise in his corporate outlook which held that the
positive actions of the government could produce through
time a greater degree of harmony and consensus. He was
now bold to declare, to the contrary, that an irreconcilable
conflict of interests and ultimately of principles obtained
within the Union:

> It cannot be denied that in a community spreading
> over a large extent of territory, and politically founded
> upon the principles proclaimed in the declaration of
> independence, but differing so widely in the elements
> of their social condition, that the inhabitants of one-
> half the territory are wholly free, and those of the other
> half divided into masters and slaves, deep, if not ir-
> reconcilable collisions of interest must abound. The
> question whether such a community can exist under
> one common Government, is a subject of profound,
> philosophical speculation in theory. Whether it can
> continue long to exist, is a question to be solved only by
> the experiment now making by the people of this
> Union, under that national compact, the constitution
> of the United States.[25]

The political prescription for dividing the enemies of the
American System, however, threatened its advocates with a
profound dilemma. As if in anticipation of the later Free-
Soil movement, Adams seemed ready to enlist the plain
republicans of the North in a crusade against the slave
power. The real enemies of freemen were not presumed
monopolists or a moneyed aristocracy, he protested, but the
small minority of southern slaveholders who sought "to rob

the free workingmen of the North of the wages of his labor, to take money from his pocket and put it into the southern owner of machinery." But success in removing the slave power obstacle in this way could not assure that corporate direction to national life would be resumed. The majority of Americans might rather remain as they were before —perversely present-minded in their outlook. "Democracy has no forefathers, it looks to no posterity," Adams once complained, "it is swallowed up in the present, and thinks of nothing but itself." The sum of its philosophy of freedom from government control, he elsewhere noted with contempt, was "comprised in the maxim of leaving money in the pockets of the people."[26] If Webster's penchant for order pointed to a "doctrine of institutions" by the 1850s, the progressive emphasis represented by Adams would tend to become absorbed into the Free-Soil crusade. The rift in the corporate outlook between the elements of past order and future improvement would then be complete and, as a fateful consequence, the vision of the nation within the process of time substantially lost to the political dialogue.

Until the end of the 1840s, however, this corporate vision remained as a real, if not always effective, foil to the affirmations of larger liberty in Jacksonian Democracy. It found lodging in the Whig party and, however chastened by the democratic spirit of the day, its spokesmen still invoked the essential idea of the earlier American System to conquer space. This meant, in their terms, giving some degree of direction to the nation's course across the continent in order to realize a more solid order and enrichment of the common life.[27]

In the dialectic of debate, many of the triumphant Jacksonians clearly embraced the policy of manifest destiny. The fundamentally timeless concept of freedom involved in their outlook provided an ample basis for this alternative course of the nation. Freedom from the prescriptions of the past and the prospects of future control, as staked out in the nullification crisis, meant essentially a freedom in the eternal present. As a political good it was not an entity pointing beyond itself to progressive development through time. It was rather a quantity to be possessed and enjoyed in its entirety at the time and to be reproduced in each successive generation. For the Union of freemen, as a consequence, the future would be a continuation of the present: its destiny would simply be more of the same. Not until 1843 did Jackson hit upon the felicitous phrase, "extending the area of freedom," but the substance of the notion inhered in his thought all along. In contrast to the Whiggish predilection for qualitative development through time, he sponsored the goal of quantitative progress across space.[28]

Classic expression of this view came from two ardent disciples of Jackson. In describing "the great nation of Futurity," it was true, John L. O'Sullivan hinted at qualitative change. But other phrases betrayed the notion of freedom as a function of space and not of time. "We are entering its *untrodden space*," he said of the *"expansive"* future, "with the truths of God in our minds, beneficent objects in our hearts, and with a clear conscience unsullied by the past." In like spirit, Representative Alexander Duncan of Ohio thought that the expansion of the nation necessarily meant the aggrandizement of freedom. World without end, as he stated the matter in 1845, the nation's true destiny had "the love of liberty for its means, liberty itself for its own reward, and the spread of free principles and republican institutions for its end."[29]

By 1848 it must have seemed to many that the manifest destiny of the country was happily in the process of being fulfilled. With the Independent Treasury, President Martin Van Buren had completed the task of divorcing federal revenue from the private banking system. The effort by the

Whigs in 1842 to re-establish the American System was
undone four years later by the Walker Tariff, a renewal of
the Independent Treasury, and vetoes by President James
K. Polk of measures for internal improvement. The flag of
the nation was, in the meantime, advancing to the Pacific
with the annexation of Texas, undisputed control of
Oregon south of the 49th parallel, and the acquisition of
New Mexico and California. With his last annual message to
Congress, Polk hopefully pronounced the epitaph of the
American System and suggested the desirability of further
acquisitions. In good earnest, then, Americans were an-
swering the call made earlier by Representative Chesselden
Ellis of New York for "filling up the grand outlines of a
territory intended for the possession and destiny of the
American race—an outline drawn by the Creator
himself."[30]

Further analysis of manifest destiny will reveal more fully
the workings of the concept of freedom in the eternal
present. For Jacksonians who regarded the people as "the
great social residuum after alien elements have been removed," the chief task of the statesman was to isolate and
banish the enemies of freedom. On the domestic level,
moneyed aristocrats were thought to comprise the chief
enemy. Their quest for special privileges threatened to
destroy the equality of pursuits, corrupt the government,
and commit the nation to the evils of time. "Legislation has
been the fruitful parent of nine-tenths of all the evil, moral
and physical, by which mankind has been afflicted," the
Democratic Review declared. By his war on the Second Bank
of the United States, Senator Thomas Morris of Ohio
claimed, President Jackson had purged the evils of the past
and thereby become "the second father of his country."
Representative David Wilmot of Pennsylvania, looking to
the future, warned anew that "the lords of the spindle"
sought with a high tariff to enslave the factory workers:

"True independence consists in freedom from restraints,"
he affirmed, "untrammeled to all things not morally
wrong."[31] Another saw in internal improvements a threat
to freedom, for one generation might so easily run up the
debt and become the "mortgagers of posterity." Horace
Greeley denounced the Jacksonian politics of conflict as a
species of "social war" and bitterly disclaimed the label of
"aristocrat" for those favoring positive legislation by the
government. But his protests merely served to underscore
the impulse to larger liberty, to essential freedom from
direction and control.[32]

The spread of freemen across the unsettled spaces of the
country was, in this view, a practicable way to keep liberty
from being lost in the toils of time. The "speedy settlement"
of the public lands, Jackson had declared in his Fourth
Annual Message, "constitutes the true interest of the Republic." Along with the removal of the Indians farther west,
his call to end federal control over the land amounted to a
domestic policy for extending the area of freedom within
the existing boundaries of the Union. Because he supposed
that "personal liberty is incompatible with a crowded population," Representative Duncan of Ohio thus joined others
in opposing all efforts to revive the American System of
policies.[33] In a somewhat "primitivist" vein Senator Lewis
Linn of Missouri likewise condemned the "high state of
civilization" which involved a compacted population, re-
finements for a few, and great corporations "enabling one
set of men to lord it over another." The "rigorous morals
and stern virtue of a republic," argued another partisan,
comprised the true alternative to overcivilization. The
"rough carol" of a Mississippi boatman or the sound of an
ax, he explained, were "better guaranties for the stability
and perpetuity of our republican institutions" than the trill
of a cavalier or the songs of the gondoliers.[34]

The praises President Polk sang to the federative nature

of the Union also expressed the predilection for timeless freedom. The Union of essentially self-governing state communities was suited to indefinite expansion, he exulted, because the decentralization of power enabled it to comprehend what it did not control. Freemen, going forth to settle new areas without direction from the center, could yet be integrated into the Union at the time of statehood. The very nature of the Union made expansion possible, and expansion in turn strengthened the Union for extending the area of freedom still farther. A policy of consolidation, by contrast, would presumably commit the nation in time and wreck the Union. "It may well be argued," Polk said in his Inaugural Address, "whether it would not be in greater danger of overthrow if our present population were confined to the comparatively narrow limits of the original thirteen states." Empty space had spared the Union the possible evils of time, and the continued expansion across the continent would enable it to reproduce this unchanging essence in the future.[35]

But the advocates of manifest destiny looked beyond the need for a rapid settlement of the empty spaces already in the Union. Since growth was "the normal state" of the young nation, Joseph J. McDowell of Ohio urged the House to support a policy of new territorial acquisitions. It constituted "the condition of our political existence," John A. McClernand of Illinois likewise argued. One of the most ardent of expansionists, John L. O'Sullivan, professed to see in every new acre of territory "an additional guaranty" for the "free development of our yearly multiplying millions." It would enable each new generation to move out to open space and reproduce the miracle of federative freedom from control. With a different view of the nature of freedom, many Whigs thought the existing boundaries sufficient, but the concept of freedom as a function of space made Representative John Reynolds of Illinois anxious to enlarge the homestead of the nation for the benefit of posterity. "This great Republic was not created for the few people who were in it at the Revolution," he warned, "nor for the few who are *now* in it, in comparison to the hundreds of millions of souls who will hereafter exist in it." Added space, in other terms, assured the freedom for each generation to recreate the essentials of the Union, to participate in the act of "extended genesis."[36]

To most partisan observers, Great Britain, by the early 1840s, appeared to be the chief external enemy to the natural and peaceful growth of American freedom. In geopolitical terms, Representative Duncan of Ohio feared, the nation was in danger of being "circumnavigated by British power" on the continent and surrounding islands. "We cannot bear that Great Britain should have a Canedy on our west as she has on the north," Jackson thus argued in behalf of annexing Texas. In like fashion McClernand of Illinois displayed "several beautifully colored maps" in the House to show how a cordon of British power stretching from Canada through Oregon and California to Mexico and the Caribbean posed a deadly peril. Senator Lewis Cass of Michigan invoked anew the law of growth. The nation's course must be onward across the continent, he warned, or else "we shall find ourselves in the decrepitude of age, before we have passed the period of manhood."[37]

But far more was thought to be involved in the enmity of the nation's ancient foe than merely stopping its outward expansion. Sam Houston of Texas advised the Senate in a speech opposing compromise over Oregon that, because of her hatred for free institutions, Great Britain actually sought to drive the nation back "within the limits of the good old thirteen States" and possibly destroy its existence altogether. One concession would lead to another, Houston predicted, until freemen were ousted "from every outpost of the Republic." It would be much better, Cass agreed, to fight for the first rather than the last inch of territory. Accepting in an aggressive way the terms of conflict defined by the external enemy of freedom, Stephen A. Douglas of Illinois vowed "to drive Great Britain and the last vestiges of royal authority from the continent of North America, and extend the limits of the republic from ocean to ocean." If the unsettled continent of the New World was to become all one thing or all another, he wanted to make it the exclusive province of freedom. A full decade before Abraham Lincoln formulated the idea of the "house divided" within the nation between slavery and freedom, the advocates of manifest destiny similarly found an irrepressible conflict in the New World between "monarchy and freedom."[38]

War to remove an obstacle to national growth would help to secure freedom for the future. To freemen in the present, moreover, war might prove very attractive as a moral equivalent, if not moral superior, to peace. Because "personal enfranchisement" was the essence of nationality in the Jacksonian view, little in the way of common purposes and common discipline remained to objectify and sustain the sense of community.[39] For negative liberals, as a consequence, a crusade against the enemies of freedom might very well serve to revive and strengthen the subjective bonds of national unity. It would in this sense fulfill the Jeffersonian prescription for a revolution in each generation. It was in this way that Jackson's dismemberment of the American System, no less than the "revolution of 1800," constituted a national revival.

War against the external enemies of freedom could promote the same end. "It was a maxim of the venerable Macon," Houston thus remarked, "that war was necessary to such a government as ours at least once in every thirty years." By calling on the people to "pay a price for their freedom," it provided a means for recreating and regenerating the first principles of the nation. If "the seeds of

Democracy were cast into the earth by the hand of the Revolution," Representative Andrew Kennedy of Indiana explained, then the tree of liberty needed to be "occasionally moistened by the blood of the patriot." In a negative way, the *Democratic Review* noted, war would discipline turbulent spirits and enable other individuals to transcend the "selfishness and mediocrity" which ever threatened to overtake a country of free individuals. "It would only be in such a conflict that the sinews and strength of freemen could be fully displayed," Representative McClernand stated more positively, "that the moral sublimity of republicanism would loom forth as a phoenix from the smoke and thunders of war." The two earlier contests with Britain, Cass agreed, had pushed the country forward "in character and position" in the world.[40] President Polk made the same claim for the Mexican War. A fuller sense of national identity would also come from the knowledge that, as Representative McDowell put it, a victory by republican arms might spark "a great moral explosion" for liberating Europe from the thralldom of priestcraft and kings. "Young America" was here beginning to contemplate more aggressive means for fulfilling the mission of freedom.[41]

Whigs confronted the affirmations of manifest destiny with a more positive appreciation of the qualitative dimensions of time. Webster, standing "as in the full gaze of our ancestors and our posterity," called for his generation in 1838 to think of itself as part of a larger corporate whole. In this perspective a contributor to the *Whig Review* could deplore the mad hostility Jacksonians were showing toward everything established. "It is high time for us to have settled something," he insisted, "to be ready to take something for granted." In opposition to the impulses for freedom in an eternal present, he protested that "this everlasting beginning will be the ruin of us." Looking to the future, Senator

Albert S. White of Indiana likewise condemned the Democrats for their reluctance to commit the nation to a positive
course. "Is this Confederated Government," he asked in
1841, "a mere machine to run in an endless cycle of
inanity?" Governor William H. Seward of New York explicitly dismissed as a "specious theory" the Jeffersonian
ideal of essential autonomy for each generation in the pursuit of happiness. The great resources of the country impressed him rather with the peculiarly collective and
cumulative nature of the nation's destiny. While working
within the context of "causes anterior to his own existence,"
Seward wanted his generation to define the nation's course
by a set of policies whose consequences would be as "distant
as its dissolution."[42]

The Whigs, who deemed order as the highest good,
expressed the strongest opposition to a policy of territorial
aggrandizement. A rapid settlement of the western lands
already placed enough strain upon the corporate Union,
Representative Joseph R. Ingersoll of Pennsylvania protested, because "a want of nationality" generally characterized the people from the newest states in the Union. To
acquire even more territory and strange peoples would
surely wreck the delicate task of building up a homogeneous nation. "What has the Rock of Plymouth or the settlement of Jamestown," he asked, "to do with Texas or the Rio
del Norte?" Another spokesman complained that "we shall
not know ourselves or know our country." In explaining his
opposition to further acquisitions, Webster confessed that
the theme of his entire career had been to make Americans
"*one people*, one in interest, one in character, and one in
political feeling." Departure from this goal would "break it
all up," he lamented, and make a "deformed monster" of
the Union. Its very existence no less than its nature was
ultimately at stake. "There must be some limit to the extent

of our territory," Webster declared in the debate over the annexation of Texas, "if we would make our institutions permanent."[43]

A resumption of domestic policies for building a "more substantial Union," according to Representative Robert C. Winthrop of Massachusetts, constituted the best alternative to indefinite expansion. A good life for the nation could be achieved, he thought, within "the old and ample homestead which our fathers bequeathed us." Henry Clay agreed that the American System alone could bring to the people "additional security to their liberties and the Union." Consistent support of its policies by the nation would, another explained, "knit together its various sections by the indissoluble bonds of a common interest and affection." A greater sense of nationality, "a fixed and decided national character," would then emerge. The appearance in the files of the *Whig Review* of an organic theory of Union to challenge the "fiction of a social compact" also underlined this urgency for order. Society was based on a contract, to be sure, but it was at first an unconscious contract rising up from the absolute moral and physical needs of man as a social being. "The aim of this contract, nay, its very essence is nationality," so the reasoning went, "the union of as many as can be bound by the ties of kindred, country, language, and a common destiny."[44] This concept of nationality obviously stood in sharp contrast to that of the Jacksonians. Whereas the latter sponsored a larger liberty for individuals from the determinations of time as the Union progressed across space, the party of order here wanted to set bounds to the Union and to thicken and make irreversible the elements of unity within.

A second group of Whigs, comprising in Seward's terms "the party of hope, of progress, and of civilization," responded to the manifest destiny of Jacksonians in a way that revealed their desire for qualitative improvement of the

nation through time. "We have a great country," Representative Luther Severance of Maine argued, "which I think it
is our 'manifest destiny' to improve." Few in this group
absolutely opposed the further enlargement of national
boundaries, but they were anxious to build up the country
as it spread out across space. Mastery over the continent,
one observed, "must be the supremacy of man over nature
as *man*." While enlarging the bounds of the nation they
were for "expanding and cultivating all the powers and
capacities of man considered as a social being."[45] In the
name of "a complete man" essentially free from time, one
Jacksonian railed against that high degree of specialization
which reduced the individual to "a supplementary being"
of society. But Whigs answered that only from "a fixed
center of thought," provided in a well developed society,
could the individual discover his true talents and realize the
fullness of his being. Thus might "the great ends of government be realized," Representative Jacob Collamer of
Vermont noted, which would "make us a homogeneous
people, all elevated and adorned with a taste and refinement becoming the members of a *glorious republic*." Henry
C. Carey summarized this position well. "The highest civilization is marked by the most perfect individuality and the
greatest tendency to union," he said in 1848.[46]

As positive liberals, some of the Whigs also hoped that a
policy of internal improvement might provide a moral
equivalent to war. Horace Mann and Abraham Lincoln
clearly analyzed the problem. The spirit of restlessness
across the land in the 1840s reflected, in Mann's view, the
"unexampled energies" set loose as the nation became lib-
erated from the force of "traditional feelings of respect for
established authority." Nor was the young Lincoln altogether sure that this spirit of the eternal present would be
able to impose upon itself a new discipline or control. It
evinced a destructive urge to tear down and reproduce the

primal drama of the fathers, he rather supposed, and not a corporate impulse to build "story to story" upon their work.[47]

But Seward was more hopeful that freemen could, by constructive and positive means, "constantly renovate and regenerate society." He clearly perceived that "action is the condition of our existence" and that action could be directed by the government "to pursuits consistent with public order and conducive to the general welfare." He revered the fathers in the first instance not as heroes who destroyed enemies of freedom, but as freemen of one generation who made great sacrifices to enrich the life of the larger corporate whole. "The principle of internal improvement derives its existence," he thus observed, "from the generous impulses of the Revolutionary age." Only with the "arts of peace," Representative George Perkins Marsh of Vermont agreed, could freemen express their nationality in the highest form. Progress was then to be measured by the fuller realization of the "dormant power" of the national mind and not by victory over trumped-up foes of freedom. "What would the money, already expended in killing those miserable Mexicans," Andrew Stewart of Pennsylvania bitterly asked in the House, "have done for the improvement of our country?"[48]

In their own terms of order and improvement, however, the Whigs had failed. While advocating a policy of "internal improvement," as Winthrop put it, they saw the nation following instead a course of "external aggrandizement."[49] The Jacksonian impulse to a larger liberty for men in time was here accompanied by the rapid spread of freemen across the spaces of the continent. A new contest with Great Britain was averted, but war came with Mexico and in its train the annexation of a vast territory westward to the Pacific. Even more fatefully, as it turned out, came a profound sectional controversy over the fruits of manifest destiny. The Free-Soil demand of the Wilmot Proviso in 1846 to prohibit slavery in the new territory soon generated the terms of a new national debate which brought to an end the old dialogue over the destiny of the nation in space and time. Elemental conflict between freedom and slavery for the right to shape the future now tended to replace the older concern for the shape which the future ought to have. In the ranks of Free Soil, as a consequence, the champions of manifest destiny would soon find an adversary far stronger than the Whigs had proved to be.

6
Free Soil and the Irrepressible Conflict

The expansion of slavery became the central issue in the national debate from the Mexican War to the outbreak of civil strife in 1861. It rapidly displaced the old debate between Whigs and Democrats over the expansion of the nation with the far more fateful conflict over which element within the nation would be entitled to expand. As they defined and forced the issue, Free Soilers saw it, not as a debate between two kinds of freedom, but rather an irrepressible conflict between freedom and slavery. "The momentous questions of liberty and slavery," Joshua R. Giddings of Ohio declared in the House, "are now before the people of the nation."[1] Only through the events of the 1850s would the irrepressible conflict mature, but the basic terms of the conflict achieved full formulation in the bitter contest over the fate of territories likely to be acquired from Mexico.

In four related ways the outlines of this irrepressible conflict can be clearly discerned. The political context in which the debate emerged was of massive import, for it heralded the disruption of the old Jeffersonian coalition of planters and plain republicans which Martin Van Buren had revived under Jackson. And, as many feared, a sundered Jefferson tended to civil conflict. Secondly, the plain republicans in the North defined the Free-Soil task before them as a "moral" no less than a "political" enterprise. In the third place, controversy over slavery expansion pressed into use the pattern of geopolitical thought which had developed in the earlier debate over the expansion of the nation itself. If advocates of manifest destiny had deemed Great Britain an external enemy to the extension of the area of freedom, the Free Soilers professed to see slaveholders in the same way. Finally, Free Soilers began to fashion, with the concept of the broker state, a northern consensus on all issues other than slavery which could draw together erstwhile Whig and Democratic foes. It served, by redressing the balance of moral idealism in the Free-Soil outlook with a healthy measure of self-interest, to forge a seemingly irresistible political force in the majority section of the country.

The emerging shape of irrepressible conflict can be seen, first of all, in the impending disruption of that coalition of planters and plain republicans first assembled under Jeffersonian Republicanism and later revived under Jacksonian Democracy. Essential to the unity of this coalition had been a common opposition to the corporate impulses of Federalism and Whiggery. Freedom from control of the central government, dominated by a would-be aristocracy, seemed to assure the good of equality to plain republicans, security to slaveholding planters, and opportunity for unchecked expansion to all identified with manifest destiny. As negative liberals, they assumed that happiness for individuals and the good of the whole nation would arise without direction from the center.[2] The chief task of statesmen was to isolate and remove whatever elements that sought by the power of government to commit the nation to an evil course through time. Thus, by the charge of a "Federalist plot" Jeffersonians had been able to close ranks and effect a settlement of the Missouri controversy.

But in the 1840s all was quite different. The reappearance of the issue of slavery expansion was accompanied by the shattering of the old formula of negative liberalism and the emergence of new formulas in naked conflict with each other. Though Whiggish corporate elements were involved in the new debate, it reflected in its basic form a bitter family quarrel within the house of Jefferson. On August 8, 1846, Representative David Wilmot of Pennsylvania, an ardent Jacksonian, introduced his proviso that any territory acquired from Mexico must be devoted exclusively to the uses of freedom. Because it came at the very end of the session the proviso provoked little debate, but its reintroduction the following year opened the controversy permanently.[3] Another Jacksonian, Jacob Brinkerhoff of Ohio, claimed that the Wilmot Proviso was nothing more than a restatement of the "Jefferson Proviso" which had banned slavery from the territories of the Old Northwest in the Ordinance of 1787. Absolutely no power had been delegated to Congress, he further argued, to give legal existence to slavery in any territory directly under national jurisdiction. Slavery did exist at the time of the Constitution, to be sure, but it remained the exclusive creature of state and local laws. The effort of the slaveholders to extend it, therefore, represented the "Federalism" of loose construction in its most flagrant form. Since the Union reposed upon the idea of individual freedom alone, the use of federal power to restrict the spread of slavery was a negative act and not a positive one. In a precise sense, it displayed a strict fidelity to the Jeffersonian principle of strict construction. With phrases soon to gain wide currency, Free Soilers thus characterized their position as one of "freedom national" and "slavery local."[4]

Responding to the Wilmot Proviso, John C. Calhoun introduced counter resolutions in the Senate on February 19, 1847, absolutely denying the constitutional power of

Congress to restrict the spread of slavery. In support of the resolutions, he likewise invoked the principle of strict construction. No power had been delegated to the federal government, in his view, to touch the existence of slavery. It was the exclusive creature of the sovereign states; and the Union, as their agent, was bound to protect whatever freemen in the states defined as property. With specific regard to the territories, jointly owned by all of the states, Calhoun argued that "the shield of the Constitution" automatically extended protection over slaves carried there.[5] To foes of this position, however, he had in effect used the old familiar argument of states' rights on behalf of the position of "slavery national." In any case, former Jeffersonian allies now pinned the label of the hated "Federalism" on each other. Free Soilers in the North wanted freedom from the control of expansionist slaveholders in the future settlement of the country, while Calhoun wanted security for slaveholders which control of the government by the Free Soilers would destroy.

Other Jacksonians brought forward the doctrine of popular sovereignty in an effort to reaffirm the relevance of the old and ambiguous idea of federative freedom to the new issue of slavery expansion. Advocates of this position rejected as equally unacceptable the claims of "freedom national" and "slavery national." They wanted instead to take the power over slavery from Congress and bestow it upon the people in the territory. Speaking in behalf of his resolutions to this effect, Senator Daniel S. Dickinson of New York argued that the "genius of our federative system" lay precisely in allowing the settlers in a new area to be free from central control in making their own decision. With his northern constituency in mind, Representative Orlando B. Ficklin of Illinois came down especially hard on the Free Soilers at this point. Their demand for restriction was another "Federalist plot," which manifested anew the contempt old Federalists had for the wisdom of the common man. "Let them decide the question," he rather affirmed, "and they will decide it right." In a similar vein Lewis Cass of Michigan feared that the Free-Soil proviso would, by provoking a bitter internal controversy, pose a fatal obstacle to the further destiny of national expansion. "In this aspect of the matter," he explained, "the people of the U[nited] States must choose between this restriction and the extension of their territorial limits."[6]

Unhappily for Cass and other Jacksonian advocates of manifest destiny, the charge of a Federalist plot simply failed to square with the facts. The new Free-Soil movement in the 1840s was not a reincarnation of Federalist restrictionism in the Missouri controversy, and in the difference lay the substance of the irrepressible conflict. With a posture of moral neutrality the Free Soilers of Federalist lineage had sought to stop the spread of slavery on the grounds of "political" expediency. As with other kinds of positive measures, they wanted to promote the corporate good of the whole. By contrast, the Free Soilers in the 1840s evinced a "moral" urgency which transcended the considerations of mere expediency. While they agreed that freedom was best suited to promote the general welfare, they placed much higher priority upon the task of restoring the nation's soul. Since they deemed individual freedom to be the essence of the national idea, the spread of slavery clearly amounted to subversion. The use of federal power to restrict the spread of slavery would thus be a negative action, for it would bring subversion to an end and restore the original design of the nation.

The contrast of two other positions will bring into clearer focus the moral imperative of Free Soil and its premises of negative liberalism. On one side stood William Lloyd Garrison and a small, but vocal, band of radical libertarians. He took the national idea of freedom, as formulated in the

Declaration of Independence, to be the universal birthright of all men. But the Union, formed in 1787, had subverted the national idea, for many of the provisions of the Constitution clearly made it a pro-slavery document. In a very precise way, then, liberty and the Union were two and totally separable things: the Union with slaveholders was rotten to the core and freedom was considered a "higher law" than the existing order. The task of restoring the nation, therefore, involved for Garrison a revolutionary act—nothing less than a dissolution of the existing Union and the creation of a new one on the basis of the universal archetype of freedom. At the opposite end of the spectrum stood Daniel Webster, among others, still identified with the older corporate concept. For him liberty and the Union remained one and inseparable, and order within the Union constituted the highest good. With a spirit of moral realism that contrasted with the absolutism of Garrison, he reckoned good and evil inextricably woven together in the web of all human affairs. In the case of the Union, slavery, no less than freedom, had been one of the historical elements that went into its formation. By timely acts of reform the government might exercise its power in limited ways to improve the existing order. At the same time Webster rejected out of hand that revolutionary impulse which sought to realize in time any absolute good.

The Free Soilers occupied the ground between Garrison and Webster. They shared with the latter the view that liberty and the Union were inseparable; with the former, the tendency to moral absolutism inspired by the idea of freedom. They considered the Constitution to be an anti-slavery document, that is, one which had incorporated the univeral archetype of freedom as lodged in the Declaration of Independence. The "higher law" of Garrison was therefore no higher law at all; it was rather the principle on which the Union had already been established. The good old

Union was hence essentially sound, and not rotten to the core as Garrison claimed. Any increase in the evils of slavery as the Union moved through time would consequently have to be attributed to some deviation from its original design. Reform, in parallel fashion, meant a restoration of the original principles. Actions by the government of freemen against aggressive slavery would, however radical they might appear to men like Webster, thus constitute the highest form of conservatism.[7]

A slave power conspiracy, in this view, was thought to be responsible for the evils that had overtaken the nation since its founding. The "Imprisoned Giant of our Constitution," Charles Sumner of Massachusetts warned, had temporarily broken his bonds. The fathers had recognized—*but not created*—slavery then existing under the laws of the original states and, in the flood tide of the love of freedom, had given them the defensive power of three-fifths representation of slaves. But the fathers also believed, according to Sumner, that, by confining slavery to its existing limits, it would in time die out completely. The end of the foreign slave trade after twenty years and the prohibition of slavery in the Old Northwest were policies designed for this purpose. Then the freemen of the nation rested after their labors, Salmon P. Chase agreed, and the essentially alien element of the slave power began to encroach upon freedom. Though totally unforeseen by the fathers, the three-fifths representation of slaves and the solidarity of sectional interests provided the lever of power whereby a small minority of slaveholders had been able to gain control of the federal government and place it on a course of expansion to strengthen and make permanent their control. In other terms, Representative John G. Palfrey of Massachusetts said that a "noxious branch" had been grafted onto the tree of liberty which threatened to overshadow and poison all the rest.[8]

The obvious task for the nation of freemen was to prune off the noxious branch or, in Sumner's terms, to drive the slave power back at once "within its original constitutional bounds." Such an enterprise would clearly resemble the dynamics of Protestant revivalism. The first need was to quicken anew in the hearts of the people the national faith of individual freedom. On the basis of this renewal, statesmen might then proceed to destroy the idolatrous constitutional creeds of the enemy and purge the evil accretions of time.[9] While Webster would add piece on piece to the old Union, and Garrison sought to create an entirely new one, the Free-Soil prescription here pointed rather to restoring or recreating, as it were, the old and timeless order of freedom. "It is the same issue which led our fathers to the battlefields of the Revolution," Giddings declared. "Our warfare," Owen Lovejoy of Illinois agreed, "is defensive as much as that of the Revolution, albeit we use different methods." In declaring independence of the slave power, the platform of the Free Soil party in 1848 invoked "the example of our fathers in the days of the first Declaration of Independence." Liberty and the Union were one and inseparable, for the restoration of the one was the only way to preserve the other. In this way Chase resisted the charge that they were "a band of fanatics" bent on destroying the Union.[10] To the popular veneration for the indissoluble Union was now being riveted the view of individual freedom as an essential.

In the practical arena of national affairs, the duty of foiling the aggressions of the slave power obviously dictated for negative liberals a politics of conflict.[11] Jacksonians had faced the moneyed aristocracy of banking and manufacture which sought to destroy freedom in the toils of time by creating in America, according to Representative Alexander Duncan of Ohio, "a European pauperism, a European aristocracy, and a European vassalage." In like fashion Palfrey pointed to the "masonry of the slaveholders." Freed at last from "the grasp of eastern capital" and the "monster bank," Wilmot thus called on former Democrats to do battle against the "money-power in the South" which, he went on to describe, was "more potent and more dangerous than all other enemies of liberty combined." The Free Soil party in 1848 accordingly invited freemen "to rescue the federal government" from the control of the slave power.[12]

Great differences did exist among the foes of the slave power about the specific policies for checking its aggressions. The most radical in the ranks of political antislavery, such as Lysander Spooner and the Liberty League, found constitutional warrant for abolishing slavery in all parts of the Union. Others, somewhat less radical, supposed that the Constitution had been subverted only by the spread of slavery beyond the original thirteen states. Consequently they called for the abolition of slavery in all states and territories brought into the Union since 1787.[13] In this perspective, the position of Free Soil proper, to which a majority in the North by the 1850s could give assent, was very modest in scope. While recognizing slavery in all parts of the Union where it currently existed, the Free Soilers insisted only in stopping its further spread into the unsettled territories. To this position, however, they brought an absolute resolve and the same basic categories of antislavery thought used by the abolitionists. For the slaveholders of the South, at any event, even this modest program defined an irrepressible conflict. It placed them under the moral ban of empire and ruled out their equal participation in the benefits of a young and growing nation.

In this specific connection, yet another dimension to the irrepressible conflict can be seen in the way Free Soilers applied the modes of geopolitical thought first used in behalf of manifest destiny. Jacksonians professed to see in monarchical Europe, and especially in Great Britain, the

enemy to national expansion and, as a consequence, to the
very existence of freedom itself. In like fashion, the slave
power posed an obstacle to freemen within the continental
Union. The exclusive claim for freedom in North America,
made in President James K. Polk's reading of the Monroe
Doctrine, found a clear parallel in the demand of the Wilmot Proviso for restricting the unsettled spaces of the nation to the uses of freedom alone. The monism of freedom,
in either case, evinced a disposition to define an irrepressible conflict with the enemies of freedom. Finally, the posture of self-defense expressed at once a moral imperative to
resolve the conflict and the assurance that power lay with
freedom to vanquish the foe.

As indicated earlier, Jacksonian expansionists thought of
freedom as in some ways a function of space. In this regard
Great Britain and at times "the conspiracy of five
monarchs" in Europe, according to Senator William Allen
of Ohio, posed a deadly threat to freedom. Senator Thomas
Hart Benton of Missouri compared the activities of the
ancient enemy in Oregon to "a vast boa constrictor."
Alarmed by other activities in Mexico, Central America,
and the Caribbean, Edward A. Hannegan of Indiana
warned the Senate that Britain was about "to hem us in and
encircle us with her possessions." Her success would, he
elsewhere noted, "hurl us from the trail of our destiny,"
thus dooming any future hopes for the eventual liberation
of the Old World. More immediately, Dickinson of New
York noted, the lack of unsettled space would prevent "the
enslaved of the earth" from immigrating to America to find
happiness under their own "vine and fig tree." Pointing to
the "American multiplication table," Representative Andrew Kennedy thought he saw an even more imminent
disaster. Without the safety valve of unsettled lands, he
feared that freemen already here would be plunged into
the thickening evils of time as they passed under the yoke of

a moneyed aristocracy ultimately controlled from Great Britain.[14]

On the "primitivist" side of their thought, manifested elsewhere in support of homesteads for actual settlers, the Free Soilers of the 1840s showed a like concern for the relation of freedom to open and unsettled space. Representative William Collins of New York favored the Wilmot Proviso because, among other reasons, "free laborers, in a few years, will be in want of land." Additionally, Kinsley S. Bingham of Michigan told the House, there would be the need of new lands in order for the United States to continue its mission as an "asylum for the oppressed" immigrants from Europe. In two closely related ways, Brinkerhoff of Ohio showed how the expanding slaveholders constituted a deadly geopolitical enemy to freedom. Their presence in a new territory kept freemen out, because the sons of freemen in his state did not want to be socially degraded by a slaveholding oligarchy. By remaining in the older part of the Union, however, they would be overwhelmed by the evils of overcivilization and the control of a manufacturing aristocracy. Without an absolute restriction on the spread of slavery, then, freedom would be crushed between the "lords of the lash" in the territories and the "lords of the loom" in the eastern part of the country.[15] Moreover, Wilmot warned that a cordon of slave states from Texas to the Pacific would forever blast the hope that freemen might enjoy a further destiny of expansion southward on the continent. "Slavery will riot in the extent of its possessions," he concluded, "and there will grow up at the south the mightiest oligarchy that the world ever saw." With such power Representative John Crowell of Ohio thought it might totally subvert the Constitution and transplant slavery in all the free states. Freedom would then truly find itself at land's end.[16]

In the exclusive claims made for freemen to the continental spaces, the advocates of manifest destiny and free soil seemed equally prepared to define an irrepressible conflict with the enemies of freedom. The "clear and unquestionable" title of the nation to all of Oregon gained its greatest sanction from the "higher law" of Providential intent for the New World.[17] Representative Stephen A. Douglas thus explained "that North America has been set apart as a nursery for the culture of republican principles, and that there is no room here for a monarchy or its dependencies." He doubtless hoped that much if not all of it would become part of the United States, but he was even more certain that all peoples on the continent outside the United States wanted to organize themselves on its model of freedom. Senator Allen, in like spirit, declared that the struggle between "the old decaying system of hereditary power" and "the new and onward system of elective authority" was the kind of conflict which "nothing human can prevent."[18] The continent could not, he supposed, remain permanently half monarchical and half free.

This monistic impulse of the expansionists found clearest expression in their response to the idea of a "balance of power" on the continent. During the final stages of the Texas affair, before its annexation as a state, French Minister Guizot suggested an intervention of European powers to check the expansion of the United States. But the premise of permanent coexistence for monarchical and free elements was rejected in President Polk's aggressive reading of the Monroe Doctrine. He rather used the doctrine to justify the claim of a virtual hegemony for the nation on the continent. The "balance of power," he tersely declared, "can not be permitted to have any application on the North American continent, and especially to the United States."[19] Senator Cass, in like fashion, wanted to give the doctrine the force of a positive congressional enactment, believing that only by such an unequivocal expression of the

nation's will would freedom gain security. He was prepared
to tolerate the "existing rights" of European powers in the
New World, but he absolutely opposed further encroach-
ment or colonization. Might was right in the case of the
United States, he reasoned, because the remarkable growth
of its power truly reflected the expansive genius of the
federative system and the energizing force of freemen lib-
erated from the trammels of the past. Providence intended
that freedom, and not the "miserable intrigues of the courts
of Madrid and Lisbon," should shape the destinies of the
magnificent regions of the continent and unlock its resources for the greater happiness of all mankind.[20]

Free Soilers looked upon the South in much the same way
that the champions of manifest destiny viewed monarchical
Europe. In the very nature of things, Representative Rock-
well of Connecticut argued, the slave labor system left the
"blight and mildew" of plundered or undeveloped resources in the wake of its march across the continent. The
added political power gained by the accession of new slave
states conduced to the same end, A. R. McIlvain of Pennsylvania told the House, for it would be used to veto tariffs and
other policies needed by freemen to develop the bountiful
resources of the country. Here was substance for the
"higher law," soon to be proclaimed by Senator William H.
Seward of New York, by which the unsettled spaces of the
continental Union were to be devoted to the exclusive uses
of freedom. By denying "that liberty and slavery have equal
rights" in the unsettled part of the Union, Representative
Luther Severance of Maine argued that the fathers had
given constitutional form to the claims of monistic freedom
and rejected any idea of a permanent "balance of power"
between freedom and slavery. Precisely because they comprised an element alien to the national idea of freedom,
Senator Hannibal Hamlin thought the slaveholders had
become aggressive. While prepared to tolerate their exist-

ing rights in the old part of the Union, he insisted upon the need of an unequivocal enactment by Congress against their expansion. Otherwise, he warned, "slavery would creep into this territory as certainly as ever Satan crept into the garden of Eden." Freedom and slavery represented "two antagonistical principles," Senator John Hale of New Hampshire concluded, and no effort by statesmen could ultimately avoid the resolution of the conflict between them. The nation would at last become all slave or all free. "It must come," he said of the conflict, "we must meet it; and the sooner we meet it the better."[21]

Finally, the position of self-defense assumed by negative ᐧ liberals reflected a moral imperative to accept the irrepressible conflict and a clear assurance that freedom was bound to win. Representative John A. McClernand of Illinois warned that "the cordon of military posts" drawn by Great Britain around the nation threatened to "crush us in her coil." The crisis of the nation's fate came in Oregon, Sam Houston said, and compromise with Britain was the certain road to disaster. Agreement to divide the territory along a compromise line would betray a moral weakness in the nation, invite new concessions, and drive freedom at last from all the outposts into the citadel itself. Cass likewise deemed it best "to defend the door sill than the hearth stone—the porch than the altar." Invoking the example of the Revolutionary fathers, Senator Hannegan would rally Americans to the defense of freedom "and leave the consequences to God."[22]

Happily most spokesmen thought the consequences would be a victory for puissant freedom. Senator David R. Atchison of Missouri gave classic expression to the notion that a successful defense of freedom pointed to its total dominion: "Sir, I would war with England, in the defence of our just rights, until she was shorn of all her power on this continent." Britain and the other despots of Europe had good reason to be frightened, Jefferson Davis of Mississippi told the Senate, because they had at last awakened "the sleeping giant of popular strength." Because the government of the United States reposed so clearly upon the "hearts" and not the "backs" of the people, Senator Allen agreed that the ultimate issue of a war would never be in doubt. Beyond the vindication of freedom in the New World, Cass also believed war "might shake the institutions of Europe to their very foundations" and compel a reorganization of them on the popular principle. But a peaceful passing of the crisis, which Cass believed more likely, would still produce the same long-run effect: the triumph of freedom in the New World meant as well the ultimate liberation of the Old.[23]

The Free-Soil pose of self-defense also involved the impulse to dominion. "We stand in defence of free soil," Hamlin said, "and resist aggressive slavery." Representative Robert McClelland expressed a sense of awe at the way a small minority of slaveholders had effectively controlled the government. "There is," he said, "a mysterious and at the same time an all-powerful influence in this institution that is incomprehensible." Senator John M. Niles of Connecticut saw in the disposition of the territory acquired from Mexico the crisis of the fate of freedom in the Union. Extending the line of 36°30' to the Pacific was hardly less dangerous than adopting the principle of popular sovereignty, in his view, because anything short of a total defeat of the slave power kept freedom in a state of total uncertainty. Equally opposed to any compromise with the slave power, Senator Hale called on freemen to do the right and "bid defiance to all consequences."[24]

But, along with this moral imperative to embrace the irrepressible conflict, came an ultimate contempt for the power of the adversary. The aggressiveness of the slave power, Representative Timothy Jenkins of New York argued, actually masked its sense of internal weakness. Because the control of the slaveholders rested upon the backs and not upon the hearts of the people, they held awful hostages to time in the prospect of slave insurrection or the political rebellion of the non-slaveholding whites. For this reason Wilmot advised his fellows not to allow the cries of disunion to keep them from the task of blocking the access of the slave power to the safety valve of unsettled space. Slaveholders depended too heavily upon the internal protection afforded by the Union, he explained, ever "to calculate its value." Should folly nonetheless drive them to secession, a war mounted by freemen to save the Union would most likely, as John Quincy Adams had ever argued, shake the peculiar institution to its very foundations.[25] Thus would be consummated in brief and violent form the final triumph of freedom which, in a more peaceful way, would come with equal certainty as slavery died out in the states when no longer allowed to spread into the territories. In either case, the firm resolve to make the new part of the Union free assured as well the liberation of the old part of the Union. Liberty and Union were becoming more than ever one and inseparable, as freemen embraced the geopolitical tactic for restoring the original design of the Founding Fathers.

In sum, there were many parallels in the thought of Free Soilers and the proponents of manifest destiny. The way the former conceived of their struggle with the slave power over the unsettled spaces of the Union clearly resembled the way Jacksonian expansionists viewed the geopolitical obstacle Great Britain and monarchical Europe generally posed to the goal of extending the area of freedom. As negative liberals, both assumed the right of freedom to dominion and the removal of its enemies as the chief condition for its full sway.

In yet another way the Free Soilers in the 1840s expressed the essential outlook of negative liberalism. They moved toward a fuller and more unequivocal embrace than others before them of the broker-state concept of the government. It was a view that blended, in some sense, the elements at issue in the preceding debate between Whigs and Democrats. Action by the government in the economic affairs of the nation was allowed, but mainly to aid and not to direct the pursuits of freemen. At the same time, it was assumed that the unplanned future for the nation would be a happy one. Gone was much of the older corporate impulse to exercise a positive, history-making power for the good. Equally missing were the fears that the actions of the government, however unsystematic, would irreversibly commit the nation to the evils of time. The government now belonged to the people for whatever they might want. "It is theirs to enjoy, to defend," Wilmot declared. "They have a right to mould it to their pleasure, to determine its policy, to direct it to the advancement of their happiness and prosperity."[26]

Tendencies in either of the older parties by the end of the 1840s undoubtedly provided substance to the broker-state idea. The hopes of winning elections often tempted Whigs to muffle their corporate impulses by an appeal, as in the "log cabin" campaign of 1840, to the present-mindedness of the people. Nor did Clay enjoy much success during the ensuing Whig administration in reestablishing the American System of policies. The Pre-emption Act undermined the earlier goal of conquering space by means of moderating the westward movement. The increase of tariff duties in 1842, at the same time, came at the sacrifice of the scheme for distributing land revenues to the states for education and internal improvements. The long campaign against executive usurpation manifested in the veto of congressional measures, moreover, tended to displace the older corporate notion of the will of all generations with the view that the "log-rolling" combinations of the present majority in Congress truly expressed the will of the nation.[27] A freshman Whig congressman from Illinois, Abraham Lincoln, thus invoked "the principle of allowing the people to do as they please with their own business." Others seemed disposed at last to accept, with little qualification, the popular concept of automatic progress for the nation. Accordingly, Representative James Dixon of Connecticut conceded that, "in spite of unwise legislation, a high degree of prosperity awaits us."[28]

Jacksonians also contributed to the cause. Intraparty quarrels, no less than victories over the American System, tended by 1846 to draw out more clearly the differences in their ranks about the precise role of the government. Representative Robert Barnwell Rhett of South Carolina sounded a doctrinaire tone of inflexible laissez faire among a growing number of southerners, a tone which contrasted with the pragmatic voice of democratic nationalism many plain republicans gave to the party. The "log-rolling" scramble for tariff bounties and legislative appropriations, he scornfully observed, amounted to nothing more than "the grand game of plundering each other." Meanwhile, the growing reality of economic consolidation and interdependence for the nation invited northern partisans to seek government aid. Stephen A. Douglas, among others from the Northwest, condemned "a general system of improvements" yet voted in an unsystematic way for particular measures to improve the rivers and harbors in their region. To the same end Senator Niles of Connecticut denied that the tariff issue came "within the province of party." Another protection-minded Democrat, Benjamin A. Bidlack of Pennsylvania, thought the government should leave the people alone, but he did not reckon it the highest virtue for the people to leave the government alone. "My rule is," he declared, "that the representative who carries out most fully the wishes of those who delegated him, gives the most conclusive evidence of the purity of his republican principles."[29]

But there were limits to heresy in the old parties. President Polk regarded his Fourth Annual Message to Congress a restatement of faith and morals. In recalling the Jacksonian strictures against the American System, he especially warned that appropriations for internal improvements would open a door through which the whole corrupt system of positive legislation might make a return. From the other side, the *Whig Review* invoked the old orthodox concern for the "general system of Union" which required the sustaining care of the statesman. Equally anxious to direct the nation's course through time, Representative Robert C. Winthrop of Massachusetts regarded measures inspired only by short-run or purely local interests as "a species of log-rolling" which lacked "form and substance."[30]

Ultimately, then, it was the debate over the issue of slavery expansion which best served to rationalize the broker-state concept of the government. The demand of the Free Soil platform in 1848 "to maintain the rights of free labor against the aggressions of the slave power" tended to make "free labor" a term as expansive as middle-class America.[31] The doctrinaire posture of laissez faire assumed by many southern spokesmen on all issues but slavery made it easier to believe that the actions of the government in behalf of freemen, however unsystematic, constituted the true interests of the nation. The opposition of the slave power to a tariff, earlier sought by some for building up the country, and to homesteads, which would spread out the country, seemed likely to muffle, if not destroy, the old debate about the nature of freedom in space and time. In the dialectical presence of an enemy who sought to commit the nation to the evils of time, freedom could rather be thought of as the kind of good immune from temporal considerations. Essential equality of opportunity for freemen in the eternal present, along with the aid, but not the direction, of a benign government, would therefore be conducive to individual happiness and the good of the whole. A strict construction of the Constitution to keep the evil of slavery from controlling the government was to be matched by a more latitudinarian spirit to accommodate the goods freemen might desire.

Movement within the ranks of political antislavery toward the broker-state concept came in two fairly distinct stages. The Liberty party, led by James G. Birney in the campaigns of 1840 and 1844, sought to separate completely the issue of slavery from the economic role of the government in the lives of freemen. While embracing the "one idea" of freedom itself, he remained totally silent on all particular measures for promoting the blessings of liberty. On practical grounds, one supporter argued that it would not be possible to write a platform on which erstwhile Whig and Democratic partisans could stand. The "incongruous materials" drawn together under the banner of freedom, Francis J. LeMoyne further explained, made it a political necessity to rule out "all collateral test questions." Another supporter of Birney likewise accepted this order of priorities. "We do not know what we want," Russell Errett of Pennsylvania said, "until we can remove the great disturber."[32] On idealistic grounds, moreover, there was the fear that the goal of true freedom might be subverted if commingled with an appeal to the selfish, short-run interests of freemen. LeMoyne warned that the party might lose its sense of mission and become "an end in itself." In this regard the political movement against slavery was reckoned to be in the nature of a self-liquidating crusade.

Joshua Leavitt thus professed to believe in 1842 that the
success of the movement would pave the way for the renewal of the old party contests.[33]

By its very nature and intensity, however, the crusade
pointed to the more likely result of transcending, rather
than of temporarily suspending, the issues in debate between the old parties. In the hierarchy of political goods,
the overriding concern of the Liberty party for freedom
itself tended, as its convention proclaimed in 1841, to reduce all other issues to the level of "comparative utility and
minor importance." The question of the protective tariff
and its related policies, once thought to involve fundamental principles about the nature of the nation's venture in
space and time, was now becoming in the presence of the
aggressive slaveholders a mere matter of political expediency. Harmony in the policies of the government and a
happy destiny for the nation would automatically come,
Birney seemed to suggest, when the irrepressible conflict
had been resolved and the labor system of the country
reduced to "a homogeneous state." Once a free-labor consensus had been achieved among Americans, Giddings
later observed in the same vein, "they will agree upon all the
great questions so vitally interesting to our people."[34]
Whereas Whigs inclined to the view of political freedom as a
function of time and Democrats as a function of space,
antislavery spokesmen here thought of it as a timeless moral
category. Without a specific concern for shaping the future
on the spacious continent, they believed the future would
be a happy one if good was free to shape it.

The dismal failure of the one idea approach in the elections of 1840 and 1844, however, invited the politically
minded within the ranks of antislavery to adopt a more
realistic strategy. "We must have some other motives to
present to people," Theodore Foster accordingly advised
Birney, "which will appeal directly to their own interests."

Only in this way, Chase agreed, could the hosts of freedom ever grow large enough to win. He therefore welcomed the opportunity to leave the Liberty party, "that forlorn hope of Freedom," and to work for a new political coalition. To the old idea that the overthrow of the slave power would make the government truly responsive to the interests of freemen, he made a crucial amendment. He now argued that a political appeal to the present interests of freemen would itself serve as an efficient means for achieving the overthrow of the slave power. What Chase and others groped for in the 1840s was that proper blend of idealism and self-interest which could command wide popular support. Success at last came, as a recent scholar has well argued, with the new Republican party in the following decade. As written into the platform in 1860, the key to success lay in the appeal to a broad range of economic interests and its restriction of the power of government over slavery to the narrow area of the unsettled territories.[35]

In this perspective, the Free Soil party in 1848 constituted a half-way stage in the development of political antislavery. By the particular form in which the elements of idealism and self-interest were combined, it looked backward to the Liberty party and forward to the triumphant Republicans. With regard to slavery, the platform could be read in a way to justify a scope of action far in excess of what Wilmot and many others in the new coalition would be prepared to support. The call for the federal government "to relieve itself from all responsibility for the existence or continuance of slavery," for example, meant for Charles Sumner the abolition of slavery in all areas directly under national jurisdiction. The "divorce" of the government from all connection with slavery necessarily involved, he thought, making the government "Freedom's open, active, and perpetual ally." Here was to be found substance for the

claim of Joshua Leavitt that the new party had remained
faithful to the cause. "The Liberty Party is not dead," he
declared, in the Free Soil convention of 1848, "but
Translated."[36] A further translation made by the Republican
party more clearly narrowed the area of action against
slavery to the unsettled territories; but within these limits it,
too, would regard action as an imperative duty prescribed
by an essentially antislavery Constitution.

On economic issues, at the same time, the Free Soil platform anticipated in considerable detail the Republican appeal to self-interest and framed the appeal in broker-state
terms. Such terms served to confound much of the cleavage
between the old parties. The demand for the improvement
of rivers and harbors drew most directly from the Whig
view of constitutional powers, though silence on any "system" of improvement might easily attract the support of
pragmatic-minded Democrats. The section dealing with
import duties could also win their approval, for it defined a
tariff tied directly to the need of revenue. As the chief
author of the platform, Chase did admit in private that a
judicious interpretation of this plank might yield a policy of
protection "least likely" to suit the free-trade tendencies of
most Jacksonians. But it lacked system, he added, and its
spirit was "so little Whiggish, in the conservative sense of
that term." Even less conservative, finally, was the provision
for a "free grant" of land to actual settlers.[37] It harkened
back to the position staked out by President Andrew Jackson during the nullification controversy when, as a part of
his effort to dismantle the American System of policies, he
proclaimed rapid movement to the West and a speedy
settlement of the lands to be in the true interest of the
nation. "Free Soil" now took on added meaning: it was to be
defined, not only by the negating presence of slavery, but
also by its opposition to the corporate impulse of John
Quincy Adams and others to use the trust fund of land

revenues for improving the quality of national life through time.

In sum, the Free Soil platform evinced no clear system with regard to the shape of the future course of the nation. Protection that might be wrested from the tariff plank and rapid movement to the West promised in the homestead measure comprised two policies which were once thought to be mutually contradictory. In this light, the new party clearly fulfilled the specifications laid down by a Birney supporter in 1845. "Our creed will be neither Whig or Democratic," Theodore Foster explained, but one in which the Whigs lost "their own identity" and the Democrats surrendered their strictures against government of "a positive character." The "system" in this outlook was to be found in the attitude of the government toward the *"paramount* question" of slavery and not in the calculation of consequences that flowed from the goods that freemen sought. On this principle, Giddings prophetically declared in 1848, "is now based a party, *or the germ of a party, that will at no distant day become dominant in this nation.*"[38]

Comment upon the new political movement by three contemporaries serves to point up the different elements in the broker-state outlook. From one side Senator Thomas Corwin of Ohio condemned it as "monomaniac Free Democracy." Its preoccupation with the issue of slavery, he supposed, ruled out any real concern for other issues. Abraham Lincoln was struck, on the other hand, by a rank opportunism in the Free Soil appeal to all interests which tended to make the government nothing more than a giver of good things in the present. "If their platform held any other (issues than slavery)," he said, "it was in such a general way that it was like a pair of pantaloons the Yankee peddlar offered for sale, 'large enough for any man, small enough for any boy'." But to such a true believer as Judge Nye, a delegate to the Free Soil convention in 1848, both Corwin and Lincoln failed to grasp the essential unity in the new faith and the hierarchy of values in its blend of idealism and self-interest. Their implicit insistence upon a system of policies and a positive history-making role for the government missed the point. "If we are wrong on the Tariff, it can be righted by legislation," the judge explained. "But if we are wrong on the subject of Slavery, it can never be righted."[39] The basic right of freemen to pursue any and all kinds of policies was of far greater importance than any consideration of the kinds of policies to be pursued.

In a number of ways, then, the ideology of Free Soil, which was to shape the national dialogue from the end of the 1840s to the outbreak of the Civil War, exhibited the distinctive form of negative liberalism. The debate over the issue of slavery expansion was not a contest between two kinds of freedom—corporate and federative—but between freedom on the one side and slavery on the other. The position of "freedom national," of individual freedom as the essential national idea, thus defined an irrepressible conflict with those who sought to expand and perpetuate slavery under the aegis of the federal government. The geopolitics of the conflict also indicated its irrepressible nature, for the containment of one meant the total dominion of the other. Success in preventing the slave power from commiting the nation to the evils of time would restore the freedom of an eternal present. Freemen might then pursue their several interests with the aid, but not direction, of the government, thereby promoting in an unplanned way the good of the whole. Chase summarized the matter well. Only "the control of the slaveholders," he argued, "holds back our country from a splendid career of greatness and glory."[40] Democracy in its first reading under Jackson had drawn planters and plain republicans together under the banner of federative freedom in common opposition to the American System. In its second reading, under the Free

Soilers, the individual, particular, and discrete elements in
the spirit of democratic nationalism assumed fuller form in
opposition to the slaveholders.

This is not to deny the presence and the influence of
many corporate elements in the Free-Soil movement. In the
name of the general welfare, for example, Representative
Jenkins of New York rejected the principle of popular
sovereignty, which gave to the people in a territory the right
to decide the question of freedom and slavery. Because it
was so fully a "national question," he rather affirmed, the
"inhabitants of the whole nation" had rights far exceeding
those claimed for "a few straggling settlers." For one thing,
the plundering of resources by an inefficient slave labor
system blasted the hopes that the national estate might be
enriched and improved. The opposition of the South to the
positive policies of the government also constituted an obstacle to the progress of the nation, and further expansion
would aggravate the evil. The equal representation in the
Senate enjoyed by new and sparsely settled slave states
served, according to Representative Truman Smith of
Connecticut, no less than the added power of three-fifths
representation to make the South nothing but "a rotten-
borough system." Nor was the Free-Soil position on particular economic issues quite as disparate and unsystematic, in
the view of some, as the broker-state concept suggests.
Horace Greeley was working toward a Whiggish synthesis
of tariff and homestead measures, and Seward would add
to it in the following decade. There is thus a good deal of
substance to the argument of a recent writer that the contest
between Free Soil and Manifest Destiny was a renewal of
the old debate between Whigs and Democrats about internal improvement versus external expansion.[41]

In exact contrast, however, to the efforts to stop the
spread of slavery during the Missouri controversy, the
force of corporate freedom at work in the Free-Soil move-

ment of the 1840s represented its minor theme.[42] The
response of many Whigs at the time demonstrates anew the
fact that the imperatives of negative liberalism constituted
the predominant theme. Representative Winthrop of Massachusetts strongly supported the Wilmot Proviso as late as
1847, it was true, and judged it to be "the great conservative
principle of the day." Its conservatism, however, lay not in
the moral impulse to purge the evil accretions of time and
restore the original design of the Union; it lay rather in the
fact that, by causing sectional divisions within the ranks of
Jacksonian expansionists, a proviso for restricting slavery
would bring to an end further territorial acquisitions and
thereby fix permanent bounds to the Union. Senator William L. Dayton of New Jersey, equally opposed to a Free-
Soil crusade for regenerating the original design of the
nation, therefore deplored the spirit of moral absolutism
with which the crusaders would "set the world on fire" for
"a mere theory." The goal of the Free Soilers, he thought,
was a good to be considered in the perspective of other
goods in the order of the Union, and not as an end in
itself.[43]

The constitutional views of like-minded Whigs also
pointed up the new and ominous way in which the issue of
slavery expansion was being debated. Representative William Duer of New York took pains to reaffirm "the true
interpretation of the Constitution" in answer to the three
separate constructions which had arisen from the splinter-
ing of the Jeffersonian heritage in the 1840s. In his view,
the Constitution did not make the prohibition of slavery
mandatory, as the position of "freedom national" supposed, nor did the shield of its protection automatically
extend over slave property carried into national territories.
The government under the Constitution assumed instead a
position of moral neutrality, for sovereign power lay in the
discretion of Congress either to prohibit or to extend slav-

ery. Though the proponents of popular sovereignty also assumed a morally neutral position, Duer could not accept their plan to devolve power onto the people in the territory. It was a national question, he insisted, and clearly within the province of congressional action. Webster was in complete agreement. He totally rejected the claims of "slavery national" put forth by Calhoun, and with the same corporate ideas would soon oppose the Free Soilers in the crisis of 1850. In both cases, the nature of his opposition constituted another measure of how the terms of the debate over slavery had been transformed since the Missouri controversy.[44]

7
The Crisis and Compromise of 1850

Angry contention over the fruits of manifest destiny brought the nation to the verge of civil war by 1850. Because the area in dispute was of such imperial dimensions, it gave special credence to the claim that the shape of the new part of the Union might reshape the whole. Stretching from Texas and the upper reaches of the old Louisiana Purchase westward to the Pacific, it included Oregon south of the 49th parallel and all of the lands acquired from Mexico in 1848. A restless and rapidly growing population in some parts of the vast domain clearly indicated the need for regular government and thus lent urgency to the call for Congress to provide territorial organization. But there was a rub. Any measure of Congress for organizing new territories would inescapably reopen the fateful controversy over the spread of slavery.

Some success had come from earlier efforts to deal with the vast and unorganized area; yet larger failures pointed to an impending crisis in the nation. A territorial government had been formed for Oregon, but the inclusion of a Free-Soil proviso embittered southern leaders. For whatever it was worth as a face-saving gesture, President Polk made it clear that he signed the measure only because all of Oregon lay north of the old Missouri Compromise line of

36°30'.[1] Elsewhere, Free-Soil opposition assured the defeat of all bills that would, in fact, extend the application of this line from the Louisiana Purchase into the new areas. Defeat also came to the Clayton compromise measure, which would have provided governments for all of the territories and left the final decision over slavery to the federal courts. As a consequence, the territories acquired from Mexico remained unorganized. In the case of the eastern portion a more imminent danger arose, for the state of Texas threatened military intervention to make good its claims to territory in New Mexico on the left bank of the Rio Grande. Meanwhile, the call for Congress to end the slave trade in the District of Columbia was matched, as the sectional debate became more wide-ranging, by the southern demand for a new fugitive slave law.[2] The prolonged and bitter struggle in the House of Representatives to choose a Speaker dramatized in another way the dimensions of the mounting crisis.

The crisis was precipitated when the people of California, acting without official authority from the central government, constituted themselves into a body politic and asked for admission into the Union as a free state. It was a fateful moment for the South, John C. Calhoun warned his fellows, because the entry of California would destroy, perhaps forever, the equality of power in the Senate heretofore enjoyed by the slaveholding states. "Events may now be controlled; but, it will be difficult, if not impossible to control their course hereafter," he wrote to James H. Hammond. Hammond agreed that the South must be able to balance the power of the free states somewhere in the common government. "If we do not act now," he said, "we deliberately consign our children, not our posterity, but *our children* to the flames." In like fashion Senator Jefferson Davis of Mississippi called on "the present generation" to meet the crisis at hand. It was a time, Representative Robert

Toombs of Georgia declared, to "carry our principles in our foreheads." Unless guarantees of slavery accompanied the admission of California he boldly spoke in favor of dissolving the Union.[3]

Apparently failing to comprehend the depth and range of the controversy, President Zachary Taylor pursued a course unlikely to resolve it in a peaceful way. He favored the admission of California on its own merits, unconnected with any compromise deal involving other issues. Not the least of its merits was the fact that, by proceeding directly from the condition of an unorganized territory to that of full statehood, the people of California had relieved Congress and the President from the need of making a decision on the issue of slavery expansion. For this same reason, Taylor recommended "non-action" in regard to New Mexico and Utah. By leaving them unorganized he could dodge the proviso question and yet hope that the people there would eventually follow the example of California. But non-action in the territories was more than balanced by the prospect of action against the state of Texas. With the self-image of an Andrew Jackson standing on the breastworks of the Union, Taylor was ready to meet by force the effort of Texas to occupy the eastern territory of New Mexico. Such a confrontation, Representative Alexander H. Stephens of Georgia warned, would usher in a civil war. The "first roar of federal artillery" in Santa Fe, he said, would rally the South to a sister state in the same way that Lexington and Concord had opened an earlier revolution against the tyranny of the British government.[4]

It was in this context that Henry Clay introduced into the Senate a set of compromise proposals for dealing in a systematic way with all of the issues in debate. The bleeding wounds in "the body politic" required "a system of measures," he argued, and not the patchwork or evasions of President Taylor. He recommended that California be ad-

mitted into the Union as a free state with the boundaries its
constitutional convention had defined. Dismissing the
Taylor plan of non-action as irresponsible, he demanded
the organization of territorial governments for New Mexico and Utah without a Free-Soil proviso. The assumption
of the state debt, by another of Clay's recommendations,
would compensate Texas for surrendering the substance of
her territorial claims in New Mexico. Laws covering two
other matters not connected directly with the issue of slavery expansion would hopefully bring peace. The slave
trade in the District of Columbia was to end, and effective
federal machinery for the return of fugitive slaves to be
established. Though subject to modifications and varied
interpretations, these proposals were the basis for the final
compromise settlement.[5]

Daniel Webster and a very small group of northern
Whigs joined hands with most party members from the
South in behalf of the settlement. For them compromise
would secure the order of the corporate Union as its highest
good. A much greater number of congressional votes for
compromise came from Jacksonians under the leadership
of Stephen A. Douglas.[6] They saw in the key compromise
measures a vindication of the principle of popular
sovereignty which would leave the people in new areas
essentially free from central control. In the perspective of
earlier arrangements for sectional concord, however, the
Compromise of 1850 fashioned a very frail and uneasy
peace. Thirty years before, southern Republican leaders
had imposed the terms of the Missouri Compromise upon
themselves, hoping thereby to restore the consensus of
planters and plain republicans under the banner of federative freedom. In similar terms President Jackson resolved
the nullification controversy with an outlook that gave form
to the national dialogue in the following years.

By contrast, little unity obtained among the Whig and

Jacksonian compromisers in 1850 to give initiative and
shape to the nation's course. As advocates of the older
concepts of corporate and federative freedom, they stood
between the stark and conflicting claims of freedom and
slavery. The compromise agreement did not therefore resolve these claims. It was only a temporary truce forced
upon the protagonists. Further analysis of the debates during the crisis of 1850 reveals instead that its basic structure
was defined by the Free-Soil terms of irrepressible conflict.
Leading southern spokesmen responded directly to the
geopolitical thought and monistic claims of "freedom national," while the Free Soilers expressed in a strong and
unequivocal way the moral imperative to regenerate the
Union on its original design.

The southern response desired, first of all, a "balance of
power." In 1845, French Minister Guizot challenged the
monism of manifest destiny and called on Europe to establish a balance of power in North America. With far greater
urgency Calhoun now demanded of Free Soilers the means
for the permanent coexistence of different political elements within the nation. He took the unchanging essence of
the Union to be a partnership of sovereign states, slave and
free, and he thought the condition of its existence lay in the
defensive power each element possessed within the Union.
If the South was on the verge of losing its power of self-
defense, Calhoun further reasoned, it had not come about
in the natural course of events. Rather it had been the result
of artificial and unconstitutional legislation, of such measures as the Northwest Ordinance, the protective tariff, and
other bounties by which the North had prospered at the
expense of the South. Secession as a constitutional right
remained the ultimate safety valve from such evils of time,
but Calhoun looked for security within the Union by restoring the equilibrium of power. In apparent despair of other
means, he vaguely suggested a constitutional amendment

which would give to the slaveholding states a permanent
veto power at some point within the common government.[7]

Very few adopted the particular policy of Calhoun for
securing a balance of power, but younger disciples hopefully sought to achieve his goal by another means. Senator
David Yulee of Florida invoked the "Liberty of Growth" to
supply the "omission in the Constitution" Calhoun professed to find. Senator Robert M. T. Hunter of Virginia
similarly regarded the greatest of all "political boons" to be
"that of bringing more slave states into this confederacy
—enough to preserve the old balance in this body; or if that
cannot be, to approach that object as nearly as possible."
Jefferson Davis had no doubt that slave labor could be used
in the areas acquired from Mexico and in others farther
south. "To the Pacific, then, I say—to the Pacific," was the
demand of Representative Richard K. Meade of Virginia.
He hoped that a cordon of slave states to the Pacific would
render the remainder of the continent to the south the
"exclusive domain" of slavery. For this reason many expansionists were willing, in contrast with Calhoun, to accept the
compromise line of 36°30′ to the Pacific. It would represent
a real concession to the South for admitting the northern
part of California as a free state, Yulee explained, "a distinct, unequivocal, unmistakable, and palpable recognition
of their full right to colonize in these and other territories
with their slaves."[8]

The alternative to the safety valve of expansion, in this
view, was the certain doom of the slaveholding South. By
surrounding it with "a cordon of free states," Representative Winfield S. Featherston of Mississippi warned, the Free
Soilers made the overthrow of slavery "inevitable." Like
"the crushings of an anaconda," John McQueen of South
Carolina explained in the House, the end might come
through the direct action of the federal government when,
by the growth of free states, a three-fourths majority would

have been attained for adopting an abolition amendment. Or, as Representative Isham G. Harris of Tennessee stated the widely professed belief, emancipation might also come by the "indirect" action of the federal government. The presence of free states and territories on all sides constituted an expanded haven for fugitive slaves and a standing invitation to insurrection. When slavery ceased to spread out into new areas, moreover, the Malthusian laws of population would at last render slave labor totally infeasible. At some point, in any case, the South would then face the gravest of all problems—the coexistence of the races. Supposing this to be impossible in a free society, Yulee believed white men had only three alternatives: they might exterminate the free Negro, be vanquished by them, or abandon the region, "leaving in the end the graves of their sires to be trodden under the heel of the African." For his section, Yulee thus concluded that the right of expansion was "the very condition of her existence."[9]

Not the least element in this existence, finally, was the feeling of sectional honor and self-respect. Senator John M. Berrien of Georgia was opposed throughout the 1840s to the policy of national expansion, yet bitterly resented the Free-Soil proviso to exclude the South from participation in the process. By placing his section under "the ban of the Republic," he said, the proviso impinged directly upon the "family circle," involving the honor of his forebearers no less than the security of his offspring. Alexander Stephens resisted in a far more militant fashion the effort to make the slaveholding states inferior partners in the Union. "I would rather that the southern country shall perish—that all her statesmen and all her gallant spirits shall be buried in honorable graves," he declared, "than submit for one instant to degredation."[10] By the demand for equal honor, if not an absolute balance of power in the Union, southern spokesmen squarely confronted the assumption of total dominion lodged in the geopolitics of free soil. The fate of the new part of the Union, in this light, vitally involved the destiny of the old.

In constitutional terms, as well, the answer Calhoun had given to "freedom national" in the preceding years gained wider currency and full expression in the crisis of 1850.[11] While couched in the old terms of states' rights, it provided to "slavery national" a solid base. "This is a proslavery Government," Toombs declared. "Slavery is stamped upon its heart—the Constitution." The Union was formed at a particular point in time, Representative Charles S. Morehead of Kentucky explained, to secure the "pre-existing rights" of the sovereign states. Lacking the corporate attributes of independent purpose or will, it was to persist in this unchanging form through all time and space as a trustee of the states. Such a Union established a moratorium on substantial change; in effect, it served to absolutize a particular moment in time. "We stand by the contract our fathers made for us," Representative Edward C. Cabell of Florida thus declared. "So long as the spirit of that contract is observed, we shall never look back to its dissolution as a remedy for existing evils."[12]

It was a contract that gave ample scope to the expansion of slavery. Under the shield of its protection, Senator James M. Mason of Virginia claimed that slavery could move as freely into new territories as it did in the interstate slave trade or on the high seas. Indeed, Senator Hopkins L. Turney of Tennessee defined the nationality of slavery in even wider terms: "it exists by the Constitution of the United States itself, in all the States and territories of the Union, except in those States only where it is expressly forbidden by state constitutions, in the exercise of State sovereignty." Where the specific need arose, Robert M. T. Hunter was therefore ready for Congress to pass a law extending positive protection to slavery in the territory.[13]

156   SPACE, TIME, AND FREEDOM

In this he clearly anticipated the call of the Southern Democratic party in 1860 for a territorial slave code.

From this position of "slavery national," then, spokesmen in 1850, no less than those of a decade later, felt compelled to reject the idea of popular sovereignty on which many were basing their support for compromise. It was "a more absurd doctrine" than Free Soil itself, Senator Turney argued, because it gave to a few straggling settlers in a new territory the power to destroy the constitutional right of slaveholders in the sovereign states. Free Soilers adduced a far more respectable sanction for violating the Constitution, by contrast, for they at least required a majority vote of the national legislature. Jefferson Davis found another reason for preferring the Wilmot Proviso to the nonintervention of Congress. By the need they felt for a positive congressional enactment against slavery, the Free Soilers indirectly admitted southern rights, whereas the advocates of popular sovereignty denied, by congressional silence on the matter, the existence of any right at all. Moreover, the assumption that the old Mexican laws against slavery remained in force served, in the view of Representative James L. Orr of South Carolina, to make popular sovereignty an efficient instrument for achieving the Free-Soil goal.[14]

Free Soil remained the ultimate enemy, however, and the idea of "freedom national" measured the degeneration of the nation from the original design of the fathers. In the ship of state, Hunter complained, "things have changed, and are changing, since the crew were first shipped." Encroachments through time upon the rights of the South, Representative George A. Caldwell of Kentucky said, had essentially subverted "*that* Union" fashioned by the founders. The will of a naked majority began to establish itself as a supreme law above constitutional restraints, Senator Jeremiah Clemens of Alabama warned, as "free democracy

degenerates into the purest federalism." Jefferson Davis
compared it to a rising flood which, swelled by the lust of
power and the spirit of fanaticism, threatened to "pour
their turgid waters through the broken Constitution." In
the same spirit, Representative John S. Millson of Virginia
rejected the pleas of those who sought by compromise to
save the Union. "We cannot have what has ceased to exist,"
he declared. "The Union, established by the Constitution,
cannot survive the destruction of the Constitution."[15]

The only way to save the Union, in this view, was to
regenerate its original and unchanging design. "The ship
of state," Thomas H. Averett of Virginia told the House,
"must be brought back to its true republican tack." This
meant, according to Representative Volney E. Howard of
Texas, that the common government recapture "the original spirit" no less than "the letter of the Constitution." In a
more fundamental sense, Meade of Virginia thought a
regeneration of the nation could not come "until the feeling
which brought the fathers together, shall reanimate the
bosoms of their sons." Then might the nation arrive at "a
new point of departure," Representative Thomas S. Bocock
of Virginia observed, and resume the task of fulfilling its
own grand destiny and of liberating the world. All the while
secession remained as a final if more limited mode of regeneration, in case all efforts to cast out the poisonous
heresy of Free Soil failed. The "spirit of 1776" aroused by
the unconstitutional effort to stop the spread of slavery
might, according to Representative Abraham W. Venable
of North Carolina, find reincarnation in a new union
formed by states still faithful to the idea of the fathers.[16]

By the contrast it presents, the reactions of many southern compromisers in 1850 points out, in another way, how
fully the proslavery spokesmen had here come to grips with
the affirmations of "freedom national." Because they were
generally opposed to a policy of territorial expansion,

158 SPACE, TIME, AND FREEDOM

Whigs in particular resisted the effort to apply geopolitical categories to the sectional controversy. Even without a Free-Soil proviso, Representative Meredith P. Gentry of Tennessee argued that slavery could not take hold in the climate and soil of the territory acquired from Mexico. Hence he deplored "the irrational excitement" generated on the subject by those who sought the addition of new slave states. Equally irrational, Christopher H. Williams of Tennessee told the House, was the anxiety for added space as the very condition for the existence of slavery. The present population of the South could live comfortably in the one state of Virginia, he supposed, while the boundaries of the entire region would easily accommodate ninety million people without any prospect of a Malthusian doom. Nor was the equilibrium of power within the Union needed to secure the existence of slavery. Pluralism, rather than a stark dualism of slave and free elements, characterized the life of the nation, Representative Edward Stanly of North Carolina said, and prescribed the true course for statesmen to follow. Real and permanent protection for slavery could best be attained, he thought, by a spirit of reciprocity among southern leaders which disposed them to support the tariff and other policies for promoting the varied interests of freemen in the North.[17]

On constitutional grounds, southern leaders in favor of compromise likewise challenged the position of "slavery national." Whig Senator George F. Badger of North Carolina reaffirmed the corporate view that slavery was a matter of political expediency and that Congress possessed equal power to prohibit or to encourage its expansion. Because Calhoun and his disciples made slavery a matter of principle and the duty of the government to protect it a mandatory one, Badger judged them to be as guilty as the Free Soilers of misreading the Constitution. From his position of popular sovereignty, which denied to Congress

either the power to prohibit or protect slavery in the territories, Democratic Senator Henry S. Foote of Mississippi
could agree. With great precision he thus condemned the
Calhoun school for seeking "a sort of southern Wilmot
proviso." Whig compromisers also rejected the idea of
peaceable secession. The Union was not the sort of thing
whose value could always be calculated, Badger protested, a
mere "mercantile partnership to transact business." Stanly
and Williams similarly thought of the Constitution as a
solemn marriage covenant from which there could be no
divorce. Secession was therefore starkly revolutionary and
not a constitutional right.[18]

Within its own terms, as a recent author has well noted,
the sectional recourse of secession as a constitutional right
seemed to contradict the general position of "slavery national" which had also been staked out.[19] But, when seen in
the dialectical presence of "freedom national," there is no
contradiction at all. The ultimate claim to sever the ties of
the Union served rather to make irrepressible the conflict
now defined in the essential frame of negative liberalism.
Proslavery spokesmen and Free Soilers alike assumed an
originally perfect design for the Union, deviation from it in
the course of time, and the need to restore it again. The
quality of timelessness in this outlook once found expression as planters and plain republicans shared a common
opposition to corporate efforts for directing the course of
the nation through time. Now each saw the enemy to freedom in the other; and only in freedom from the control of
the other did each suppose it possible to avert the multiplying evils of time. Expansion across space under the full and
honorable sanction of the Constitution, it was hoped, might
bring security to the South's awful hostage from the past. As
a declining minority in a Union increasingly disposed to
meddle, however, the failure to gain immunity from time
by the safety valve of expansion pointed at last to the neces-

sity of secession. In a formal sense, they might be compelled
to regenerate the idea of the fathers by creating a new and
separate union.

By contrast, the latent and growing majority which Free
Soilers hoped to fashion prescribed a totally different
course. For them the enterprise of regeneration was to be
accomplished only within the existing Union. If secession
brought on a crisis, as a consequence, the real question
confronting them would be a simple one: not a concern for
the preservation of the Union, but for the kind of Union to
be preserved. Instead of temporising expedients or a
patchwork of compromises with the evil of slavery, they
would invoke anew the principle of timeless freedom on
which they supposed the Union to repose. Liberty and the
Union had become one and inseparable, in the view of Free
Soilers, and they stood ready to use force for resolving the
irrepressible conflict which they had helped to define. By
1850 the ideological terms of the Civil War had thus gained
full expression. One of the best gauges of this historic
juncture in the affairs of the nation can be found in the
position assumed by Daniel Webster. As the following
analysis seeks to demonstrate, his plea for compromise in
behalf of the order of the Union "as it is" serves to place in
sharp relief the impulses to larger liberty and the urgency
of regeneration in the Free-Soil movement.

During the crisis Webster addressed himself chiefly to
fellow congressmen of the North who stood inflexibly opposed to the compromise measures.[20] Because the constitutional obligations with regard to fugitive slaves seemed so
clear, he condemned as "guilty of treason" those who appealed to a higher law. He deplored as well their blood
thirst in refusing concessions to Texas in the boundary
dispute with New Mexico, for the threat of that state to
occupy the area with troops brought the nation to the brink
of civil war. Most of all, Webster resisted the effort of the

Free Soilers to apply the Wilmot Proviso to bills for organizing the territorial governments of New Mexico and Utah.
Since soil, climate, and the prior laws of Mexico had already
interdicted slavery, he could only regard the proviso as a
"mere abstraction." Webster expressed the desire to stop
the spread of slavery, and he favored a positive enactment
of the proviso "whenever there is a particular good to be
done." But what he opposed here was an abstract politics
which made the proviso a political good or end in itself. In a
more general way, he attacked the spirit of moral absolutism which informed that kind of politics. "They deal
with morals as with mathematics," he complained, "and
they think what is right may be distinguished from what is
wrong, with the precision of an algebraic equation."[21]

Free Soilers readily accepted the challenge of Webster.
Thaddeus Stevens of Pennsylvania told the House that
"There can be no fanatics in the cause of genuine liberty."
Questions involving the morality of slavery and freedom,
Representative Charles Durkee of Wisconsin agreed, "are
more clear than any question in algebra." Absolutists, in
such a case, embody political realism in its truest sense. But
the realism lay in the fact that the idea of freedom to which
they appealed was not a "higher law" as Webster claimed,
but the established principle of the Union itself. It was "the
great idea," Congressman Kinsley S. Bingham of Michigan
explained, which the fathers adopted "in the earlier and
better days of this Republic." The Wilmot Proviso thus
embodied the most fundamental idea of the nation, Representative George W. Julian of Indiana added, "the very
life blood of freedom." While Webster dismissed the proviso as a needless taunt to the South, Julian held that its
periodic affirmation served the salutary purpose of national rededication. "Sir," Thomas B. Butler of Connecticut
accordingly declared in the House, "we stand where our
fathers stood—we abide by their principles."[22]

Underlying this debate between Webster and the Free Soilers were profoundly different concepts of time. Webster, keenly aware of the irreversible flow of events, tended to see the destiny of freemen chiefly within the temporal process. He could not, therefore, accept the dictum of Lord Bolingbroke that history was only philosophy teaching by example. While something of natural rights and a universal human nature undoubtedly persisted through time, Webster was struck most by the "concomitant rush of altered circumstances" within which the life of each generation transpired. As a practical political good, he ever supposed that freedom in America had "an ancestry, a pedigree, a history." The Union, formed to secure the blessings of liberty, likewise possessed temporal dimensions. Webster thought of it as a grand corporation which organized and gave meaning to freemen in each passing generation. Hopefully, as well, qualitative improvement might mark its career through time. But he observed that progress would come in the form of a gradual redress in the balance of good and evil; for, unlike the restive Free Soilers who insisted "that nothing is good but what is perfect," he thought that life caught up in time was an inescapable mixture of plural and imperfect elements. In the crisis of 1850, Webster especially sought to make his fellows see themselves in the proper historical perspective. "Let us make our generation one of the strongest and brightest links," he implored, "in that golden chain which is destined, I fully believe, to grapple the people of all the States in this Constitution, for ages to come."[23]

Free Soilers, by contrast, displayed in the crisis of 1850 a decidedly ahistorical temper. Their appeal was more to "nature" than to "history," to a timeless good and not to the good shaped and determined in time. Whereas Webster looked to the pedigree of American liberty, Senator Salmon P. Chase of Ohio sought for a universal sanction. The

Revolutionary War, he pointed out, "was waged not to vindicate privileges, but rights; not the rights of any part or class of people, but the rights of all men—'the rights of human nature'." Representative David Wilmot agreed that the "great doctrine of the universality of freedom" constituted "an established article of the republican creed." Since slavery and not freedom partook of the temporal process, Senator John P. Hale of New Hampshire took the role of statesmen to be an essentially defensive one. They were not to perfect or improve the quality of freedom through time by the history-making power of the government, but rather to assure the natural progress of the free principle by keeping the government from falling into the hands of the negating element of slavery. They should be as "the vestal virgins" in Rome, Representative Peter H. Silvester of New York thus noted, guarding "the holy fire" in the temple of liberty. Finally, the ultimate strength and security of the temple of the Union lay less in its corporate and institutional presence than in the love of freedom created anew in each successive generation of the people. "And the voice of that people," Charles E. Clarke of New York declared in the House, "is the voice of God."[24]

The differing concepts of time found more particular manifestation in the way each side conceived of the crisis and the proper way to deal with it. For Webster the crisis represented a temporary derangement of the plural elements composing the Union. He supposed that the many parts making up the Union had ceased for the time to perceive their true relation to the corporate whole. As a consequence, the "imprisoned winds" of agitation had escaped to set "the whole ocean in commotion." In their preoccupation with the "one idea" of a Free-Soil proviso, northern demagogues neglected the many other goods to be achieved by attending all interests. Their politics of abstractions, Webster complained, glossed over the great truth that in the pursuit of solid benefit "men go from step to step, according to the exigency of the case." Nor were the people any longer content, he feared, to do good "in that sphere of life in which we are placed."[25] They seemed unable to realize how the concrete blessings of daily life depended upon the grand order of the Union which past generations had achieved by toil and sacrifice. But it was only in the Union, he solemnly advised, that "their daily labor, their daily employment, their daily means of living and of educating their families may continue undisturbed." Webster here assumed that the pursuits of happiness were cumulative and corporate in nature, and that the failure to perceive the true dimensions of the Union placed everything in jeopardy. "If a house be divided against itself," he warned in a language which anticipated Abraham Lincoln's formula of crisis in 1858, "it will fall, and crush everybody in it."[26]

Unlike the Free-Soiler Lincoln a decade later, however, Webster believed that only by compromise could the crisis be happily reached and passed. "I speak today," he told the Senate, "out of a solicitous and anxious heart, for the restoration to the country of that quiet and that harmony, which makes the blessings of this Union so rich and so dear to us all." This involved the task of composing anew the many elements which had initially gone into the Union. In answer to the Free Soilers, he protested that the "spirit of union which actuated our ancestors" was not the kind which sought to vanquish one of the constituent elements. Webster hoped by compromise to restore the nation to the concrete course of development which the crisis had interrupted and to make Congress once more "an active, beneficial, and parental legislature for the whole country."[27]

But Webster warned his fellows in the Senate that the god-like task of restoring order would not be easy. They must withstand the popular pressures, he warned, and reject the vulgar counsels of the "common mind." In a powerful philippic against the right of state legislatures to instruct their representatives in the Senate, he contended that "all the world out of doors is not so wise and patriotic as all the world within these walls." Once harmony had been reestablished by the actions of those who understood the matter best, Webster predicted that the people would sing hosannas anew to the Union as they had done after the crises of 1820 and 1833. The "virtue," the "patriotism," and the "Americanism" of statesmen would discipline the people to a vision of their destiny within its true corporate and temporal dimensions.[28]

The Free Soilers saw the crisis in a radically different way. "Sir," Senator William H. Seward of New York said, "the agitations which alarm us are not signs of evils to come, but wild efforts of the commonwealth for relief from mischiefs past." In like spirit, George W. Julian resisted Webster's idea that the "disease in the body politic" was nothing more than a temporary disorder of constituent elements. He deemed it rather to be a fateful illness caused by the incursion of "an alien and hostile element."[29] Equally disposed to view the crisis as a drama of cosmic proportions between good and evil, Ohio Representative John Crowell welcomed "the turbulence of freedom" as the herald of the final ripening of the irrepressible conflict. Agitation could not be stopped, Joshua R. Giddings warned those inclined to compromise, any more than one could hold back the tumbling waters of Niagara. "This progress in morals, and in political intelligence," he declared, "is in strict accordance with the law of our being, and cannot be prevented." For this reason Chase predicted failure for the efforts of Webster and a congressional elite to compose the political elements. The people, he triumphantly claimed, "will unsettle your settlement."[30]

Because Free Soilers regarded the crisis as a joyful opportunity to be seized and not a dreadful moment to be passed, they rejected all compromise appeals. In practical terms, Representative Clarke warned, past compromises had been "shortsighted, temporising, ruinous expedients," for they had brought not a new era of sectional harmony but further aggrandizement of the slave power. The contest over the territory acquired from Mexico was especially important, Wilmot thought, because it held the key to the remainder of the continent to the south and, in consequence, the fate of freemen "to the remotest posterity." In ideological terms, most of all, Free Soilers discounted the very possibility of compromise. Unlike "the ordinary questions of the day," where differences might be accommodated, Representative William A. Sackett of New York protested that there could be no harmony between the "absolute right" of freedom and the "absolute wrong" of slavery. Julian agreed that the moment had come to make an irreversible commitment to the national idea of freedom. "In the very nature of things, slavery and freedom are irreconcilable foes to each other," he explained, "and therefore their conflicts cannot cease until justice shall assert her supremacy, in the subjection and overthrow of the latter." The crisis, as Lincoln later put it, would then be properly passed, and the house would cease to be divided. "Then our fair country will be glorious indeed," Thaddeus Stevens added, "and be to posterity a bright example of the true principles of government—of universal freedom."[31]

The difference between them found clear expression in the way each conceived of the alternative to compromise. The failure to reach a settlement struck Webster as horrible and stark. It presented the prospect of nothing less than the total destruction of the Union as a historic order of freedom. "We have established over us a much better form of government than may ordinarily be expected in the allotments of Providence to men," he warned those who blandly assumed the Union an eternal entity. Though it possessed grand corporate dimensions, Webster yet believed that one generation might bring it down in ruins. "But, alas, gentlemen," he observed, "human structures, however strong, do not stand upon the everlasting laws of nature." A "perpetual darkness" or the "return to chaos" would, with disunion, displace the good of order which the "unthinking and careless" people took so much for granted. Or, to change the figure, he wanted freemen to see themselves as passengers on the ship of state and to realize that the preservation of the vessel in the storm constituted the highest good. "I speak today for the preservation of the Union," he pleaded at the outset of his famous Senate speech. "Hear me for my cause."[32]

For Webster, liberty was a good which had been gained and disciplined by the past and which might become more nearly perfect through time. The American Revolution, in this view of things, secured that degree of freedom established during the colonial period. The "great and wise Constitution" provided an order within which the nation might then enjoy its freedom. Webster could only dismiss as "a new species of patriotism" the appeal which Free Soilers were apparently making to a higher law. "I profess to love liberty as much as any man living," he protested, "but I profess to love American liberty, that liberty which is secured to the country by the government under which we live; and I have no great opinion of that other and higher liberty which disregards the restraints of law and the Constitution."[33] To be sure, Webster did invoke the spirit of universal liberty in response to the charges of the Austrian minister Hulsemann that the United States was displaying too much sympathy for the Hungarian rebels. But even here, as he privately admitted, the appeal in the public letter was calculated to arouse patriotic feelings for preserving his kind of Union. "I wished to write a paper which should touch the national pride," he said, "and make men feel *sheepish* and look *silly* who would speak of dis- union."[34]

Webster did not suppose, of course, that the peculiarity of American liberty was so complete as to rule out all uni- versal significance. In the case of slavery, and presumably of all other political issues, he professed to discover a dialogue between a "natural right" and an "established relation" in society. Progress, in these terms, involved a redress in the balance of the two. But it was a process which took time, he protested, because men in every generation were "subject to be influenced by what appears to them their present, emergent, and exigent interest." On these grounds Webster regarded as far too facile the Free-Soil charge that the machinations of the slave power had caused the spread of the peculiar institution since the adoption of the Constitution. The invention of the cotton gin had opened new prospects of enterprise to the slaveholders, he argued instead, and "gratified their desire for improve- ment and accumulation." He therefore refused to con- demn their actions as unusually selfish and dishonest. "All that has happened has been natural," Webster concluded, for time had unfolded new possibilities and fixed new limits within which the freemen of the nation might at any par- ticular moment shape their destinies.[35]

Webster resisted, consequently, the call of the Free Soil- ers to abolish the products of time and start over again. From his corporate point of view, he had always denied that each generation possessed a separate identity or the power to achieve a complete regeneration. The undeniable fact of daily births and deaths belied the Jeffersonian claim of autonomy and separate nationality for each generation. It suggested, to the contrary, that the common life occurred in a larger temporal process. Regeneration, in this case, could mean the attainment of lasting good through the

course of time. Webster thus refused to "co-operate in
breaking up social and political systems" on the hope of
achieving instant and absolute good. Christianity itself had
won its way into the hearts of men very slowly, he reminded
an abolitionist minister, and had yet to enjoy a complete
victory. "But what are two thousand years," he asked, "in
the great work of progress of the regeneration and redemption of mankind?"[36]

If Webster professed to see in the failure of compromise
the likely destruction of the order of the Union, Free Soilers
opposed concessions to slavery precisely because they
wanted to recreate the true order of freedom. The position
they took represented a blend of two elements. On the one
hand, the assurance of their potential power led them to
scoff at threats of disunion. Webster and others might
conjure the spirits of the "vasty deep," Henry Bennett of
New York declared in the House, but the Union would
endure. The cry of the Union-savers was "a threadbare
humbug," Representative Orin Fowler of Massachusetts
agreed, addressed to "cowering doughfaces." The Union
reposed so absolutely in the hearts of the people, he said,
that it would forever be preserved by "their clear-headed,
strong-handed, lion-hearted power." Connecticut Congressman Chauncey F. Cleveland noted that the issue ultimately lay between "seventeen millions of free people and
three millions of slaves" and "less than five hundred
thousand slaveholders." Such figures clearly tended to
render absurd the southern claim that the fathers had
created the government for the purpose of protecting
minorities. The right of the majority, Representative Lewis
B. Peck of Vermont rather affirmed, was "*the* principle on
which the Constitution is based." The growing interdependence and consolidation of the common life, once con-
sciously sought as the object of government policy, provided another basis for the feeling of the people. "The

people must govern," Thomas Booth of Connecticut thus
told the House, "they *will* govern; and in their hands the
Union is safe."[37]

To accompany this sense of power, however, was a moral
imperative that the will of the people be properly informed
with the principle of timeless freedom.[38] Unlike Webster's
faith in the redeeming quality of time, the Free Soilers were
struck by the degeneration which time had wrought in the
original good proclaimed by the fathers. The "politically
orthodox in 1787," Julian complained, had become in the
age of slavery propagandism and compromise "the rankest
heresy in 1850." Chase made the same discovery. "Sir, this is
a great change, a sad change," he said. "If it goes on, the
spirit of liberty must at length become extinct, and a
despotism will be established under the forms of free institutions." He rejected out of hand Webster's contention
that the cotton gin had been mainly responsible for the
change. Instead, Chase argued that a malignant slave
power had sought to commit the nation irreversibly to a
course calculated to subvert freedom. In like spirit Representative Cleveland charged "the *South* with aggressing
upon the *North*, by every addition of slave territory since the
adoption of the Constitution."[39]

In this way, Free Soilers expressed the need to regenerate
the original design of the fathers. It was, Thaddeus Stevens
declared, the "crisis of the fate of liberty." Except for the
"bloody conflict which gave birth to the nation," Wilmot
likewise noted, no issue had been so "momentous" as the
challenge presented by the slavery propagandists. Though
Webster termed the proviso against slavery a mere abstraction in 1850, Representative Clarke of New York insisted
upon an absolute affirmation of the principle of freedom.
"The Wilmot proviso is only a reassertion under this new
name, of a great principle of human liberty older than the
Republic," he said, "a principle which will last as long as the

Republic.endures." George W. Julian gave similar formulation to the enterprise of national regeneration. Even where
no need existed for positive congressional action against the
spread of slavery, he said with Webster and other compromisers in mind, "I would still insist on the proviso, as a
wholesome and needful reassertion, in the present crisis, of
the principles on which the Government was founded and
was designed to be administered—as a means of restoring it
to its early policy, and animating it anew with the breath of
freedom which bore our fathers through their conflict, and
made us an independent nation."[40]

The "new birth" of freedom Lincoln later spoke of was
here already articulated by Webster's adversaries in the
crisis of 1850. By a communal "owning of the covenant," a
revival of the faith of the fathers, they hoped to purge the
evils that had crept in through time and make a fresh new
start.[41] "This struggle may be considered the Second
American Revolution," Charles Durkee of Wisconsin said
in a very revealing language. Representative Bingham similarly avowed that "we are only walking in the footsteps of
the patriots and statesmen who have preceded us." In removing the "only blot" on the nation's fame, Cleveland
believed they would forever secure the freedom of posterity and push forward the mission to liberate the world:
"By this course we could transmit to our children the rich
inheritance bequeathed to us by our fathers, and by our
example ultimately overthrow all of earth's tyrants."[42]

During the crisis of 1850, in sum, the claims of "freedom
national" and "slavery national" starkly encountered one
another in all their fullness and form. To the belief of each
in an unchanging design for the Union fashioned by the
fathers was now joined the belief that the other presented
an absolute threat to the design. Regeneration in either case
necessarily scorned the arts of temporising and accommodation. It willed the total elimination of the opposing claim.

Open space had once provided a solid basis for freedom in the federative Union from the corporate efforts to give some direction to the nation's course through time. That same space had now become the very arena in which the contention of timeless principles ripened to irrepressible conflict.

The peace enforced upon the extremes in 1850 was chiefly the work of the protagonists of the old debate over the destiny of the nation in space and time. On the Whig side, the virtually unanimous support of southern partisans gained small, but vital, reinforcement from the North when Millard Fillmore, upon replacing the deceased Taylor in the White House, threw the force of executive power in the balance of compromise. Agreeing with Webster that the proviso was an "instrumentality" and not an end in itself, Representative William Duer of New York condemned the abstract politics of the Free Soilers and their "superstitious veneration" for a ban on slavery, where no real need existed. Representative George Ashmun of Massachusetts equally condemned the "one idea" approach of the Free Soilers, for it not only gave "gratuitous offence" to the South, but also injured all of the other interests of freemen in the North. He calculated that the embarrassments suffered by business in a single month of agitation amounted to a far larger sum than was needed to compensate Texas for relinquishing her territorial claims on New Mexico. In a more general way, Senator Badger shared Webster's vision of man in time and heartily recommended for the consideration of the absolutists of the South no less than of the North "the Divine procedure in the past history of the world."[43]

Henry Clay, to whom much credit for the compromise was due, based his support at last on an appeal to the order of Union as the highest good. Its dissolution would be, he warned, "the greatest of all calamities." He rejected the view that the leaks in the ship of state bespoke a condition of fundamental degeneration. They reflected, instead, the work of party passion and the loss of patriotic vision. In addition to his efforts in the Senate Clay sought to stop the leaks by encouraging non-partisan Union meetings across the country, anxious only that they appear as "local and spontaneous" in nature.[44] Throughout the crisis he invoked the awful presence of the corporate Union. At one point, indeed, its majesty tended to reduce to an "atom," a "second in time," or a "grain of sand" the stature of individual freemen within it. "Shall a being so small, so petty, so fleeting, so evanescent," he asked, "oppose itself to the onward march of a great nation, to subsist for ages to come—oppose itself to that long line of posterity which, issuing from our loins, will endure during the existence of the world? Forbid it, God!"[45]

In terms of numbers and leadership, the Democratic party made a greater contribution than the Whigs to the Compromise of 1850. Many northern Democrats, inclining toward the Free-Soil proviso out of bitterness for the defection of southern votes to Taylor in the election of 1848, now returned to the platform of popular sovereignty on which their candidate, Lewis Cass, had run.[46] With a heart big enough to embrace the whole Union, at the same time, Senator Sam Houston of Texas gave voice to compromise sentiment in the South. The "solid population" of yeomen in his section remained unagitated at home, he advised the ardent proslavery spokesmen, and in the pursuit of happiness under "the broad aegis of the Union." Another observer from Kentucky likewise warned Senator Hunter that "the boys up the hollows and in the brush" would not countenance a dissolution of the Union. Meanwhile, the failure of the Omnibus Bill, by which Clay had combined several compromise proposals, opened the way for the effective leadership of Senator Stephen A. Douglas of Il-

linois. By a strategy that disrupted the solid opposition of
the extremes, he pushed each of the compromise proposals
through Congress as a separate measure and, by the middle
of September, could claim complete success.[47]

On the central issue of slavery expansion, moreover,
Democrats provided the key principle of popular
sovereignty. To be sure, many Whigs plausibly justified
their willingness to forego the application of the Free-Soil
proviso on the ground that the old Mexican laws against
slavery remained in operation. But this basis of support was
seriously undercut by the fact that the final measures for
organizing the territories of New Mexico and Utah did,
while leaving the old Mexican laws untouched, indeed em-
power the territorial legislatures to decide the matter of
slavery.[48] In support of the principle of these measures,
Douglas appealed to the past experience of the nation, no
less than to its conformity to the federative genius of the
Constitution. Even in the territory covered by the Northwest Ordinance of 1787, he contended that the final decision had, in fact, been made by the actual settlers there.
That slavery had existed for many years in Illinois was a
reality which seemed to discount the efficacy of central
power to determine a local matter. The decision for freedom in Oregon and California had been reached in a similar way. "It was done in obedience to that great Democratic
principle," Douglas concluded, "that it is wiser and better to
leave each community to determine and regulate its own
local and domestic affairs."[49]

Other arguments in support of popular sovereignty
showed the continuing vitality of the concept of federative
freedom and its related vision of a manifest destiny for the
nation. Representative Willis A. Gorman of Indiana condemned the "Federal-toned" efforts of Congress to decide
the matter of slavery expansion because it showed the same
old contempt for "the capacity of the people to govern

themselves." Another congressman from the same state, Cyrus L. Dunham, similarly denounced the "doctrine of trusteeship" asserted by Free Soilers over new territories as a new species of British colonialism. The right of the people in a new territory to determine matters vital to their common life, Senator Cass therefore affirmed, was "the very cardinal doctrine of American freedom." In answer to critics who argued that whatever sovereign power a territorial people possessed had originally come from Congress, he made a simple counterclaim: "They got it from Almighty God." Possessed with an intelligence equal to the people left behind, new settlers moving to the open spaces of the West carried an even greater love of freedom which was the vital element in "national identity." There they started the human enterprise over again, created new states, and reproduced the miracle of federative freedom. By extending the area of freedom, old Jacksonian expansionists could still find in space the true arena for national regeneration. In this same spirit Douglas equally rejected the southern claim for an equilibrium of power and the Free-Soil urge to total dominion. The Union was neither a monism nor a dualism of elements, he insisted, but a growing community of diverse and essentially self-governing states and territories.[50]

In a number of ways, however, the Compromise of 1850 was an uneasy peace. For one thing, the protagonists of the old debate who fashioned the compromise lacked any principle of unity, such as Jacksonians possessed after 1833, to give shape to the nation's course. With the passing of the sectional crisis, most Whigs wanted to focus attention anew on other domestic matters. Democrats, especially those identified with Young America, looked rather to a bolder foreign policy and further territorial acquisitions. But even here, as the position of Douglas indicates, a profound dilemma obtained. He condemned the Free-Soil proviso as an "insuperable" obstacle because the controversy it generated within the nation diverted energy from its outward expansion.[51] With a tactic of ending the bitter debate over slavery by taking it out of Congress, Douglas hoped that the principle of popular sovereignty would remove this obstacle to manifest destiny. But if contention over the fruits of manifest destiny had brought on the crisis of 1850, which in turn had escalated and matured the terms of conflict, then further acquisitions would surely provoke a new contest between Free Soilers and slavery spokesmen over which element should enjoy the benefits. The furor that greeted the Kansas-Nebraska bill would soon emphasize the limits of this outlook. If the removal of sectional controversy opened the way to new expansion, expansion would, in its train, bring on a renewal of sectional controversy. Space ceased to be a safety valve from the evils of time; for, inevitably, the death struggle of two timeless principles would now take place over the space itself.[52]

Another evidence of uneasy peace lay in the varied and contradictory ways congressmen embraced the doctrine of popular sovereignty. Dunham, with many of the northern Democrats, avowed his support on the grounds of expediency, holding, to the consternation of Southerners, that Congress did possess the power to interdict slavery. In much the same way, Representative William A. Richardson of Illinois adduced the "positive law" interpretation. A Free-Soil proviso against the spread of slavery was superfluous, so the reasoning went, because, in the absence of any positive laws of protection at the very beginning of settlement, slaveholders would not risk taking their valuable property into a new territory. Representative Edson B. Olds of Ohio therefore asserted that popular sovereignty, and not Free Soil, provided "the most effectual estoppal to the extension of slavery."[53] Here was added substance for the demand made by the Southern Democratic party in

1860 that Congress pass a positive slave code for all territories.

Nor was there agreement among southern and northern
partisans about the precise time when the people in the
territory might act. Senator Foote of Mississippi and Representative Howell Cobb of Georgia supposed that no action would be taken until the people organized into a state.
Cass claimed, to the contrary, that the people could decide
the issue of slavery at some point during the territorial stage
itself.[54] By its direct challenge to the claims of "slavery
national," which the Dred Scott decision was later to adopt,
this northern interpretation defined the lines along which
the Democratic party at last split in 1860.

Finally, the stringent provisions of the new fugitive slave
law cast a shadow over the prospects for permanent peace.
There would probably have been no civil war over the
matter of fugitive slaves alone, for the issue of expansion
was central to the controversy. But it did possess great
symbolic value. For the South, the new measure seemed to
vindicate the claim that the Constitution was a proslavery
document. By contrast, many Free Soilers regarded the
fugitive slave provision a compact between the states and
not the basis for federal action. As a consequence, the new
fugitive slave law struck them as another evidence of a slave
power conspiracy to subvert the idea of "freedom national"
which was taken to underlay the Constitution. Most of all,
isolated efforts by the federal government to return fugitive slaves were to generate profound feelings and redouble
the moral resolve of the North against any new slaveholder
aggressions. *Uncle Tom's Cabin* at once reflected and reinforced these feelings which, in all their force and fury,
would be ready to oppose the Kansas-Nebraska bill. There
was thus some truth in the observation attributed to President Lincoln that Harriet Beecher Stowe was the little lady
who had caused the Civil War.[55]

8
Progress and the Irrepressible Conflict

The Kansas-Nebraska bill must be reckoned one of the most important measures ever passed by Congress. Designed by Stephen A. Douglas to organize a new territory in order to accommodate the rapid growth of the nation, it quickly became entangled in the sectional issue of slavery expansion. In the first draft of the bill, Douglas would place under one government all of the remaining territory in the Louisiana Purchase still without organization, namely, the area north of Oklahoma and west of Missouri, Iowa, and Minnesota. With regard to slavery, he offered a very ambiguous solution. While leaving untouched the old Missouri Compromise ban on slavery north of 36°30', he also incorporated the doctrine of popular sovereignty which had been used in the Compromise of 1850. By the old law the central government had prohibited slavery in the territory; by the new principle the people in the territory would be free to make the decision for themselves. Any resulting conflict between the two rules for regulating slavery was to be resolved in the federal courts.[1]

But a new sectional crisis soon arose as the bill for organizing the territory assumed a different and far more significant form. Whig Senator Archibald Dixon of Kentucky demanded that the ambiguity in the first draft be removed by an explicit repeal of the 36°30′ line. The continuation of the old ban on slavery was totally unacceptable to the South, he argued, for it rendered meaningless the principle of popular sovereignty. It prevented slaveholders from venturing with their valuable property into a territory during the initial stage of settlement and, therefore, from any real opportunity to participate in the decision for or against slavery. Mounting pressure from other southern spokesmen, especially Democrats fearful of being upstaged by the Whigs, finally compelled Douglas to follow the logic of his doctrine to the point of declaring the 36°30′ line "inoperative and void." At some stage in these proceedings the agreement was also reached to form two territorial governments instead of one. In accepting the repeal of the Missouri Compromise line Douglas reportedly felt it would raise a "hell of a storm," but he apparently believed he would be able to weather it. One important reason for his success, in any case, was the pledge of support he had extracted, at the outset, from President Franklin Pierce.[2]

The great number and variety of interpretations constitute one indication of how important the measure was. Many of these explanations, especially the ones which focus directly on Douglas, have tended to reflect the polarized judgment of his contemporaries. On the one hand, he was taken to be the tool, however unwittingly, of the slave power; on the other, he was considered a statesman seeking a permanent solution to the slavery issue which stood in the way of the nation's imperial destiny. A wide range of motives has also been brought into question. Was he acting under the strong influence of proslavery forces in Missouri, led by Senator David B. Atchison, and with the hope of southern support for the Presidency? Or was he genuinely concerned for encouraging westward settlement, opening a way for the Pacific railroad, and more generally for promoting national expansion? In this connection Harry V.

Jaffa has argued that the effort to establish the principle of
popular sovereignty was the "minor premise" in the outlook of Douglas, and that manifest destiny remained his
"major premise." Though he condemned Douglas for im-
pulsiveness and "dim moral perceptions," Allan Nevins
invited historians to consider other and less personal forces
at work—the need for new territorial organization, the
rising anxieties of the South, and the floundering of the
Pierce Administration. Roy F. Nichols has stressed the dis-
array in the old party organizations and especially the tug
and pull among the Democratic factions.[3]

If interpretations thus vary about the causes of the
Kansas-Nebraska bill, far greater consensus obtains with
regard to its consequences. Politically, it represented the
point of no return. A flood of outrage in the North swept
away the remains of the old Whig party, seriously eroded
the Democracy, and left in its wake a South more solid than
ever before. Most importantly, the new Republican party
came into being, based on the thoroughly sectional platform of Free Soil and resolved to shape the nation in its
image. In ideological terms, as the escalating sequel of
events was to show, the Kansas-Nebraska bill "let slip the
dogs of war." The moral outrage of the North was not
influenced by the repeal of an old compromise formula,
since Free Soilers had successfully opposed in the preceding years the application of the 36°30′ line to other areas. It
was rather in response to the immediate, massive, and
stunning fact that a vast area once thought secure for freedom was to be opened to the possible uses of the slaveholders. It now became easy for Northerners, in numbers
far greater than ever before, to believe that the government
was run by the slave power and that the advocates of popular sovereignty merely subserved its evil designs. Many who
had supported compromise in 1850 on the old grounds of
corporate or federative freedom now embraced the Free-

Soil view that the only issue before the nation was freedom versus slavery. More than any other single event the Kansas-Nebraska bill set in rapid motion the forces which transformed the Free-Soil minority of the 1840s into a triumphant majority.[4]

The reaction of many conservatives at the time registered the critical juncture at which the nation had arrived. The repeal of the Missouri Compromise was an act of "extreme radicalism," Senator Truman Smith of Connecticut protested. It was not practicable to undo the old settlement, first of all, because interests had become vested beyond the hope of perfect recall. The slave states south of 36°30′ could not be returned to a territorial condition, J. Wiley Edmands of Massachusetts explained in the House, nor was it just to suspend the absolute guarantee of freedom which prospective settlers north of the line had been given.[5]

Others feared the ideological consequences. The repeal was a radical act, Pennsylvania Representative Joseph R. Chandler argued, because it went a long way toward undermining that temporising spirit of compromise and accommodation upon which the order of the Union reposed. "Ours, sir, is a nation of compromises," he declared. Time had hallowed the agreement, Senator James Cooper of the same state argued, for the acquiescence of the nation for thirty-four years possessed a higher sanction than any presumed constitutional right. In this perspective the Kansas-Nebraska bill represented a revolutionary appeal from history to nature, from the prescriptive force of a consensus worked out in the past to an unchanging truth thought to inhere in the Constitution. Dialogue, in other terms, now gave way to a naked and immediate confrontation of negative liberals. Each of the protagonists gave a different meaning to the larger liberty he claimed from the determinations of the past. But here was precisely the rub, according to Representative Charles W. Upham of Massachusetts. On the vital and controversial matter of slavery, the oracles of nature spoke a varied language, and the appeal to this source of truth would not likely lead to a new consensus short of force. "The country will swing from its moorings," he predicted, "and we shall embark, with all the precious interests, all the glorious recollections, and all the magnificent prospects of this vast republican empire, upon an untraversed, unknown, and it may well be feared, stormy, if not fateful sea."[6]

One fateful confirmation of Upham's prophecy was near at hand in the new posture which the logic of events was forcing the advocates of popular sovereignty to assume. As one of the chief authors of concord in 1850, Douglas now seemed guilty of creating discord. While professing only the desire to apply the principle of peace in 1850 to the Kansas-Nebraska bill, he was in fact disrupting the sectional peace which a much older compromise had established. In this context the doctrine began to lose much of its force as a compromise formula for mediating the conflicting claims of "freedom national" and "slavery national." It was becoming instead merely one of the competing principles of nature seeking to replace the prescriptive force of a historical settlement. More than ever before, as a consequence, Douglas sounded like a doctrinaire: "this was the principle upon which the colonies separated from the Crown of Great Britain; the principle upon which the battles of the Revolution were fought, and the principle upon which our republican system was founded."[7]

Others in support of the principle professed to regard its inclusion in the Kansas-Nebraska measure as a final regeneration of the nation. "It was a returning from a gross departure in 1820 back to the first principles asserted by us in the days of the Revolution," Samuel A. Bridges of Pennsylvania declared in the House. "I go for it," Senator Moses Norris of New Hampshire likewise argued, "because it brings us back to and reasserts the original and true principle upon which this Government was originated and finally established." To Senate critics who invoked the hallowed sanctity of the Missouri Compromise, John R. Thompson of New Jersey replied that "Time gives no title to wrong." From temporising expedients he appealed anew to "the seminal principle" of local self-government. But an equivocal element remained in the claims of having reaffirmed the true principles of the nation. By making the power of the people over slavery in the territory "subject only to the Constitution," the authors of the Kansas-Nebraska bill clearly invited a court ruling. Moreover, the reluctance with which Senator Lewis Cass supported the measure suggests that events, far more than a positive or burning zeal, also brought other northern advocates to the crusade of restoration.[8]

In a more hearty fashion, by contrast, many southern spokesmen welcomed the prospects of a final regeneration. The Union made by the fathers was not "a Government of compromises" but "a Government of the Constitution," William S. Barry of Mississippi reminded his fellows in the House. "Let us go back to the original charter of our rights," Representative Alfred H. Colquitt of Georgia agreed, "and make that the bond." Senator Robert Toombs thus hoped that the Kansas-Nebraska bill would put an end to "temporary expedients" and enable the nation to "restore the true principles of the Constitution." Meanwhile, blunt-spoken Albert G. Brown of Mississippi left no doubt in the Senate that these principles were, as used in this study, those of "slavery national." In this perspective the task of restoration was only half complete. The repeal of the 36°30′ line lifted the unconstitutional ban Congress had imposed on the spread of slavery, but the doctrine of popular sovereignty as generally understood in the North still enabled the people in a territory to violate the constitutional right of slaveholders. With the Dred Scott decision in 1857, as a consequence, Brown and others of like mind would feel that the nation approached a final regeneration of the original design of the Founding Fathers. They took this decision to mean that the property guarantee of the fifth amendment automatically extended the shield of federal protection over slavery in all national territories. It was on this basis, finally, that Southern Democrats in 1860 would call for Congress to enact a positive slave code for the protection of property.[9]

With the very same terms that southern spokesmen used to measure the regeneration of the nation, however, the Free Soilers saw the nation degenerating from its original design. Through the promising instrument of the new Republican party they were to meet the crisis of declension and restore the nation. One key to success lay in toning down that note in the Free-Soil voice of the 1840s which struck many as still too radical. Another key was the appeal of the party platform to a wide range of selfish economic interests by the promise of such broker-state goods as free homesteads, tariff protection, railroad grants, and internal improvements.[10] But the moral element remained essential to success. At the risk of some repetition it will be the burden of the rest of the present chapter to analyze the way Republican spokesmen after 1854 refined upon, while remaining faithful to, the imperatives of "freedom national." Specific focus upon the concept of progress will place in sharp relief the quality of timelessness and the monistic impulse in the Free-Soil movement which at once defined and proposed to resolve the irrepressible conflict.

As the rapid growth of science in early modern Europe gave substance to a more general concept of progress, it also bequeathed two fundamentally different interpretations of the concept. One of them, inspired by Descartes' theory of knowledge, held that the good or the true was something to be possessed in its entirety, all at once. If somehow lost by a violent stroke or the process of degeneration, it might be recovered in the same dramatic way. Implicit in this view were the notions of moral "primitivism" and cyclic movement through time. In contrast to this essentially revolutionary and ahistorical interpretation was another one ultimately derived from Pascal's theory of knowledge. It supposed that the good or the true came by degrees in a more linear fashion through time. Progress involved the ongoing task of "civilization," of building upon the work of the past, and the prospects for the future were for gradually enlarging good.[11]

In Europe these two interpretations tended to define the terms of debate between revolutionaries and conservatives, but in the United States the result was a paradoxical blend. Here the predominant revolutionary concept took on a conservative cast and generated what Daniel J. Boorstin might call the "preformation theory," that is, the belief of successive generations that their country began its existence with a design perfect and complete from the very outset. Puritans by the end of the seventeenth century, the Revolutionary fathers, and the Jacksonians alike manifested, according to Wesley Frank Craven, "the common inclination of the American people to look back to the origins of their country for an explanation of its essential character." Indeed, without an extended past to draw on Americans have found it necessary, as Hans Kohn well noted, to define their nationality in some measure by identification with a timeless and universal idea.[12] Progress through time, in these terms, meant the working out of the national idea, the fuller realization of unchanging truth. If the nation had moved, was moving, and would move in a desirable direction, to use the formula of J. B. Bury, it was at last because of its fidelity to "primitive" principles. Conversely, movement through time in an undesirable direction bespoke di-

vergence and gave to the idea of progress the more proxi-
mate meaning of return to original truth.[13]

It was this concept of progress which, in a peculiarly
urgent and vital form, found expression in the Free-Soil
outlook of the 1850s.[14] Pervading the outlook of leading
spokesmen, as the following passages indicate, was the
theme of restoration and return. "It is our mission," David
Wilmot of Pennsylvania told fellow Republicans in 1860,
"to restore this Government to its original policy, and place
it again in that rank upon which our fathers organized and
brought it into existence." Senator John P. Hale of New
Hampshire agreed: "We ask that the country shall come
back to the point from which it started." Pennsylvania Representative Joseph Allison demonstrated "the degeneracy
of the times" by comparing the "pigmies" of his day to the
"statesmen" of the past. Yearning in like fashion for "the
pure fresh, free breath of the revolution," Abraham Lincoln wanted to "readopt the Declaration of Independence."
In answer to the southern charge that the effort of the
North to stop the further spread of slavery was revolutionary and aggressive, Representative E. P. Walton of
Vermont clearly summarized the Free-Soil credo of identity with the faith of the fathers: "We *are* revolutionary, as
they were, against tyranny and wrong, for liberty and right.
But it is a counterrevolution that we have inaugurated to
roll back the government of the nation and the states to the
principles and the policy of our revolutionary fathers."[15]

In this light, the victory of Lincoln on a Free-Soil platform in 1860 took on immense significance. One supporter
savored the prospect of his inauguration "amid the joyous
greetings of a regenerated people." Another well-wisher
noted that "The Constitution has been vindicated and its
principles reinaugurated in the hearts of the people."[16]
Compromise with expansion-minded slaveholders at such a
moment, William Herndon warned, would be an "implied

atheism." Senator William Pitt Fessenden of Maine was, in like spirit, urged to make no concessions "involving the slightest taint of the Constitution." The "apparent jostling of the arc" to be seen in the threats of disunion, he was assured, could not be steadied by the "profane hand of slavery." A constituent, whose father and grandfather had both fought in the Revolutionary War, told Senator Benjamin F. Wade of Ohio that his son was ready to fight, if necessary, "to achieve a second independence."[17]

Involved here were three closely related propositions about time and the Union which gave rounded form to a cyclic concept of progress. At the outset, it was thought, the Union began its career in a state of fullness and perfection, informed by the timeless principle of freedom. But in the course of time degeneration came as spokesmen for the negating and temporal element of slavery sought to gain the status of permanent coexistence, if not of total ascendancy, in the Union. A crisis would therefore arise at some later point in time as the conflict matured in the body politic between its monistic principle of freedom and the ideologically alien element of slavery. At this point the nation ought to choose, as the alternative to irreversible corruption and decline, to reaffirm its seminal principle and generate anew its original and perfect design.

In this general form—with its emphasis on original perfection, declension through time, and regeneration—the Free-Soil outlook evinces a kinship with what Mircea Eliade has called, in his study of early religious thought, "the myth of the eternal return." Basic in his analysis is the view that the people of past times have possessed "a terror of history," a deeply ingrained fear of the pain, ambiguity, and prospective annihilation involved in the irreversible flow of time. In its most archaic form this fear of things temporal found expression in the denial to "profane" time of any reality at all and in the imperative to identify instead with unchanging "archetypes." On a somewhat more advanced level, time was accorded some greater degree of reality, Eliade noted, yet even here degeneration from the archetype essentially marked its course. Periodically, as a consequence, ritualistic means had to be applied to purge the evil accretions of time and to generate society anew. One aspect of ritualistic regeneration involved a scapegoat mechanism and another one the effort to imitate the original act of creating the world. This is what Eliade meant by the process of "collective regeneration through repetition of the cosmogonic act."[18]

Such ideological conservatism and the companion sense of timelessness did not rule out, it was true, the capacity for responding to changing realities. Eliade argued, to the contrary, that a belief in the removal of the evil accretions of time was one way of coming to terms with the irreversible products of time. Thus the Puritan "jeremiads," the outcry of the Revolutionary fathers against a corrupt ministry conspiring to subvert their freedom, and the crusade mounted by Jacksonians in the name of old Republican virtue against the monster Bank all served in their turn to build community anew under radically altered circumstances.[19] In like fashion, the appeal of the Free Soilers to a presumably unchanging national idea enabled them to create a new consensus amid the swirl of forces—vast territorial expansion, rapid movement to the West, the influx of immigration, the quickening pace of industry —which were disrupting the relatively stable order of the late eighteenth century and generating leveling tendencies to a degree unknown to the fathers.[20] Here could be seen a pattern of creation by destruction, of cyclic regeneration that made possible further movement in time, of progress forward by looking to the past.[21]

In the case of the Free Soilers, however, this frame of thought for apprehending and acting upon reality possessed a fateful limitation. The unchanging national idea to which they appealed was one that gained specific content by the dialectical presence of a presumed enemy of freedom, the aggressive slaveholders. This meant in practical terms that they were building a new consensus by destroying a negative element. But the element to be denationalized was one vast in magnitude, capable of identification along geographical lines, and itself moved by a belief in fidelity to the fathers. In short, the Free Soil mode of progress by regenerating the national idea involved a "cultural purge" which, with the alternative of disunion ruled out, truly defined the terms of irrepressible conflict. For all the pragmatic and conservative temper Boorstin has found in his consensus view of the "preformation theory," it was yet a consensus in which there necessarily inhered the potential for genuine conflict.[22] No matter if the revolutionary concept of progress in Europe had been "established" in the United States, something of its wildness still remained. While professing only the desire to save the Union made by the fathers, the Free Soilers were actually in the process of transforming the Union which the fathers had made.

A fuller analysis of the Free-Soil outlook, with particular focus on the ideas of original perfection, degeneration through time, and the need for restoration, will make clearer the terms of irrepressible conflict. The first task of the Free Soilers in the 1850s, as before, was to demonstrate that the Union had been originally designed upon the archetype of freedom. The cosmogonic act of the fathers had come during the Revolutionary era, according to Senator Hale, when "their locks were hoary with the frosts which had fallen upon them as they stood sentinel round about the camps of liberty." As to a more specific date, Senator Salmon P. Chase of Ohio found the "first bond" of the Union in 1774 when the Articles of Association singled out the slave trade for special consideration. Lincoln pointed to the same event in his First Inaugural, but elsewhere he found the primal act of nationality in the Declaration of Independence. Many others, likewise, fixed upon this moment. The Declaration contained the "baptismal vows" of the new nation, Senator Charles Sumner of Massachusetts declared. In quarrying the stones of its foundation from "the mountain of truth," Representative Aaron H. Cragin of New Hampshire noted in a different figure, the fathers "recognized the rights of human nature as universal."[23]

Nor did the writing of the Constitution, in their view, represent a conservative reaction to the spirit of the Revolution. The "principles promulgated in the Declaration of Independence," affirmed the Republican platform in 1860, were "embodied in the Federal Constitution." As the "formal" cause of the Union, in other terms, the Constitution gave better organization to the "final" cause of freedom. Liberty was "the apple of gold," according to Lincoln, later framed by a "picture of silver" in the constitutional charter. "The *picture* was made *for* the apple," he insisted, "*not* the apple for the picture." In the very nature of things, Representative Sidney Dean of Connecticut declared, "liberty and slavery could not have a common nationality in one common government or upon one common soil."[24] The Union was founded as a monism of freedom and not as a partnership of slave and free elements designed for permanent coexistence.

There were certain stubborn facts about the nation's early history, however, which seemed to belie Free-Soil claims. Slavery existed almost everywhere at the beginning; slaveholders played a leading part in winning independence; and certain clauses in the Constitution also reflected their presence and handiwork. It was on these bases that southern spokesmen could argue that the Union had been founded as a dualism of slave and free elements. Many of the fathers personally disliked slavery, to be sure, but

Senator Toombs carefully distinguished between their "individual opinions" regarding the morality of slavery and their "collective will" written into the national covenant. "I repeat," he said in 1854, "these clauses of the Constitution provided for the perpetuity and not the extinction of slavery." Nor was this view restricted entirely to the South. William Lloyd Garrison among one group of abolitionists also interpreted the Constitution as a proslavery document. Supposing, as a consequence, that liberty and the Union were separable goods and liberty more dear, Garrison placed the slogan, "No Union with Slaveholders," upon the banner of freedom.[25]

By the contrast it presents, the Garrisonian position serves to illuminate further the Free-Soil belief in original perfection. Garrison held to a truly revolutionary concept of progress, for he wanted to gain and to establish in its entirety for the first time the unchanging good of freedom. The Free Soilers, on the other hand, professed to believe that the good had been instituted in the beginning, and that the task was merely one of restoring what had been lost. Liberty and the Union were inseparable and the preservation of the one inextricably bound up in the other. "In seeking the reform of existing evils," Sumner explained, "we also seek the conservation of the principles of our fathers." Representative Edward Wade of Ohio was equally explicit: "Sir, in order to preserve the Union, necessity is laid upon us to go back to the birth of the Union, prior to and under the Constitution—to catch and hold the spirit which animated those great and good men, and apply it now, and for all time, to the administration of this Government."[26]

With two basic lines of argument the Free Soilers defended the belief in the perfection of the original design against the challenge presented by the historical facts of the existence of slavery. First of all, they placed stress upon the federative nature of the Union; and, however strange this might appear for men of such intense moral nationalism, it served the purpose well. Because slavery stood in violation of the common law and the laws of nature, it was reckoned to be the sole and exclusive creature of positive, man-made law. In the United States this meant that slavery existed only by the force of local legislation in the several states. Since no power was delegated by the Constitution to the federal government to create slavery, the Constitution represented an antislavery document and the government of the nation reposed exclusively upon the archetype of freedom. The slogan "freedom national" and "slavery local" precisely expressed this position, which enabled Representative Joshua R. Giddings of Ohio to claim that the Union, in effect, had experienced a virgin birth: "This line of demarcation, which separates the natural rights of all men from human legislation, was clearly drawn by the fathers of our Republic."[27]

To the Free Soilers of a more radical cast of thought, this meant that none of the slavery provisions in the Constitution touched the national soul. The clause forbidding Congress to end the foreign slave trade for twenty years represented a temporary concession for securing the good of the Union. The three-fifths clause could be interpreted as an actual penalty upon the political power of the South, for all persons might otherwise have been fully represented in national councils. They also tended to regard the provision on the return of fugitive slaves a compact between the states and not a substantive grant of power to the federal government. At the very time the fathers were writing the Constitution, moreover, Congress was passing the Northwest Ordinance absolutely prohibiting the introduction of slavery into the unsettled territory north of the Ohio River. Since the Old Northwest was at that time the only area under the exclusive jurisdiction of the federal government, the ordinance clearly applied the principle of "freedom national" there. "Up to the time of the adoption of the Constitution," Chase thus concluded, "there was not a single slave in America, made such or held such, under any law of the United States."[28]

For moderate Free Soilers who could not deny the substantial nature of the three-fifths and fugitive-slave provisions of the Constitution, a second line of argument yet served to vindicate the essential purity of the original Union. They attributed to the Founding Fathers the geopolitical idea, widely professed in both North and South by the 1850s, that when slavery ceased to spread out into new and unsettled areas it would in time die out in the old areas where it already existed. Representative Hiram Warner of Georgia gave to the prevailing idea its most concise formulation: "There is not a slaveholder in the House or out of it, but who knows perfectly well that, whenever slavery is confined within certain specified limits its future existence is doomed; it is only a question of time as to its final destruction." The press of an increasing slave population against the available resources in the restricted area, so the reasoning went, would at last render slave labor of little value and compel the slaveholders to set their bondsmen free. By the restrictive policy to be found in the Northwest Ordinance and the provision for ending the foreign slave trade, Lincoln claimed, the fathers had placed slavery "in the course of ultimate extinction." Whatever practical taint the existence of slavery gave to the original Union, founded on the idea of "freedom national," would thus in the course of time be totally removed. It was therefore no accident that the word "slave" was omitted from the charter of national government, Lincoln rejoiced, for in the generations and centuries to come "the Constitution should not show that there ever had been a slave in this good free country of ours."[29]

At some point in time after the Union came into being, however, the Free Soilers believed that a process began which was calculated to subvert rather than fulfill the originally perfect design. In their view, degeneration from the principles and policies of the fathers was marked by the reciprocal action of two forces: the growing indifference of freemen invited the slave power to become aggressive. On the one side, as Representative Francis P. Blair of Missouri noted, "the impulse which the love of liberty received" in the Revolution began to wane. Their "diversified pursuits and general prosperity," moreover, tended to make northern freemen "oblivious to the hateful aggressions" of the enemy. On the other hand, Senator Sumner compared the necessarily aggressive slave power to the serpent of old. Its "loathsome folds," he warned, were "coiled about the whole land." Except for this foul spirit, Senator Charles Durkee of Wisconsin agreed, "our federative Union might have remained a political Eden to this day."[30]

In practical political terms, the social cohesion of the slaveholding class, its unity of interests, and its great wealth assured complete dominion over the vast majority of freemen in the South. The three-fifths representation of slaves, contrary to expectations, served to enhance the power of the slaveholders in the national councils. At the same time, the diversity of economic interests in the North made it easier for the slave power to divide and conquer. The key to its final conquest lay in the ability to suborn northern "doughfaces" by the prospects of patronage and political preferment. Representative Reuben A. Fenton of New York compared this corrupting influence of the slave power to the black magnetic mountain in ancient fable which drew out the bolts of every passing ship: "The principles of earlier years instilled in the land of freedom, with too many of our public men, as they approach this power, one by one are withdrawn until they fall a disjointed wreck."[31]

While there was general agreement among the Free Soilers about the fact of degeneration, differences did exist with regard to the timing of the process and other details. Roughly speaking, two theories emerged. In 1854 Senator Chase of Ohio gave to the more radical of the two theories its most systematic formulation. With categories informed by great moral clarity, he divided the history of the nation into three distinct eras. In the first one, the Era of Enfranchisement, the fathers placed the power of the government actively on the side of freedom and against slavery. The work of their period culminated in the two great acts of 1787—the constitutional charter of freedom and the Northwest Ordinance.

But very soon after the Constitution went into effect, the process of degeneration began. In 1790, to be exact, Chase noted how the principles of monistic freedom had been undermined when the federal government accepted from the state of North Carolina the cession of the Tennessee territory on the expressed condition that slavery not be abolished there. From this cession Chase dated the second period of the nation's history, the Era of Conservatism. During this phase the federal government ceased to work actively on the side of freedom, as its original principle required, and assumed instead a position of moral neutrality, that is, one of lending support, indifferently, to slavery and to freedom, wherever they happened to exist. As in the case of Tennessee, the government did not bring slavery into existence, but it did place its protective power over the slavery already there. During the next three decades the government also acquired the slave territories of Louisiana and Florida, admitted several new slave states into the Union, and extended the shield of its protection over slavery in the District of Columbia, on the high seas, and in interstate commerce. In this same spirit of conservatism, the Missouri Compromise line of 36°30' divided the actual areas where slavery and freedom then existed; yet even here Chase thought it marked "a wide departure" from the policy of the fathers.[32]

By imperceptible degrees, after the Missouri Compromise in 1820, Chase further explained, the emboldened slave power began to demand that the government drop its position of moral neutrality and act more exclusively on the side of slavery and against freedom. Intimations of this new Era of Propagandism could be seen in the nullification controversy, the fight in Congress over the "gag rule," and the Seminole War. The annexation of Texas revealed in fuller dimensions the aggressive spirit of the slave power; and the new acquisitions from Mexico in 1848, duly secured to slavery by the compromise two years later, presaged a more ambitious plan of expansion which included Cuba, the remainder of Mexico, and Central America. In this perspective, Chase regarded the Kansas-Nebraska bill in 1854 as the boldest step thus far of slavery propagandism and the most brazen example, as well, of treason by northern "doughfaces." Passed under the leadership of Senator Douglas and supported by President Pierce, it lifted the ban on slavery north of 36°30' and gave to the settlers in the territory the right to decide the issue of slavery or freedom. It was "an atrocious plot," Chase charged with burning eloquence, to convert a vast area of freedom "into a dreary region of despotism inhabited by masters and slaves."[33]

For others in general agreement with Chase's theory, the rampant slavery propagandism of the Kansas-Nebraska measure brought the nation to the point of no return. The rapid degeneration of the nation from its original principle of freedom had reached the crisis stage, in their view, and the choice for them lay between a willful act of regeneration or the irreversible triumph of the negating element of slavery. The measure opened to the tread of slaves "a garden of God" larger than "the original thirteen States," Sumner warned, and pointed to the triumph of slavery in the entire Union. Representative Israel Washburn, Jr., of Maine agreed that "From the irresistible promptings of self-preservation the time had come when slavery must be crippled, or freedom go to the wall." Because he regarded the moment to be "the crisis of our country's fate," Senator Wade saw the alternative still more starkly and the moral imperative to action commensurately urgent: "Slavery must now become general, or it must cease to be at all."[34]

While Chase developed the radical theory of degeneration, Lincoln gave rounded form to a more moderate interpretation. His theory differed from that of the Ohio senator in significant ways. Chase supposed declension had begun as early as 1790, and he placed great stress upon the agency of a malignant slave power. By contrast, Lincoln traced degeneration back no further than the Kansas-Nebraska bill itself, and he tended to place more stress upon the moral indifference of freemen. In substance, however, the morphology of degeneration in Lincoln's theory and the sense of moral urgency made it strikingly similar to the theory of Chase. Though it came in a much shorter period of time, Lincoln saw regression from original truth proceeding through stages paralleling the three Eras Chase professed to find in the nation's past.

Until 1854, Lincoln supposed the nation had remained essentially faithful to freedom. But the Kansas-Nebraska bill represented a fundamental change. "The spirit of seventy-six and the spirit of Nebraska, are utter antagonisms," he declared at Peoria, "and the former is being rapidly displaced by the latter." With the principle of popular sovereignty Douglas did not totally reverse the policy of the fathers, Lincoln admitted, for he did not place the power of the government actively on the side of slavery and against freedom. The principle contained nothing more than that attitude of moral neutrality, Douglas rather boasted, with which God had presented to Adam and Eve the choice of good and evil. But Lincoln rejected out of hand the assumption that freedom in this case meant a procedural right to choose wrong and not a substantive right to affirm the absolute good. The support freemen gave to the doctrine of popular sovereignty represented "a dangerous dalliance," Lincoln feared, "a sad evidence that, feeling prosperity we forget right—that liberty as a principle, we have ceased to revere." This degeneration from "our ancient faith," he also warned, might open the way for the South to become even more aggressive.[35]

Indeed, Lincoln more than half suspected that the "*declared* indifference" of the Kansas-Nebraska measure masked a "covert *real* zeal for the spread of slavery." In the eyes of other Free Soilers, the events of the four years that followed seemed to bear out this expectation, as the executive and judicial branches of the government moved beyond the moral neutrality of Congress to an active propagandism for slavery. Senator Henry Wilson of Massachusetts charged that the filibustering foreign policy of President Pierce was calculated, not only to acquire new slave territories, but also to divert the attention of freemen from their internal enemy.[36] Senators Jacob Collamer of Vermont and William Pitt Fessenden of Maine equally deplored the way Pierce used executive patronage and the Army to abet David Atchison and the "Border Ruffians" of Missouri in stamping the territory of Kansas with a proslavery mold. Pierce's successor, James Buchanan of Pennsylvania, pursued this same line of policy to even bolder conclusions. He persisted in the effort to make Kansas a slave state under the Lecompton Constitution even after the approximately 6,000 votes in its favor had been overmatched by the votes of 10,000 freemen. But this only served as a true measure, Representative William Kellogg of Illinois said, of how far "the policy of the fathers of the Republic has been debauched."[37]

Most of all, Free Soilers thought the Dred Scott decision marked an advanced stage in the course of degeneration. "Our Government is vibrating between freedom and despotism," Giddings declared. Fessenden expressed the belief, shared by many others, that the decision had been reached in conspiratorial concert with the other branches of government and that it represented a logical progression from preceding events.[38] From an attitude of moral neutrality proclaimed in the Kansas-Nebraska act the decision now placed the government actively on the side of slavery and against freedom. To this end, the Supreme Court argued that the Constitution, of its own inherent force, carried slavery into all territories. More precisely it gave to the due-process clause of the fifth amendment a substantive meaning in behalf of slave property. The decision consummated what Senator James R. Doolittle of Wisconsin later called the "Calhoun Revolution" in constitutional interpretation. The effect would be to project across the unsettled spaces of the Union and to secure for all time an evil which the fathers had reckoned transitory, local, and foreign to the national idea.[39]

In his House Divided speech in 1858, Lincoln gave system and form to these prevailing ideas about conspiracy and degeneration. The events of the four preceding years evinced "a common *plan* or *draft*," he charged, "drawn up before the first lick was struck." The position of moral neutrality officially taken in the Kansas-Nebraska bill served, in this design, to create a "don't care" attitude among freemen and thus to prepare them for further steps. Meanwhile, the very language of the bill invited a constitutional ruling from the Supreme Court, for the power it

accorded to a territorial legislature to pass on slavery matters was made "subject only to the Constitution." But the
Dred Scott case, which had been initiated in a lower court at
the precise time the Kansas-Nebraska bill was passing
through Congress, was not finally decided by the high
tribunal until after a national election had presumably
given a mandate to the conspirators. In this fashion the
inauguration of Buchanan brought in its train the ruling by
the Court that the Constitution carried slavery into all national territories. Only one more decision was needed, Lincoln warned, to break down the barriers of freedom in the
northern states themselves and to make slavery national
everywhere.[40]

By 1858, then, Lincoln came to share the view, expressed
more generally by radical Free Soilers four years earlier,
that the nation approached the point of no return. Degeneration had advanced to such a point that it threatened
totally to subvert a nation designed on the archetype of
freedom. As the alternative to an irreversible commitment
to slavery, there was the imperative need to place the nation
back upon a course that would eventually realize its true
principle. Regeneration in this case involved a purge of the
negating element and a repetition, in Eliade's phrase, of the
"cosmogonic act" of the fathers.

In very revealing phrases the Free-Soil spokesmen conceived of the task in these terms. George W. Julian of
Indiana called on freemen to "eradicate the sentiment of
tyranny" from their hearts and to animate the nation "anew
with the breath of freedom which bore our fathers through
their conflicts, and made us an independent nation."[41]
After "the unclean spirit of slavery propagandism" had
been exorcised from the Union, Representative George W.
Palmer of New York wanted to "reinvest it with something
of the purity, the justice, the civilization, the Higher Law,
with which it was clothed at its birth."[42] Representative

Mark Trafton of Massachusetts believed that, in practical political terms, to win an election on the "primitive principles" of the fathers would be to "hurl this usurper from its seat, and with loud acclaim hail the second instauration of freedom and equal rights." Anticipating the "new birth" of freedom he was later to proclaim during the Civil War, Lincoln called for a national commitment in the 1850s to "reinaugurate the good old 'central ideas' of the Republic." By that means, Chase noted, the nation could reverse the course of degeneration, cast off "the old and wrinkled skin of corruption," and "wax young again."[43]

With regard to the specific policies needed for generating "the new era," as Chase put it, differences once more obtained among radical and moderate Free Soilers.[44] Both groups subscribed to the idea of "freedom national" and took it to mean, in a general way, that the government should no longer use its power to promote and perpetuate slavery. Where they reckoned a vital matter to be involved, moreover, both groups brought to their policy an uncompromising moral temper. It was in the range of their policies, then, and not in their spirit that the differences existed.

Most radical Free Soilers contemplated a relatively wide scope of action. Charles Sumner defined its limits in this fashion: "*first*, the divorce of the National Government from all support or sanction of slavery, and, *secondly*, the conversion of this *Government*, within its constitutional limits, to the cause of Freedom, so that it shall become Freedom's open, active, and perpetual ally."[45] Since slavery was solely the creature of local legislation in the several states, in this view, the federal government was bound to withdraw all connection with slavery under its direct jurisdiction. This meant the immediate abolition of slavery in the District of Columbia and the territories, the end to the use of slave labor in federal arsenals or other installations, the cessation of efforts to recapture fugitive slaves, and the withdrawal of protection in the interstate slave trade. But Chase, in basic agreement with this plan to "denationalize" slavery and drive it back exclusively within the limits of the slaveholding states, took pains to show that such actions, in a federative Union, were purely negative and not positive in nature. Because no power was given to the federal government to create or sustain slavery, all previous acts to do so in the District of Columbia or elsewhere were necessarily usurpations by the government. Abolition, in this perspective, simply meant the repeal of previous unconstitutional measures and the restoration of the principle of Free Soil to every square inch under national jurisdiction. By peeling off the evil accretions of time, the original design of the fathers would be restored.[46]

In contrast to the radicals, Lincoln defined for himself and other Free Soilers of moderate persuasion a much narrower course of action for the government to follow. He agreed with the radicals that no warrant could be found in the Constitution for touching slavery in the states where it then existed. But he opposed their call for the use of government power against slavery then existing in all areas under direct national jurisdiction. He focused rather on the task of stopping absolutely the further spread of slavery into the free and unsettled territories of the United States. Whereas the radicals defined Free-Soil responsibility to include all areas of the Union outside the existing slave states, Lincoln was directly concerned only with that part of the Union that lay ahead in space and time.

Involved in this outlook was a concept of two Unions, but it was, even in the narrower range of actions, an outlook that shared with the radicals the spirit of moral absolutism and the urgency of regeneration. In the old Union, composed of the present states and settled territories, Lincoln was prepared to accept for the time being the coexistence of slave and free elements. In the new and unsettled Union that lay before him, on the other hand, he absolutely insisted upon applying the monistic principle of "freedom national." Even in this limited form, however, with its distinction between the old Union of the past and the new Union of the future, Lincoln still claimed to reproduce in a strict and faithful way the cosmogonic act of the "blessed fathers": "To me it seems that if we were to form the government anew, in view of the actual presence of Slavery, we should find it necessary to frame just such a government as our fathers did; giving to the slaveholder the entire control where the system was established, while we possessed the power to restrain it from going outside those limits."[47]

It cannot be doubted, of course, that this concept of the two Unions easily lent itself to a very conservative reading. Onto the unsettled possibilities of the new Union could be projected the profound debate in the old part of the Union. In a real sense the frontier here could serve as an ideological safety valve. Put another way, the prospect of coexistence with slavery for an indefinite period of time in the old part of the Union might be made more tolerable to the rising antislavery sentiment of the North where it could be plausibly argued that something was being done somewhere to realize the national idea of freedom. Indeed, Lincoln's own phrasing of the matter often suggested less concern for the substantive goal of removing the evil of slavery than for the subjective task of restoring to a peaceful frame of mind the agitated opinion of the North. The Union had existed for eighty-two years half slave and half free, he said in 1858, "because during all that time, until the introduction of the Nebraska Bill, the public mind *did rest*, at the time, in the *belief* that slavery was in the course of ultimate extinction." Presumably, then, the crisis of the house divided would pass when the public mind came to rest once more.[48]

But at last moderate Free Soilers regarded their policy less a safety valve for radical opinion than a substantial mode of national regeneration. This was true because of the uniquely strong belief held by Americans in the 1850s that the nature of the new part of the Union would ultimately determine the nature of the whole. Such a climate of opinion had developed, according to a recent study, because of the remarkable growth of the nation since the time of the Founding Fathers. Its rapid spread across the unsettled spaces of the continent and the proliferation of new states provided the basis for the view that the newest part of the Union would control and redefine the whole. The potentiality of the future became the most real of things, as a consequence, for it literally suggested that "the society of the future was being determined by the small scale institutional beginnings of the present." The statesmen in such an expanding Union were therefore very anxious to "seed" the future with proper principles. "Never forget," Lincoln said in 1859, "that we have before us this whole matter of the right or wrong of slavery in this Union, though the immediate question is to its spreading out into the new Territories and States."[49]

In a negative way this belief in the decisive influence of the new part of the Union found expression in the widely held view, noted earlier in the essay, that slavery would die out in the old and settled part when it ceased to spread out over the new. Representative David Wilmot would, by surrounding the existing areas of slavery with a cordon of freedom, place in operation "certain great laws" of population. "Sir," he said in response to the charges of abolitionism, "I would not obstruct the operation of God's laws." Lincoln also made it clear that he was interested in arresting the spread of slavery for a more substantial reason than merely that of placing the public mind at rest. When slavery ceased to expand, he said, "It *would be* in the course of ultimate extinction." He believed, in effect, that the absolute refusal to implant the evil of slavery in the new part of the Union would assure the final destruction of that vested interest from the past. In all territories where no vested interest from the past obtained, he embraced the imperative duty to act. "There we should in every way resist it as a wrong," he said, "treating it as a wrong, with the fixed idea that it must and will come to an end."[50]

On the positive side, the Free Soilers wanted to inform the unsettled possibilities of the future with the archetype of freedom. In arguing the case, consequently, they sounded less like legislators dealing with the ordinary affairs of a foreseeable future than constitution makers engaged in what Eliade called the cosmogonic act. "In our new free territories," Lincoln noted, "a state of nature *does* exist." Sumner professed to approach "with awe" the "transcendent theme" of the unsettled domain. "As the twig is bent the tree inclines," he declared, "and the influences impressed upon the early days of an empire—like those upon a child—are of inconceivable importance to its future weal or woe."[51] In its influence over "untold millions, to the remotest time," Senator Wade of Ohio remarked how much greater was the power of the United States Senate than that of imperial Rome. "She could dispose of conquered nations," he said, "but had not the shaping and moulding of a nation in its infancy—such a duty belongs to America alone." In founding new states "*de novo*," Senator James Harlan of Iowa believed, the American Congress legislated by its influence "for the whole human race." Representative Cragin of New Hampshire betrayed this same urgency in the fate he was helping to cast for Kansas. "The hopes of unborn millions survive or perish by your

votes!" he exclaimed. "Action in such a case becomes god-
like, and voting rises to the solemnity and dignity of a
prayer."[52]

Similar quotations by the score could be drawn from the
speeches and letters of other Free Soilers, but they would
only serve to strengthen this impression of the pervasive
sense of their productive power. Standing at a uniquely
significant point in space and time, they would make the
future part of the Union a monism of freedom and thereby
regenerate the whole. Theirs would be, in Eliade's phrase,
"a copy of the primordial act of the creation of the world."[53]
Lincoln thus appeared to act as if God and all posterity were
peeping over his shoulders: in legislating for the unsettled
part of the Union, he legislated for the whole and for all
time to come. While avowed conservatives in the 1850s were
disposed to compromise in order to save the Union, Lincoln
wanted to make it "forever worthy of the saving." He went
on in a very significant language to add: "We shall have
saved it, that succeeding millions of free happy people, the
world over, shall rise up and call us blessed, to the latest
generation." It was a particular kind of Union he wanted to
save, and he believed it could only be saved by reaffirming
the archetype of freedom with which the fathers had originally informed it.[54]

No wonder Alexander H. Stephens of Georgia was later
to observe that "with Lincoln the Union rose to the sublimity of religious mysticism." The Union in this regard was
less a product of history than an emanation of nature. To be
sure, Lincoln possessed something of Daniel Webster's feel
for the Union as a grand historical corporation which or-
dered the life of successive generations and took on much
of its own character in the very contours of this experience
through time.[55] But its essence was to be found at last in the
archetype of freedom, and the highest task of statesmen
was a periodic removal of the negating elements that crept

in through time. Cyclic regeneration, in this sense, conformed to the Jeffersonian ideal of freedom in the eternal present for each successive generation. In his famous Cooper Union speech, Lincoln did evoke a Whiggish savor for the historical past and a disposition to seek in the twists and turns of the nation's course some sanctions for the present. But a temper of moral absolutism underlay the entire speech and found extreme expression in the conclusion. It was there that Lincoln made his own appeal from history to nature. He called on the nation to cast off its fear of disunion threats, act on the basis of principle in the matter of slavery expansion, and leave the consequences to God: "Let us have faith that right makes might, and in that faith, let us, to the end, dare to do our duty as we understand it."[56]

As it turned out, the consequence of the policy of moral regeneration for the nation was secession and conflict. Most spokesmen from the slaveholding South professed themselves absolutely unwilling to accept the Free-Soil concept of the two Unions, clearly affirmed in the Republican platform of 1860, or the double standard it involved.[57] Conceiving of the Union rather as a partnership of elements, slave and free, they assumed that the coexistence of these elements might mark the Union's course across all of its unsettled spaces and through all time to come. The Free-Soil resolve to fix upon a present point in space and time, beyond which a monism of freedom totally displaced a dualism of slavery and freedom, therefore struck them as a revolutionary design to subvert the Union which their slaveholding fathers had helped to make.

Shortly after Lincoln had won the presidential election of 1860, South Carolina began the movement of secession. The only real hope for keeping the other states of the lower South from leaving the Union lay with the compromise proposals brought forth by Senator John J. Crittenden of

Kentucky in late December, 1860. His plan rejected the monistic claims of Free Soil, for its key provision would, by a constitutional amendment, extend the line of 36°30′ westward to the Pacific and allow slavery to exist in all territories south of the line presently in the Union or to be later acquired.[58]

But President-elect Lincoln stood adamantly opposed to the Crittenden scheme, or to any other compromise proposals that might trench upon the Free-Soil position. "Let there be no compromise on the question of *extending* slavery," he wrote to Senator Lyman Trumbull of Illinois. "The tug has to come & better now, than any time hereafter." He gave the same advice to two of the state's representatives in the House and to Thurlow Weed. "It acknowledges that slavery has equal rights with liberty," he explained to another correspondent at the time, "and surrenders all we have contended for." Lincoln here took his election on a Free-Soil platform to be the crisis in the nation's course reached and hopefully passed, and he thus supposed that any surrender of that platform would postpone, if not permanently dash, all hopes of national restoration. In a letter to Alexander Stephens, the wording of which rather closely anticipated a passage in his First Inaugural, he defined the ultimate issue very clearly: "You think slavery is *right* and ought to be extended; while we think it is *wrong* and ought to be restricted. That I suppose is the rub. It is certainly the only substantial difference between us."[59]

The difference was irreversibly there, however, and that which made it so substantial was at last the stark moral terms in which the issue was cast. Harry V. Jaffa has well argued that the "one idea" emphasis placed by the Free Soilers on the task of stopping the spread of slavery was essentially foreign to the temper of the Founding Fathers. Nor did they hold the concept of the two Unions with the same degree of intensity or to the same purpose as did Lincoln's generation. The idea that the newest part of the Union ultimately shaped the whole was one which became firmly rooted only after new territorial acquisitions and the rapid spread of the nation across the unsettled spaces of the continent. With specific regard to the effect of the process of expansion upon the fate of slavery, moreover, Allan Nevins has seriously questioned whether the fathers really supposed the institution would die out when it ceased to grow. Their expectations were "much more equivocal," he believed, than their hopes. For that matter, Jefferson voiced a rather widespread notion as late as 1820 that the diffusion of slavery across space and into the hands of many owners would be more likely to promote emancipation than the tactic of restriction.[60]

Finally, the constitutional interpretation Free Soilers claimed to share with the fathers will not bear close analysis. The contention that the guarantees of liberty in the fifth amendment carried freedom only into all national territories represented a divergence from the fathers no less distinct than the counter claim of southern expansionists that the guarantees of property carried slavery into all of the common domain. Until the controversy over slavery expansion grew intense by the end of the 1840s, only one view had generally prevailed. According to this view the Constitution had given to the federal government exclusive jurisdiction over territorial matters. In the exercise of that power, Congress might choose to prohibit the entry of slavery into a territory, or it might allow slavery to enter and receive the protection of the government. Since it was a matter of political expediency and not of absolute principle, in other words, the federal government officially occupied a position of moral neutrality. In actual practice the policies of the government from the beginning were informed with a spirit of compromise whereby an equilibrium of slave and free elements had been generally maintained.[61] The coexis-

tence of slave and free elements had thus issued out of the
original Union of thirteen states and begun its march across
the continent.

   While professing only the desire of following the policy
of the Founding Fathers, the Republican Free Soilers in the
1850s were actually bent on fundamental change. They
claimed that the policy would restore the Union which the
fathers had made; but it was precisely this belief which
inspired the political movement to transform the Union of
the fathers. In the thought pattern of negative liberalism,
the Free Soilers supposed the nation had begun its existence with a design perfect and entire. The activities of
expansion-minded slaveholders, in this view, necessarily
constituted an alien and negating element which brought
regression from the national idea. Progress in turn dictated
the need to peel away the evil accretions of time and to
reaffirm the primitive principles of the republic. It was true
that, for Lincoln and others of like mind, the actual political
task of regeneration would be restricted to the unsettled
territories. Yet, in a young and growing country, even this
modest progress would define and precipitate an irrepressible conflict.

9
Seward and the
Repressible Conflict

In the same year that Lincoln gave final form to his Free-Soil position with the "house divided" speech, Senator William H. Seward coined the phrase, "irrepressible conflict," to characterize the struggle between freedom and slavery. Many contemporaries, as well as later historians, claimed to find a strong family resemblance in the way these two leading Republicans perceived the issue of slavery expansion. But there was also a profound difference. It is the burden of the present chapter to focus upon that difference. Lincoln embraced a moral imperative to resolve the conflict, and he supposed the resolution of it ultimately involved the restoration of the nation's soul. Progress meant an absolute determination to end the further spread of slavery and to reaffirm the original and perfect design of the fathers. In the political arena, as it turned out, this project of restoration brought secession and war.

Seward's concept of progress, by contrast, indicated nothing so dramatic or traumatic. With an outlook blended of corporate, federative, and individual ideas of freedom, he tended to see the issue of slavery expansion in "political" more than "moral" terms. The defeat of efforts to extend slavery into Kansas by 1858 suggested to him that, in substance, the irrepressible conflict had been resolved in favor

211

of freedom. The nation might thus move on to other concerns in the ongoing corporate task of progress and development. The coming of the Civil War, in these terms,
pointed up the limits of Seward's outlook, if not the measure of his failure. For this very reason, however, a close
analysis of his statesmanship during the years of intense
sectional controversy leading to secession will serve especially well to illuminate the course which the nation at last
pursued. It will also help to summarize the pattern of the
political debate among freemen for the entire National
Period.

Something of the enigmatic will probably always remain
in any effort to explain the course Seward followed in
regard to the issue of slavery expansion. In the very same
speech which proclaimed a "higher law" of freedom in 1850
he also indicated a willingness, under certain conditions, to
admit California as a slave state. Though identified with the
Free-Soil principle that Congress ought to prohibit the
introduction of slavery into new territories, he gave tenta-
tive approval later in the decade to the doctrine of popular
sovereignty whereby a territorial legislature and not the
Congress exercised power over slavery matters. In 1858,
Seward defined the conflict between slavery and freedom
as irrepressible, yet most of his subsequent actions seemed
designed to repress it within the order of the Union. His
disposition to conciliate the slaveholding section during the
secession crisis of 1860-1861 thus stood in contrast to the
opposition he mounted against the compromise ten years
earlier. Finally, when the failure of peaceful efforts to save
the Union made civil war a virtual certainty, Seward favored instead a foreign war as the means of repressing the
domestic conflict.

Historians have explained this pattern of actions in various ways. Frederic Bancroft, the best of Seward's earlier
biographers, thought that the senator "had undertaken the

impossible task of being politician, statesman, and radical."
He reflected in many ways a blending of contradictory
elements, a mixture of the idealism and the realism separately derived from the two men he claimed as mentors,
John Quincy Adams and Thurlow Weed. James Ford
Rhodes found his course "full of inconsistencies." It was
one, he thought, that could be charted along a line from
that of a "radical of radicals" in 1850 to that of a Whiggish
compromiser by the end of the decade.[1] Seward trimmed
his actions to the political exigencies of the time, in the view
of others, and a supple rhetoric that masked as much as it
revealed seemed calculated to enhance party fortunes and
his own hopes for higher office. Students of the period have
actually disagreed less about Seward's inconsistency than
about the point of view from which it sprang. Some have
supposed that his deviations proceeded from an essentially
radical outlook; but the greater weight of authority leans to
the view, well expressed by Allan Nevins, that Seward's
radicalism was more rhetorical than real, and that his compromising tendencies by the end of the 1850s marked the
emergence of his "natural conservatism."[2]

Much can be explained in these ways, yet a greater consistency marked Seward's course than is suggested in many of
these studies.[3] He never took the Free-Soil task of stopping
the further spread of slavery as a political end in itself, to be
promoted in an inflexible way. For one thing, his faith in
the inherent power of freedom ruled out any urgent sense
of moral imperative or the need for rigid means of political
action. Flexibility also came from seeing freedom in its close
and reciprocal relation to other goods in a growing nation
destined, as he believed, to realize a grand imperial sway.
Like other goods, moreover, it was to be achieved in a
cumulative fashion as each successive generation contributed to the corporate pursuit of happiness whatever the
peculiar circumstances of the time placed within its power.

At bottom Seward held to a concept of progress which generated great optimism and gave to the statesman a wide latitude of action on the issue of slavery expansion. If there were flaws in his statesmanship, the difficulty is to be found in his basic premises far more than in any inconsistent application of them.

To be sure, Seward contributed not a little of his rhetorical skill to the Free-Soil cause and to the concept of progress embraced by Chase and Lincoln. His formulation in 1850, indeed, served to place the concept in broad philosophical perspective. "There is a sound maxim," he declared, "which teaches that every government is perpetually degenerating towards corruption, from which it must be rescued at successive periods by the resuscitation of its first principles and the reestablishment of its original constitution." Such phrases as the "higher law" and "irrepressible conflict" obviously invited people to think about political matters in moral categories. His opposition to the compromise in 1850 as "radically wrong and essentially vicious" resounded in later speeches and doubtless strengthened the posture of no-compromise with slaveholders.[4] But a closer analysis of his words and deeds at critical moments during the sectional controversy reveals a course governed in the main by a second and more conservative concept of progress. If he contributed to the forces making for irrepressible conflict, he also acted as if it could be peacefully resolved.

Pervading Seward's outlook in the two decades before the Civil War was the optimistic belief that, to paraphrase the formula of J. B. Bury, freedom had moved, was moving, and would continue to move in a desirable direction. He invoked "a higher law than the Constitution" which devoted the unsettled national domain to freedom, yet he often tended to regard this law as more descriptive than prescriptive in nature.[5] Right led to might, in this view, and the degree of freedom already established was bound to extend its own dominion. "Freedom organizes all the great springs of the human system," he declared, and this inherent power to outdistance slave labor in a growing nation gained daily accessions of strength from a redundant population in the Old World drawn irresistibly to the unsettled spaces of the New. In "obedience to laws which, I should say, were higher than the Constitution," he elsewhere noted how immigration would help to make the future even more decidedly the era of freedom. The call of John C. Calhoun for a constitutional amendment guaranteeing the slave-holding section a "political equilibrium" of power in the Union struck Seward as absurd, because the South had lost its "physical equilibrium" by the time of the Constitution and further decline had marked its subsequent course.[6]

Indeed, Seward regarded the irrepressible conflict itself as a sign of the progress of freedom through time. The thrust of free labor in the increase of population, the settlement of the open spaces, and the thickening of internal patterns of trade and transportation contributed to a process of consolidation in national life that would eventually require a uniform system of labor, slave or free. The new aggressiveness of slaveholders was a reflex of this tendency, he believed, an admission of their relative decline. Seward never took the conflict to be one of highest moral urgency because he simply never supposed the final fate of freedom to be in doubt. The resolution of the conflict was a problem of means far more than a matter of ends. "The laws of political economy," he explained, "combining with the inevitable tendencies of population, are hastening emancipation, and all the labors of statesmen and politicians to prevent it are ineffectual."[7]

Even in his most "radical" phase during the crisis of 1850, Seward did not apply the higher law with that degree of zeal which more doctrinaire Free Soilers deemed desirable. Senator Salmon P. Chase of Ohio among them did admit that Seward favored a Free-Soil proviso in all territorial bills that came up, but he criticized the New Yorker for taking no initiative in bringing such bills forward. Even worse, in Chase's view, Seward failed to use his great influence over President Zachary Taylor for securing a positive national commitment to the Free-Soil cause.[8] Instead he gave his main support to the President's plan of "non-action," whereby no territorial governments would be organized for New Mexico or Utah and thus no opportunity would be presented to Congress for acting on the issue of slavery expansion at all. Seward could point, as did Daniel Webster and Henry Clay, to the continuing force of the old Mexican laws against slavery; yet others under the lead of Calhoun equally maintained that the Constitution abrogated those laws and carried slavery into the new areas. Thus a degree of ambiguity remained in the plan of non-action, and to that extent it must be reckoned a compromise position. By his support of it, in any case, Seward should not be associated with that school of abstract politics which Webster condemned at the time for making the Free-Soil proviso a political good or end in itself.[9]

Seward's course later in the decade evinced even greater flexibility on the issue of slavery expansion. There are some grounds for believing that, in the fashioning of the Kansas-Nebraska bill in 1854, he actually encouraged southern Whigs under the leadership of Senator Archibald Dixon of Kentucky to force upon Senator Stephen A. Douglas and the Democratic party an outright repeal of the Missouri Compromise ban on slavery north of 36°30'.[10] But, in any event, the opening of these territories under the principle of popular sovereignty did not cause alarm. "Since there is no escaping your challenge," he told southern leaders, "I accept it in behalf of the cause of freedom. We will engage you in competition for the virgin soil of Kansas, and God give the victory to the side which is stronger in numbers as it is in right."[11] The mighty force of freedom, he supposed, would surely vindicate the right.

Events in "Bleeding Kansas" during the next four years served to justify Seward's faith in the power of freedom. By 1858, indeed, he thought the crisis in the conflict with expansive slavery had been reached and passed. The failure of President James Buchanan's administration to make Kansas a slave state under the Lecompton Constitution seemed decisive. Popular sovereignty had been "an epic in two parts," he noted: part one portrayed freedom lost by the repeal of the Missouri Compromise, while part two showed freedom regained on the plains of Kansas. Seward hailed the leadership of Douglas in the Lecompton fight and gave assent to the doctrine of popular sovereignty. As for the future, he shared with Eli Thayer the belief that the superior energy of free labor would, under the doctrine, outdistance the masters of slave labor even in the imperial race for Mexico and Central America. Southern efforts to continue the expansion of slavery, Seward thus noted in the spirit of a Tallyrand, would "fail to be a great crime" because "a stupendous imbecility." It only remained for the South to determine when and in what manner freedom "shall enjoy her already assured triumph."[12]

One might well suspect that it was this tone of assurance which excited southern spokesmen the most. Even in the case of the conservative John Bell it seemed to be true. With "an oracular mien and air," the Tennessee Senator complained of Seward, "he read to us, as from the book of fate, the decrees which he seemed to think it concerned the South to know."[13] It was a degree of assurance, however, which would later enable Seward to face the secession crisis with a spirit of conciliation. The imperative of the higher law tended to become less categorical as freedom progressed toward a fuller triumph.

Flexibility of another sort came by seeing the issue of

slavery expansion in the larger context of national expansion. Though freedom was in some part a good or end in itself, it was also a means for promoting the progress of the nation toward a grander destiny. "Our twenty millions are expanding to two hundred millions," Seward exulted, "our originally narrow domain into a great empire."[14] While radical Free Soilers tended to divide the past into stages of degeneration from the original principle of freedom, he most often regarded it as "the drama of our national progress." In his eulogy to the departed Clay in 1852, Seward noted how past generations in the ongoing national venture had in turn colonized the country, won independence from Great Britain, organized effectively under the Constitution, and used the new instrument of government for bringing order and consolidation to the young and growing republic. He would, in this perspective, have his own generation rightly perceive the task that lay before it: "We are rising to another and more sublime stage of national progress—that of expanding wealth and rapid territorial aggrandizement." Seward also recognized the positive contribution which slave labor had made to the past progress of the nation. Only in the more advanced stage, as he thought, was the exclusive use of free labor necessary "to make a State already great the greatest of all States."[15]

In a general way Seward thought of national progress, no less than that of freedom, as the dictate of a higher law. He dismissed the fear of old Whigs that continued expansion would dismember the Union, for he believed its federative nature suited the republic for indefinite extension. Even more fundamentally he rejected the assumption that the nation had possessed any real choice in the matter. The past career of aggrandizement, he argued, "has been shaped, not so much by any self-guiding wisdom of our own, as by a law of progress and development impressed upon us by nature itself." The decline of European power in the New

World since the eighteenth century had opened the way for the growth of the United States, and the future promised a virtual hegemony on the continent. Many expansionist Democrats of the time wanted to give official congressional sanction to the Monroe Doctrine and, by defining an irrepressible conflict with European powers, make it the basis for a bolder program of aggrandizement. But Seward regarded the doctrine in a way similar to the Free-Soil proviso—less an imperative to action than "a sagacious discovery of the tendency of the age."[16] He believed the vital force of free labor and free institutions would in a peaceful fashion continue to exert a gravitational pull on the surrounding areas and assure at last a Union of grand dimensions.

Seward felt a greater imperative for action in the Pacific area of imperial opportunity. This helps to explain his willingness in 1850 to admit California, even as a slave state, if the alternative were to be a decision by her people to slip from the orbit of the Union and draw the entire Pacific slope after them. He ever professed to believe that the Rocky Mountains or the Sierras, and not the Mason-Dixon line, constituted the only fissure or fault line likely to destroy the integrity of a continental Union. Thus, congressional deadlock in the crisis of 1850 or the humiliation involved in the Clay proposal for linking the fate of California in a compromise package with other matters might, he feared, cause the people of that distant region to snap the ties of Union. The sense of priorities expressed in the title of his speech, "California, Union, and Freedom," scandalized the more doctrinaire champions of freedom, yet it was some indication of his anxiety for a firm grasp upon the Pacific. "And now it seems to me," he said, "the destiny of the empire hangs on the decision of this day and of this hour."[17]

Seward attached such importance to California because

he deemed it indispensable for the future role the United States might play in the affairs of the world. In the "westward course of empire" through the centuries he supposed that "the Pacific ocean, its shores, islands, and the vast regions beyond, will become the chief theatre of events in the world's great hereafter." It was in this area that the final showdown would come between Great Britain and the United States for the scepter of commercial supremacy and with it the power to shape the destinies of the world. The many efforts Seward later made as Secretary of State in behalf of Pacific empire were anticipated in the range of measures that won his support in the Senate. Among other things he wanted to open Japan to trade, push new explorations, seek new colonies and bases, open the gates to Asian immigration, subsidize the mail steamers on the Pacific, and promote the construction of telegraph and rail links to the Pacific and beyond.[18] Many Free Soilers at the time would promote the nation's mission by making it a more nearly perfect model of freedom at home. Seward contemplated, in addition, a positive role in regenerating the world. "If, then, the American people shall remain an undivided nation," he said, "the ripening civilization of the West, after a separation growing wider and wider for four thousand years, will, in the circuit of the world, meet again, and mingle with the declining civilization of the East on our own free soil, and a new and more perfect civilization will arise to bless the earth, under the sway of our cherished and beneficent institutions."[19]

It was this imperial vision, in turn, which gave form to Seward's system of domestic policies for rearing "a high commercial structure." A policy of tariff protection would develop "our yet unelicited manufacturing capacity," while bounties to steamers and the fisheries would strengthen these elements needed for commercial rivalry with Great Britain. In order to increase the agricultural surplus, he

looked to "the settlement in the shortest space of time" of
the great continental interior. For this purpose free homesteads to actual settlers, an open welcome to immigrants,
and a network of internal improvements were designed.
The high priority he placed on completing a railroad to
California especially reflected the Pacific orientation to his
policies. In a very revealing passage Seward neatly summarized the relevance of his system of domestic policies to
the imperial goal:

> Open a highway through your country from New York
> to San Francisco. Put your domain under cultivation,
> and your ten thousand wheels of manufacture in mo-
> tion. Multiply your ships and send them forth to the
> East. The nation that draws most materials and provi-
> sions from the earth, and fabricates the most, and sells
> the most of productions and fabrics to foreign nations,
> must be, and will be the greatest power of the earth.[20]

In effect, Seward's policies added up to a course of peaceful aggrandizement for the nation. Steadily and surely, he
thought, the resources of the country would be developed
and other areas of the continent drawn into the Union.
Such a continental Union, in turn, provided the solid base
for commercial ascendancy and world power. Seward resisted the "one idea" platform of freedom, because he believed it best to advance the antislavery cause in the political
forum as "collateral" if not "subordinate" to other issues.[21]
Measures designed to promote the good of free labor
would thus be expected to promote the larger progress of
the nation. He could, in this light, give a balanced reading to
the Republican platform of 1860, and his own disposition to
compromise after the election contrasted with the "one
idea" impulse of others who would stand firm on the Free-
Soil plank.

Something of this same relation between freedom and national progress came through in many of the speeches he delivered in the West during the presidential campaign of 1860. "Seward must have breathed the air of 'manifest destiny' as he journeyed into the wilderness of the Northwest," one student has observed of his appearance in St. Paul, Minnesota. This relation gained a very precise definition in his speech at Lawrence, Kansas. He rejoiced in the freedom they had won for themselves, yet he reminded them that their "pivotal position" on the continent also made their decision of controlling importance for the remainder of the unsettled empire. ". . . I think you will find that the whole battle was settled to the deliverance of Kansas," he said, "and that henceforth Freedom will be triumphant in all the Territories of the United States."[22]

A third element in Seward's concept of progress complemented the flexibility that came from his belief in the power of freedom and its relation to the goods of empire. This was his steady vision of the national venture in its institutional and corporate dimensions. In the spirit of Edmund Burke, whom he often quoted, Seward rejected as a "specious theory" the Jeffersonian ideal that each generation was a separate nation with the autonomy to define and achieve its own goods. The Union was to be thought of rather as a grand partnership of all generations and the pursuit of happiness as an ongoing and cumulative enterprise. A true patriot was always aware that he participated in a reality far greater than his own "mortal" self, in an entity that enjoyed a "continuous identity" through the ages and the capacity for indefinite improvement. In this same perspective, Seward would have the statesman grasp the relation that obtained between his present actions and the corporate whole. "He is conscious," Seward hoped, "that every important measure of government in which he may be engaged is in some degree the result of causes anterior to his own existence, and may be productive not only of consequences immediately affecting himself and his contemporaries, but of others pervading the whole state and distant as its dissolution."[23]

The statesman, in this view, could best be regarded as a steward and his duties as a paradoxical blend of two elements—an urgency to action and the spirit of moderation. On the one hand Seward thought the responsibilities of the steward "to the generation which is living, and to the generations which are to come into life" ruled out the posture of inaction that came from a conservative reading of the corporate existence. Invoking rather the authority of John Quincy Adams at this point, he affirmed "that the tenure of human power is on condition of its being beneficently exercised for the common welfare of the human race." Seward could not, in other terms, accept a conservative "doctrine of institutions" which would make the established order an end in itself. He wanted rather to use the existing order in some degree as the means of effecting progressive change.[24] "The law of progress does not require changes of institutions to be made at the cost of public calamities, or even of great inconveniences," he told an audience at Plymouth, Massachusetts, in 1855. "But that law is, nevertheless, inexorable."[25]

With regard to imperial expansion, Seward argued that the "popular passion" for territorial aggrandizement reposed on the solid record of past growth and reflected as well a legitimate hope for the future. The real task of the statesman was not to resist this passion, but to give orderly expression to it. The alternatives might otherwise be an unchained spirit of filibustering, recurring wars, the annexation of "subjugated provinces," the acquisition of slaveholding areas, and the loss of that degree of homogeneity needed to make the empire a permanent one. By prudent and positive action, Seward thought, "we become co-laborers with our fathers, and even with our posterity throughout many ages."[26] Free labor constituted an efficient cause and the federative nature of the Union a formal and institutional means for the peaceful and progressive realization of the goods of empire.

Seward also saw the need for some degree of corporate action to promote the good of freedom. The call of avowed conservatives for an end to antislavery agitation struck Seward as useless, if not irresponsible. The rising temper of agitation, in his view, reflected a conflict between slavery and freedom that came inescapably as the forces of greater centralization in national life dictated at last a uniform system of labor. Seward deplored as well the predilection of conservative "Union savers" to compromise a vital matter in the name of preserving the order of the Union. He thought, to the contrary, that the very forces making for irrepressible conflict were also producing an indissoluble Union. "If it could be dashed to atoms by the whirlwind, the lightning, or the earthquake, today," he reminded Webster and Clay in 1850, "it would rise again in all its just and magnificent proportions tomorrow." The fathers had founded the Union by voluntary agreement, but economic, social, and political developments thickening through time had made it "a globe accumulating on accumulation, and not a dissolving sphere." Here, as elsewhere, can be found little in the way of constitutional interpretation, for it was the fact of the nation's irreversible progress through time that exerted the greatest influence on Seward's thought about the Union.[27]

With specific regard to action on the issue of slavery expansion, Seward claimed a wide range of choice. He had no doubt that Congress possessed the constitutional power to prohibit slavery in new areas of settlement, or that the exercise of this power would secure the "lasting interests" of the present and future generations of freemen. Seward also professed the widespread belief that the Free-Soil policy amounted to a geopolitical tactic for permanently resolving the slavery problem. With a language in 1850 that anticipated Lincoln's later formula, he noted how a Free-Soil proviso would, by drawing a cordon around slavery, "circumscribe its limits and favor its ultimate extinguishment."[28] To the states that would thereafter adopt their own plans for gradual and compensated emancipation, Seward offered the financial aid of the national government. His own plan, in 1850, for emancipation in the District of Columbia might be seen as a pilot project for the later action of the states. One of its provisions called for adequate compensation, and another assured that the process would not get under way until the owners had given their assent.[29]

But Seward was not absolutely wedded to the Free-Soil proviso as a means for corporate action. His support for Taylor's plan of non-action in 1850 and his leanings toward popular sovereignty later in the decade displayed greater flexibility as to means. This did not rule out other modes of action on the national level, however, because he could never accept a morally neutral position about the outcome of the conflict in the territories between slavery and freedom.[30] The higher law, in this sense, had a prescriptive no less than a descriptive force. Freedom did possess the inherent power to triumph over slavery; yet victory could only be certain if freemen were properly alerted to the nature of the conflict which they faced. While not dictating the precise policy which the government ought to adopt, the higher law of freedom did require the nation to clearly perceive the good and to fashion the will for achieving it.

It was for this reason that Seward emphasized the role of public opinion in the ongoing life of the nation. He regarded it as the only legitimate force higher than the Constitution. He furthermore supposed that the process of shaping opinion was itself a vital part of the institutional structure of a free society. Seward would have the statesman use his position in some degree as a forum for informing the public mind, and many of his own words and deeds were calculated to have that effect. In larger part, the division of labor between reformer and statesman called for the latter to take the given state of opinion and put it to work within the peculiar configuration of circumstances at the time.[31] The discretion which this gave to the statesman was clearly used by Seward on the issue of slavery expansion, yet his willingness to dispense with the Free-Soil proviso reposed on the assurance that the work of forming the national will had been well done. In other words, the opinion shaped by the moral urgency of the Free-Soil goal made it possible to achieve that goal by the means of popular sovereignty.

If the vision of the nation in its corporate dimensions called for some degree of purposeful action, Seward also thought it served to place realistic limits upon the goods which any generation might hope to achieve. He could thus confront those champions of "manifest destiny" who seemed compelled to realize the fullness of imperial glory all at once. Too exclusive a preoccupation with the goods of empire, he feared, would not only endanger other goods, but also tend to subvert the goal of a grand destiny itself. His phrasing of the matter also expressed very well his general concept of progress:

> Thus believing, let us not indulge the discouraging thought, however reverential, that our fathers were wiser or even better than we can be; or that other disheartening fear, that our children, or their children, will degenerate. Let us rather trust and hope in the Future, within whose veil Providence directs that every Anchor shall be cast. Let us be assured that although

the career of civilization is well begun, yet it shall only end with Time, and that even our feeble hands may somewhat regulate its velocity and guide its course.[32]

Seward gave the same basic advice to the ardent champions of freedom who sought for a speedy consummation of the good they reckoned absolute. "Circumstances determine possibilities," he characteristically observed, and thereby prescribed the extent of the good that could be achieved at any point in time. He would do all that was in his power and then suppose that a "superior wisdom" had reserved the remaining tasks for other times and places. "To us," he elsewhere affirmed, "who forget that though we perish, time does not perish with us—that though we die, our country is immortal—the abolition of slavery seems slow."[33]

Underlying this advice was the belief that the order of the Union constituted, finally, the highest good. On one side, Seward challenged the premise of impatient Garrisonian abolitionists that liberty and Union were separable goods and liberty far more dear. He rather regarded the Union as an indispensable means for securing all other goods, including the eventual emancipation of slavery itself. Nor was the slogan, "Union and Liberty," which he adopted for the campaign of 1860 anything new, for he had expressed the same sense of priorities twelve years earlier to a strong antislavery audience in Cleveland. "The first principle of our duty as American citizens," he said, "is to preserve the integrity of the Union."[34]

On the other side, the peculiar emphasis which many Free Soilers were giving to the opposite premise, namely that liberty and Union were inseparable goods, also clashed with Seward's corporate view of the Union. It was their belief that the Union could only be preserved by reaffirming its basic principle of freedom. In terms of policy, this

meant an inflexible stand on the principle of Free Soil for
the territories; in ideological terms, it involved a return to
the spirit of the fathers. "Sir," Representative Edward
Wade of Ohio declared, "in order to preserve the Union,
necessity is laid upon us to go back to the birth of the Union
prior to and under the Constitution." Because of the different elements in his concept of progress—the inherent
power of freedom, its relation to other goods, and especially the temporal dimensions within which he viewed the
life of the nation—Seward could rule out the need for such
a dramatic or revolutionary mode of national redemption.
In the long run, he supposed, "the noblest objects of national life must perish, if that life itself shall be lost . . ."[35]

Seward's outlook, in sum, enabled him to occupy a position during the debate of the 1850s somewhere between
Lincoln and Douglas. In the case of Lincoln, a preoccupation with the issue of slavery expansion disposed him to
make the Free-Soil policy a moral imperative for the nation.
From his initial reaction to the Kansas-Nebraska bill in
1854, until the outbreak of the Civil War, he consistently
conceived of the issue in moral categories.[36] Douglas, on the
other hand, deplored this excessive concern for the issue of
slavery expansion, because he deemed it a stumbling block
to further national expansion. Continual debate in Congress over the status of slavery in the territories would tend
to divide the nation so bitterly that no new areas could be
acquired at all. It was for the purpose of removing this
obstacle that Douglas sought, by the doctrine of popular
sovereignty, to take the power over slavery out of Congress
and place it in the hands of the territorial legislatures. The
way would then be open for a bolder posture in foreign
affairs and rapid imperial aggrandizement.[37]

Seward, by contrast, embraced both the good of freedom
in the territories and the good of national aggrandizement.
He supposed freedom to be both an end in itself and an

indispensable means for other goods. True progress for the nation required the agency of free labor; yet an absolute commitment by the government to freedom was not a necessary precondition to further advancement. Seward shared with Lincoln the strong feeling that freedom ought to win and with Douglas the view that it was ultimately bound to win. He embraced with other Free Soilers the task of shaping the opinion of the nation in favor of freedom, but he reserved to the statesman a great latitude in acting upon the matter. He never doubted that it would be best for the government, in advance of settlement, to assure freedom a monopoly in the new territories. At the same time, he felt almost as certain that aroused freemen would, under popular sovereignty, claim victory for their cause after the process of settlement got under way. Seward praised the leadership of Douglas in the successful fight against the Lecompton Constitution, and he believed the victory in Kansas cast the fate for the remainder of the continental Union. It was a true measure of progress for freedom and empire, he said, "an important stage in the advance of civilization on the continent."[38]

In another and more distinctive way, finally, Seward might be regarded as a mediator. He sometimes expressed the hope that his system of domestic policies for building up the country and for peacefully aggrandizing the empire would serve as a moral equivalent to foreign or civil war. The evil of "military ambition" inhering in too rapid a fulfillment of the nation's manifest destiny and the danger of "civil commotion" that lay in the intensity of the sectional conflict alike reflected, he thought, something of the rawer energies of a young and dynamic society in need of greater discipline. The way he formulated the problem in 1858 clearly suggested the search for a salutary discipline:

Sir, activity is the law of a community so strong, so

vigorous, and prosperous. I mean activity beyond the
mere daily occupation in domestic trades and profes-
sions, in mining and in agriculture, and in manufacture and commerce—an activity which constituted the
exterior life, if I may so call it, of a State, and which
forces it on some career of improvement or aggrandizement; that political activity which, carrying one
nation forward after another, or many along together,
constitutes what we recognize as the world's progress
or the advance of civilization. Political activity is a law of
nations.[39]

In these terms of analysis, Lincoln's mode of "political
activity," with its emphasis on the imperative of Free Soil,
involved at last a moral regeneration of the nation—a reaf-
firmation of its principle of freedom as the indispensable
condition for whatever future role the nation might play in
the progress of the world. Douglas would, on the contrary,
promote progress for the nation and the world by a tactic of
rapid aggrandizement and a bold foreign policy. But inescapably the one involved a mounting risk of violent conflict
at home, while the other form of "political activity" ran the
danger of aggressive war abroad.

Seward hoped his course of peaceful aggrandizement
might serve as a constructive alternative. "The passions of
the American people find healthful exercise," he noted, "in
peaceful colonizations, and the construction of railroads,
and the building up and multiplying of republican institutions." To be sure, the settlement of new territories under
the doctrine of popular sovereignty might not be altogether
peaceful, yet the experience in Kansas convinced Seward
that the process could be kept within tolerable bounds. Nor
did projects for the internal improvement of the existing
empire comprise a mode of "political activity" as dramatic
and exciting as that of moral regeneration or foreign war.

But Seward did argue, with a good deal of plausibility, that a well-directed settlement across the continent and the building of a railroad to the Pacific were actions that bore directly upon the progress of the nation and the world. Within the corporate dimensions of the process, indeed, such actions contributed their part to the progressive realization of a grand destiny. Seward would therefore have Americans become more aware of how the ordinary rounds of economic activity and the offices of daily life pointed to a larger meaning and reality in which they actually participated.[40]

If the foregoing analysis is valid, then secession and the Civil War defined the limits of Seward's outlook and the measure of his failure. With the quality of flexibility which he used during the 1850s, however, Seward responded to the crisis at the end of the decade. At the outset of the crisis he searched for a peaceful way to secure the good of Union, and this disposed him to compromise with the slaveholding section.[41] While the evidence is more circumstantial than definitive, there are grounds for believing that Seward was prepared in late December, 1860, to support the Crittenden plan, which, in the opinion of most historians, held out the best hope for keeping other slave states from following South Carolina out of the Union. Its key provision obviously violated the Republican principle of Free Soil, for it would extend the line of 36°30' to the Pacific and permit slavery to exist in all areas south of the line then in the Union or to be "hereafter acquired."[42] But Seward's faith in the power of aroused freemen remained, and, with the victory in Kansas, he simply did not believe that Mexico or Central America would ever come in to the Union as slaveholding areas.

The inflexible opposition of President-elect Lincoln to the Crittenden proposal, however, helped to destroy whatever chances existed for its success. Seward turned, as a

consequence, to other efforts at compromise. He especially
sought ways to keep the border states loyal, in the belief that
they would provide the base for rallying the Union sentiment in the seceded areas. Among other things he called
for the repeal of the personal liberty laws in the northern
states, an amendment specifically guaranteeing slavery in
the states where it then existed, a southern railroad to the
Pacific, and a plan for admitting all the territory west of
Kansas into the Union as two states. The presumption was
that the more southerly of the two would be a slave state.[43]
Although none of his proposals was adopted, the fact that
he had made them doubtless exerted a soothing influence.
The Union which Lincoln came to preside over on March 4,
1861, at any rate, could still count on the loyalty of half the
slaveholding states.

By that time the prospects for reuniting the whole by
peaceful means could not have been very bright. Yet Seward, now Secretary of State, clung to the hope of a peaceful
and voluntary reconstruction of the Union. He refused to
believe the separation of the states could be a permanent
thing, for he had always supposed that physical, social, and
political necessities made the Union absolute and indissoluble. The subjective sentiments for Union which accompanied its objective reality would surely assert themselves in
the seceded areas, he thought, if only an interlude of peace
could be gained.[44] This was precisely the weakness of his
outlook. The mounting crisis over Fort Sumter and
Lincoln's resolve to use force, if necessary, ruled out the
possibility of a peaceful interlude, certainly one as long as
the two years he believed necessary. His dealings with the
Confederate commissioners and his opposition in Lincoln's
cabinet to the Sumter expedition were therefore unavail-
ing.

By April 1, the range of choices for saving the Union had
become even more narrow. Peace or war no longer re-

mained as alternative means for the purpose. The only real choice lay between one kind of war and another. In "Some Thoughts for the President's Consideration," Seward thus urged President Lincoln to make war on at least two European powers, Spain and France. The news that the Spanish had just annexed San Domingo, with the approval of France, seemed to Seward providentially timed. He would also have had the President "seek explanations from Great Britain and Russia, and send agents into Canada, Mexico, and Central America to rouse a vigorous continental spirit of independence on this continent against European intervention."[45] During the 1850s, Seward had resisted the inclinations of Douglas and others for too rapid or forceful a course of imperial aggrandizement, for he believed that the natural progress of the nation pointed to hegemony on the continent. Within the narrower range of choices that came with the crisis of Union, however, he preferred this form of "political activity" to that of forcing the conflict at home to the point of civil war.

Lincoln followed another course and Civil War was the result. When it came, Seward threw his support to the cause; yet in the perspective of his previous career it represented his last choice of action. For two decades he had wanted by peaceful aggrandizement to promote in a close and related way the goods of liberty, Union, and empire. When the fact of secession ruled out that possibility, Seward sought by compromise peacefully to save the Union as a good indispensable to the realization of all others. Because the corporate dimensions of the nation's existence tended to make civil war the worst of all possible evils, finally, he turned to the alternative of unifying the nation by an aggressive war for empire after peaceful efforts had failed.

In sum, Seward presents the seeming paradox of a leader who proclaimed an "irrepressible conflict" and then acted as if it were in fact a repressible one. His idea that progress

gave the statesman a wide range of choice determined the
course he took. If it led him to overrate the forces of unity in
national life and to underestimate the morally disruptive
force of slavery, something of this failure might also be
attributed to the fact that Lincoln's moral imperative of
Free Soil tended to make the conflict truly irrepressible. In
either case, it must be one of the great ironies of the nation's
history that many Americans, and the delegates to the Republican national convention in 1860, regarded the New
York Senator more radical and inflexible on the issue of
slavery expansion than Abraham Lincoln.[46]

In the perspective of the preceding decades, Seward's
career in the 1850s constitutes in many ways a good summary of the entire period from 1815 to the outbreak of the
Civil War. His own sense of the nation's destiny within the
temporal process stood in clear contrast to the timeless
quality of outlook lodged in the moral categories of the
Free-Soil movement and in the Jacksonian predilection for
open space. The effort to synthesize these elements, no less
than the order of priorities he followed in the final crisis of
the Union, were a microcosm of the National Period succes-
sively shaped by the concepts of corporate, federative, and
individual freedom. Alexis de Tocqueville had seen the
democratic revolution as a providential fact, and he hoped
his vision might enable thoughtful Europeans to impose
some form upon its ultimate triumph. In this context, the
failure of Seward's statesmanship serves as a chart to measure the course of larger liberty through its incarnation in
Jacksonian Democracy to the fateful conflict Free Soilers
defined with the negating element of slavery.

A final word on the sequel of events will help to place the
findings of the present study in further perspective. If the
impulse to larger liberty in the Free-Soil movement
brought on the Civil War, many recent works suggest that

the experience of the war itself severely chastened the disposition of Americans to perceive the common life as relatively free from temporal and institutional constraints. Allan Nevins made much of the fact that the actual task of prosecuting the war compelled the Union to organize in an effective fashion the varied elements of the national existence. The process was irreversible and it served, in many ways, to fulfill the goals of consolidation long nurtured by spokesmen with a corporate outlook. By vindicating itself in the "blood and iron" of war, Paul C. Nagel noted how the Union took on the character of an absolute institutional presence, which stood over and set limits to the area of freedom. Many avowed conservatives in the 1850s, according to George M. Fredrickson, embraced the war precisely for this end. To them, the forceful preservation of the Union meant more than a punishment for rebellious slaveholders. It would also discipline the lawless and anarchistic tendencies of the freemen in the North. Much that was noble in the aspirations of transcendentalists and social reformers was stamped out, Fredrickson felt, as the nation gave itself over to a new age of business and material pursuits. Alexander Hamilton tended to displace Thomas Jefferson as the political idol, and formal thought in the new age was shaped principally by the categories of organic nationalism.[47]

While much of this is beyond dispute, the warning of David M. Potter to students of nationalism still seems relevant. Nationalism must ultimately be regarded as a subjective thing, he insisted, the sustaining faith of a people in its common destiny. Preoccupation with objective and institutional elements, as a consequence, often serves to obscure as much as it reveals.[48] The hope of President Lincoln for a "new birth" of freedom gave voice to a profound belief that the nation might truly be restored. If the Union appeared to many as an absolute, it was for the very good reason that

the Union embodied once more the national idea of freedom. Artificial weights had been lifted from the shoulders
of labor and greater equality assured in the race of life. To
be sure, black freedmen would not, in fact, become
freemen in the aftermath of reconstruction; but it must be
remembered that most Free Soilers in the 1850s gave to the
national idea of freedom the substantive political meaning
of equality for free *white* men. The abolition of slavery, in
this view, had destroyed the base of the aristocratic
slaveholding class and achieved this goal. Freemen might
henceforth pursue their several interests with the aid, but
not direction, of a broker-state government reposing on
their will. Any new evils that might creep in through time
could be dealt with by the succeeding generation. As they
saw it, many Populists and Progressives would later mount a
new crusade to restore the free design of the nation.

A full exploration of these matters clearly lies beyond the
scope of the present study. In the terms here used to chart
the course of the debate among freemen during the National Period, however, there is much to be said for the view
that the Civil War fulfilled more than it thwarted the impulses of larger liberty. The prolonged political effort of
freemen to remove the slave power obstacle surely tended,
by its moral and emotional intensity, to deepen the American faith in the tenets of automatic progress. Good would
come when evil and subversive forces had been removed.
The idea that the good of the whole arose automatically out
of the interaction of freemen, each in the pursuit of his
separate and short-run interests, was an idea that had a
considerable degree of relevance for an agricultural nation
rapidly spreading across unsettled spaces. But the quality of
timelessness in the outlook would seem, in retrospect, ill-
suited for a people on the threshold of an irreversible
commitment to the toils of industrialization. Many contem-

poraries and later historians would take Mark Twain's term, "the Gilded Age," to mean that something had gone wrong with the nation. It might be more accurate to suppose that the age expressed rather than betrayed the concept of freedom which emerged from the National Period.

Notes

Chapter 1

[1]By his approach to the subject from the "Union" side, Paul C. Nagel has provided many useful insights into the growth of nationalist thought. In the beginning the Founding Fathers regarded the Union as an "experiment," as one possible means for achieving the goals of the common life. But as technological development tended through time to forge irreversible bonds of physical unity, the commanding presence of Union took on the character of an end or "absolute." *One Nation Indivisible: The Union in American Thought, 1776-1861* (New York: Oxford University Press, 1964). By the approach taken in the present study from the "Liberty" side, the effort has been made to focus upon the meaning which the debate over freedom gave to the Union and not upon the limits which an "absolute" Union placed on freedom.

[2]By analyzing American liberalism in the context of the European experience, Louis Hartz found that a fundamental consensus obtained. This did not rule out, however, the possibility of a meaningful debate among liberals in the nineteenth century, nor does it relieve the historian from the task of tracing out the elements of conflict. The damaging admission that his "liberal society analysis" cannot account for the conflict over slavery points up the limits of the consensus view, for it is thus unable to explain the most "liberal" event in the nation's history since the Revolution. *The Liberal Tradition in America: An Interpretation of American Political Thought Since the Revolution* (New York: Harcourt, Brace, 1955), 19.

[3]Richard D. Birdsall, "The Second Great Awakening and the New England Social Order," *Church History*, XXXIX (September, 1970), 345-64; Clifford S. Griffin, *Their Brothers' Keepers: Moral*

Stewardship in the United States, 1800-1865 (New Brunswick, N. J.: Rutgers University Press, 1960); Perry Miller, *The Life of the Mind in America from the Revolution to the Civil War* (New York: Harcourt, Brace, 1965), 116.

⁴For an analysis of the conservative call by the 1850s for a "doctrine of institutions," see George M. Fredrickson, *The Inner Civil War: Northern Intellectuals and the Crisis of the Union* (New York: Harper and Row, 1965), 23-35. Hezekiah Niles was one of the most zealous spokesmen for the development of a "national character." An early statement of the goal can be found in *Niles' Weekly Register*, VII (September 10, 1814), 1-2.

⁵Guido de Ruggiero (trans. R. G. Collingwood), *The History of European Liberalism* (Boston: Beacon Press, 1959), 347-69.

⁶Most recent students of Jacksonian Democracy have, by focusing too exclusively upon the Bank war, missed the significance of the nullification controversy as the context in which can best be explained the considerable mixture of slavery in the freedom blend of democracy in its first reading. Two important studies help to redress the balance: Richard H. Brown, "The Missouri Crisis, Slavery, and the Politics of Jacksonianism," *South Atlantic Quarterly*, LXV (Winter, 1966), 55-72; William W. Freehling, *Prelude to Civil War: The Nullification Controversy in South Carolina, 1816-1836* (New York: Harper and Row, 1966).

⁷Marvin Meyers, *The Jacksonian Persuasion: Politics and Belief* (Stanford: Stanford University Press, 1957).

⁸Boorstin, *The Genius of American Politics* (Chicago: University of Chicago Press, 1953), 8-35; Craven, *The Legend of the Founding Fathers* (Ithaca, N. Y.: Cornell University Press, 1965), *v*; Noble, *Historians Against History: The Frontier Thesis and the National Covenant in American Historical Writing Since 1830* (Minneapolis: University of Minnesota Press, 1965), 3-17.

⁹Rush Welter, "The Idea of Progress in America: An Essay in Ideas and Methods," *Journal of the History of Ideas*, XVI (June, 1955), 401-15; Merrill D. Peterson, *The Jefferson Image in the American Mind* (New York: Oxford University Press, 1962), 69-87.

¹⁰Eliade, *Cosmos and History: The Myth of the Eternal Return* (New York: Harper and Row, 1959); Dudden, "Nostalgia and the

American," *Journal of the History of Ideas*, XXII (December, 1961), 515-31; Berthoff, *An Unsettled People: Social Order and Disorder in American History* (New York: Harper and Row, 1971); Somkin, *Unquiet Eagle: Memory and Desire in the Idea of American Freedom, 1815-1860* (Ithaca, N. Y.: Cornell University Press, 1967); Smith, "Anxiety and Despair in American History," *William and Mary Quarterly*, 3rd. series, XXIV (July, 1969), 416-24; Elkins, *Slavery: A Problem in American Institutional and Intellectual Life* (Chicago: University of Chicago Press, 1968). More on the anxiety theme can be found in Paul C. Nagel, *This Sacred Trust: American Nationality, 1798-1898* (New York: Oxford University Press, 1971) and in Bernard Wishy, *The Child and the Republic: The Dawn of Modern American Child Nurture* (Philadelphia: University of Pennsylvania Press, 1968).

[11]Niebuhr, "The Protestant Movement and Democracy in the United States," James Ward Smith and A. Leland Jamison (eds.), *The Shaping of American Religion* (Princeton: Princeton University Press, 1961), 20-71; Mead, *The Lively Experiment: The Shaping of Christianity in America* (New York: Harper and Row, 1963), 111; Tuveson, *Redeemer Nation: The Idea of America's Millennial Role* (Chicago: University of Chicago Press, 1968), 10, 43.

[12]McLoughlin, "Pietism and the American Character," *American Quarterly*, XVII (Summer, 1965), 168; Donald G. Mathews, "The Second Great Awakening as an Organizing Process, 1780-1830: An Hypothesis," *ibid.*, XXV (Spring, 1969), 23-43.

[13]Miller, *The Life of the Mind in America*, 11; "From the Covenant to the Revival," Smith and Jamison (eds.), *Shaping of American Religion*, 322-68; *Nature's Nation* (Cambridge: Belknap Press, 1967), 279-89.

[14]Robert V. Remini, *Martin Van Buren and the Making of the Democratic Party* (New York: Columbia University Press, 1959), 130-33.

[15]Jackson to Aaron V. Brown, February 9, 1843, John Spencer Bassett (ed.), *Correspondence of Andrew Jackson* (7 vols., Washington: Carnegie Institution of Washington, 1926-35), VI, 201. John William Ward, *Andrew Jackson; Symbol for an Age* (New York: Oxford University Press, 1955), 133-49, and Frederick Merk,

Manifest Destiny and Mission in American History: A Reinterpretation (New York: Alfred A. Knopf, 1963), 24-60, note the expansionism inherent in the concept of federative freedom.

[16] A good introduction to the shift in the national debate is given in Joseph G. Rayback, *Free Soil: The Election of 1848* (Lexington: University Press of Kentucky, 1970).

[17] Leon Litwack, *North of Slavery: The Negro in the Free States, 1790-1860* (Chicago: University of Chicago Press, 1961); Eugene H. Berwanger, *The Frontier Against Slavery: Western Anti-Negro Prejudice and the Slavery Extension Controversy* (Urbana: University of Illinois Press, 1967).

[18] *Congressional Globe*, 31 Cong., 1 Sess., Appendix, 942 (July 24, 1850). The middle-class ideology emerging from the controversy over slavery expansion is dealt with at length in Eric Foner, *Free Soil, Free Labor, Free Men: The Ideology of the Republican Party Before the Civil War* (New York: Oxford University Press, 1970), 1-39.

[19] Parrington, *The Beginnings of Critical Realism* (New York: Harcourt, Brace, 1930), 17-26. The laissez faire that Sidney Fine dealt with in *Laissez Faire and the General Welfare State: A Study of Conflict in American Thought, 1865-1901* (Ann Arbor: University of Michigan Press, 1956) would seem to be the negative liberal position here defined as broker-state individualism.

[20] Foner has rightly given Salmon P. Chase much of the credit for developing this pattern of Free-Soil thought by the end of the 1840s. *Free Soil, Free Labor, Free Men*, 73-102. Further perspective upon the novelty of Free-Soil thought is provided by: Arthur Bestor, "The American Civil War as a Constitutional Crisis," *American Historical Review*, LXIX (January, 1964), 327-52; Robert R. Russel, "Constitutional Doctrines with Regard to Slavery in the Territories," *Journal of Southern History*, XXXII (November, 1966), 466-86.

[21] Edwin S. Corwin, "The Dred Scott Decision, in the Light of Contemporary Legal Doctrines," *American Historical Review*, XVII (October, 1911), 60-61.

[22] Holman Hamilton, "Democratic Senate Leadership and the Compromise of 1850," *Mississippi Valley Historical Review*, XLI (December, 1954), 403-18; Robert R. Russel, "What Was the

Compromise of 1850?" *Journal of Southern History*, XXII (August, 1956), 292-309.

[23]Two works clearly underscore the moral imperative in Lincoln's outlook: Harry V. Jaffa, *Crisis of the House Divided: An Interpretation of the Issues in the Lincoln-Douglas Debates* (Garden City, N. Y.: Doubleday, 1959); Don E. Fehrenbacher, *Prelude to Greatness: Lincoln in the 1850s* (Stanford: Stanford University Press, 1964). The essentials of Lincoln's outlook can be found in the two speeches touched upon here. Speech at Springfield, June 16, 1858, and Address at Cooper Institute, February 27, 1860, Roy P. Basler *et al.* (eds.), *The Collected Works of Abraham Lincoln* (9 vols., New Brunswick, N. J.: Rutgers University Press, 1953), II, 461-69; III, 522-50.

[24]Albert D. Kirwan, *John J. Crittenden: The Struggle for the Union* (Lexington: University of Kentucky Press, 1962), 379-84.

[25]In addition to the work of Kirwan cited above, two other works argue at some length that Seward was disposed to compromise. Frederic Bancroft, *The Life of William H. Seward* (2 vols., New York: Harper and Brothers, 1900), II, 30-37; David M. Potter, *Lincoln and His Party in the Secession Crisis* (New Haven: Yale University Press, 1942), 183-84.

Chapter 2

[1]The best single work on the Missouri controversy is Glover Moore, *The Missouri Controversy, 1819-1821* (Lexington: University of Kentucky Press, 1953).

[2]*Niles' Weekly Register*, XVII (December 4, 1819), 220. King's speeches on the Missouri question in the second session of the Fifteenth Congress were not recorded in the *Annals of Congress*, but the substance of them was printed by Niles and many other newspapers in the country.

[3]Tyler to Dr. Curtis, February 5, 1820, Leon G. Tyler, *The Letters and Times of the Tylers* (2 vols., Richmond: Whittet and Shepperson, 1884-1885), I, 316; Jefferson to John Holmes, April

22, 1820, H. A. Washington (ed.), *The Writings of Thomas Jefferson*
(9 vols., New York: John C. Riker, 1853-1857), VII, 159; Charles
Francis Adams (ed.), *Memoirs of John Quincy Adams, Comprising
Portions of His Diary from 1795 to 1848* (12 vols., Philadelphia: J. B.
Lippincott, 1874-1877), IV, 502 (January 10, 1820).

[4] A word of explanation is needed on the approach here taken
to the basic sources of the Missouri debates. While Free Soilers of
all kinds shared much in common, there was, yet, a significant
difference. Most of those identifiable as Federalists in 1820
seemed clearly aware of the distinction between the political and
the moral argument. By contrast, the northern Republicans vo-
cally opposed to slavery expansion mingled the two far more
fully. As a consequence, the substance of the Federalist Free-Soil
position described here might have been extracted from their
speeches in Congress. But the opposite procedure would not
have been possible. Only in the thought of the Republicans was
the moral argument developed into a rounded concept of the
Union distinctly different from that concept yielded by the pri-
mary emphasis Federalists placed on the political argument.

[5] *Annals of Congress*, 16 Cong., 1 Sess., 245 (January 25, 1820);
1183 (February 9, 1820).

[6] Shaw, "Slavery in the Missouri Question," *North American
Review*, X (January, 1820), 165; Webster and others, Memorial to
Congress on Restraining the Increase of Slavery, December,
1819, Webster, *The Writings and Speeches of Daniel Webster* (National Edition, 18 vols., Boston: Little, Brown, 1903), XV, 60.

[7] *Annals of Congress*, 16 Cong., 1 Sess., 180 (January 19, 1820);
211 (January 20, 1820).

[8] *Niles' Weekly Register*, XVII (December 4, 1819), 220; Webster,
Memorial to Congress on Restraining the Increase of Slavery, 56;
Annals of Congress, 16 Cong., 1 Sess., 1216 (February 9, 1820).

[9] *Niles' Weekly Register*, XVII (December 4, 1819), 218. The
biographies of two leading Federalists involved in the Missouri
controversy stress this political approach to the question: Robert
Ernst, *Rufus King: American Federalist* (Chapel Hill: University of
North Carolina Press, 1968), 369; Samuel Eliot Morison, *The Life
and Letters of Harrison Gray Otis: Federalist, 1765-1848* (2 vols.,
Boston: Houghton Mifflin, 1913), II, 224. Both clearly show that

King did not use the moral argument until February, 1820, a full year after the controversy had begun.

[10]Boston *Daily Advertiser*, March 6, 1820; *Niles' Weekly Register*, XVII (December 4, 1819), 219; *Annals of Congress*, 16 Cong., 1 Sess., 217 (January 20, 1820). For perspective on the issue of the three-fifths representation, see Albert F. Simpson, "The Political Significance of Slave Representation, 1787-1821," *Journal of Southern History*, VII (August, 1941), 315-42.

[11]*Annals of Congress*, 16 Cong., 1 Sess., 185 (January 19, 1820); 253 (January 25, 1820).

[12]Raymond, *The Missouri Question* (Baltimore: Schaeffer and Mound, 1819), 7; King to Mr. Giles, March, 1820, Charles R. King (ed.), *The Life and Correspondence of Rufus King* (6 vols., New York: G. P. Putnam's Sons, 1894-1900), VI, 325.

[13]*Annals of Congress*, 16 Cong., 1 Sess., 1215 (February 9, 1820); Raymond, *The Missouri Question*, 3; Walsh, *Free Remarks on the Spirit of the Federal Constitution* . . . (Philadelphia: A. Findley, 1819), 103.

[14]Richmond *Enquirer*, February 26, 1820; *Annals of Congress*, 16 Cong., 1 Sess., 1219 (February 10, 1820).

[15]Richmond *Enquirer*, December 21, 1819; *Annals of Congress*, 16 Cong., 1 Sess., 1385 (February 17, 1820); 1081 (February 4, 1820).

[16]Opponents of slavery restriction also developed a strong argument by appealing to the treaty of 1803, whereby France ceded the Louisiana Territory, including Missouri, to the Union. One provision in the treaty guaranteed the rights of property in the territory, and another assured to the people the right of admission into the Union as a state. Since this was peculiar to the debate in 1820 and not as relevant to the later controversy over slavery expansion, it will not be dealt with here.

[17]*Annals of Congress*, 16 Cong., 1 Sess., 1225 (February 10, 1820); 397 (February 15, 1820); 355 (February 1, 1820).

[18]Taylor, *Construction Construed and Constitutions Vindicated* (Richmond: Shepherd and Pollard, 1820), iii; *Annals of Congress*, 16 Cong., 1 Sess., 223 (January 20, 1820).

[19]*Ibid.*, 1320 (February 14, 1820); 255 (February 1, 1820); 174 (January 19, 1820); 1393 (February 17, 1820).

[20]Two works cited in Chapter 1 clearly demonstrate the basic belief of many Americans that the nation had commenced its career with a perfect and complete design: Boorstin, *The Genius of American Politics*, 8-35; Craven, *The Legend of the Founding Fathers*, v.

[21]Taylor, *Construction Construed*, 2; John W. Eppes to James Barbour, May 3, 1820, Lyon G. Tyler (ed.), "Missouri Compromise: Letters to James Barbour, Senator of Virginia in the Congress of the United States," *William and Mary College Quarterly*, X (1901-1902), 22; *Annals of Congress*, 16 Cong., 1 Sess., 220 (January 20, 1820).

[22]Richmond *Enquirer*, January 1, 1820; Jefferson to Mark Langdon Hill, April 5, 1820, Washington (ed.), *Writings of Jefferson*, VII, 154. From the perspective of European thought, the Federalist concept of progress was conservative and the formula of the Jeffersonian Republicans radical. For an analysis of the difference see J. B. Bury, *The Idea of Progress: An Inquiry into Its Origin and Growth* (New York: Macmillan, 1932), 68-69; Charles Frankel, *The Faith of Reason: The Idea of Progress in the French Enlightenment* (New York: King's Crown Press, 1948), 3-38; Welter, "The Idea of Progress in America: An Essay in Ideas and Methods," 401-15.

[23]Jefferson to John Holmes, April 22, 1820, Washington (ed.), *Writings of Jefferson*, VII, 159-60.

[24]*Annals of Congress*, 16 Cong., 1 Sess., 1534-35 (February 25, 1820). Good background for this matter can be found in two articles by Joseph J. Spengler: "Malthusianism and the Debate on Slavery," *South Atlantic Quarterly*, XXXIV (April, 1935), 170-89; "Population Theory in the Ante-Bellum South," *Journal of Southern History*, II (August, 1936), 360-89.

[25]Joseph Blunt, *An Examination of the Expediency and Constitutionality of Prohibiting Slavery in the State of Missouri* (New York: C. Wiley, 1819), 18.

[26]Philip F. Detweiler, "Congressional Debate on Slavery and the Declaration of Independence, 1819-1821," *American Historical Review*, LXIII (April, 1958), 602; King to Christopher Gore, February 17, 1820; King to John A. King, February 11, 1820, King (ed.), *Life and Correspondence of Rufus King*, VI, 276; 270.

[27]*Annals of Congress*, 16 Cong., 1 Sess., 254 (January 25, 1820); Otis to William Sullivan, February 13, 1820, Morison, *Life and Letters of Otis*, II, 226; David Hackett Fischer, *The Revolution of American Conservatism: The Federalist Party in the Era of Jeffersonian Democracy* (New York: Harper and Row, 1965), 33.

[28]Charles Francis Adams (ed.), *Memoirs of John Quincy Adams*, V, 4, 11 (March 3, 1820).

[29]Edward Stanwood, *A History of the Presidency from 1788 to 1897* (Boston: Houghton Mifflin, 1928), 291. Detweiler's work is inadequate at this point, for he failed to see that the higher law of the Declaration was in the process of being assimilated into the Constitution during the Missouri controversy. "Congressional Debate on Slavery and the Declaration of Independence," 598-616.

[30]*Annals of Congress*, 16 Cong., 1 Sess., 125 (January 17, 1820); 1112 (February 4, 1820).

[31]*Ibid.*, 1397 (February 17, 1820); Message to Congress in Special Session, July 4, 1861, Basler (ed.), *The Collected Works of Abraham Lincoln*, IV, 433-35.

[32]*Annals of Congress*, 15 Cong., 2 Sess., 1182 (February 15, 1819); 1211 (February 16, 1819); 16 Cong., 1 Sess., 1111 (February 5, 1820); 1438 (February 21, 1820).

[33]*Ibid.*, 1379 (February 16, 1820); Memorial of the Inhabitants of Hartford to the Senate and House, December 3, 1819, Noble E. Cunningham (ed.), *The Early Republic, 1789-1828* (Columbia: University of South Carolina Press, 1968), 105; Stanwood, *History of the Presidency*, 293; *Annals of Congress*, 16 Cong., 1 Sess., 136 (January 17, 1820); 1174 (February 15, 1820).

[34]*Ibid.*, 1438 (February 21, 1820); 15 Cong., 2 Sess., 1223 (February 17, 1819).

[35]For typical statements of strong Unionist sentiment among Republican Free Soilers, see the House speeches of Joshua Cushman of Massachusetts and Daniel P. Cook of Illinois. *Ibid.*, 16 Cong., 1 Sess., 1307 (February 14, 1820); 1106 (February 4, 1820). Cook's views are especially revealing, for they anticipated the Unionism of Lincoln. In addition to all other reasons for opposing dissolution, he clearly saw how the geographical location of the Old Northwest, in its relation to the Atlantic and the

Gulf of Mexico, made political unity a physical necessity and his region the ultimate guarantor of the Union.

[36]*Ibid.*, 1376 (February 16, 1820); William Plumer, Sr., to Daniel Tomkins, January 29, 1820, Plumer Letterbook (Manuscript Division, Library of Congress, Washington, D. C.); Speech of Representative Claggett to a meeting in Portsmouth, December 14, 1819, Portsmouth *New Hampshire Gazette*, December 21, 1819; *Annals of Congress*, 16 Cong., 1 Sess., 1397 (February 17, 1820).

[37]Taylor, *Construction Construed*, 2.

[38]Editorial in the Richmond *Enquirer*, February 10, 1820.

[39]*Annals of Congress*, 16 Cong., 1 Sess., 227 (January 20, 1820); 326 (February 1, 1820); 260-69 (January 26, 1820); Richmond *Enquirer*, February 10, 1820; *Annals of Congress*, 16 Cong., 1 Sess., 408 (February 15, 1820).

[40]By an analysis of crucial votes, Glover Moore demonstrated that the compromise reflected the majority will of the South and the minority of the North. While some spokesmen in either section regarded the compromise a solemn and binding compact, Moore also showed that a greater number at the time did not look upon it in that way. *The Missouri Controversy*, 111-12.

[41]Spokesmen from western slaveholding states were generally more inclined to accept the constitutional right of Congress to prevent the spread of slavery into a territory not yet opened to settlement. See the speech of Representative Hardin of Kentucky, *Annals of Congress*, 16 Cong., 1 Sess., 1091 (February 4, 1820); letter of John H. Eaton to Jackson, March 11, 1820, Bassett (ed.), *Correspondence of Andrew Jackson*, III, 18; an editorial in the Nashville *Whig*, March 8, 1820. This was also the position held by Henry Clay during the controversy.

[42]A sharp clash in the House between Cook of Illinois and William Lowndes of South Carolina dramatized the importance of this point. Cook strongly urged that the ban on slavery north of 36°30' would last "forever," that is, it would operate not only during the territorial stage but also after statehood. Lowndes just as strongly argued the opposite view. *Annals of Congress*, 16 Cong., 1 Sess., 1111 (February 4, 1820).

[43]Pinckney to the editor, March 2, 1820, Charleston *City Gazette and Commercial Advertiser*, March 10, 1820; King to Oliver Wolcott, March 3, 1820; Robert Goldsborough to King, May 30, 1820, King (ed.), *Life and Correspondence of King*, VI, 287-88; 342.

[44]Moore, *The Missouri Controversy*, 218-57; Richard H. Brown, *The Missouri Compromise: Political Statesmanship or Unwise Evasion?* (Boston: D. C. Heath, 1964), 84; Shaw Livermore, Jr., *The Twilight of Federalism: The Disintegration of the Federalist Party, 1815-1830* (Princeton: Princeton University Press, 1962), 88-96; George Dangerfield, *The Awakening of American Nationalism, 1815-1828* (New York: Harper and Row, 1965), 97-140.

[45]Nelson to Charles Everette, February 26, 1820, Hugh Nelson Papers (Manuscript Division, Library of Congress); Stokes to Governor John Branch, February 27, 1820, cited in Walter B. Stevens, "The Travail of Missouri for Statehood," *Missouri Historical Review*, XV (October, 1920), 14. For a fuller analysis of the Missouri Compromise in these terms see the article by Richard Brown cited in Chapter 1: "The Missouri Crisis, Slavery, and the Politics of Jacksonianism," 55-72.

[46]Jefferson to General Dearborn, August 17, 1821, Washington (ed.), *Writings of Jefferson*, VII, 215; Letter from a Gentleman in Washington, February 12, 1820, Richmond *Enquirer*, February 17, 1820; Jackson to Andrew J. Donelson, April 16, 1820, Bassett (ed.), *Correspondence of Jackson*, III, 21. Glover Moore believed the "gentleman" in Washington cited above was none other than President James Monroe, or at least someone very close to him at the time. Though the President pursued a vacillating course, he apparently gave the compromise some active, if covert, support at the end. *The Missouri Controversy*, 235-39.

[47]*Ibid.*, 106; Ernst, *Rufus King*, 273; Homer C. Hockett, "Rufus King and the Missouri Compromise," *Missouri Historical Review*, II (April, 1908), 211-20.

[48]This pattern of thought among northern compromisers came out clearly in the statements of three of them: John Holmes, Letter to the People of Maine on the Missouri Compromise, April 10, 1820, Cunningham (ed.), *Early Republic*, 110-17; speech of Representative Charles Kinsey of New Jersey, *Annals of Congress*,

16 Cong., 1 Sess., 1578-83 (March 2, 1820); Representative Jonathan Mason of Massachusetts to David Sears, March 18, 1820, Boston *Columbian Centinel*, March 25, 1820.

[49]A wealth of newspaper material cited by Glover Moore shows how the northern compromisers dealt with the charge of a Federalist plot. *The Missouri Controversy*, 193-97. Senator Otis, who had been a central figure in the Hartford Convention, keenly felt the force of this appeal. In part for the purpose of combating it, he tried, by a series of newspaper articles published widely across the country, to demonstrate that disunion had been totally foreign to the purposes of the ill-fated convention. Otis to William Sullivan, February 13, 1820, Morison, *Life and Letters of Otis*, II, 227.

[50]Charles Francis Adams (ed.), *Memoirs of John Quincy Adams*, IV, 492-93 (December 27, 1819).

Chapter 3

[1]Glyndon G. Van Deusen, *The Life of Henry Clay* (Boston: Little, Brown, 1937), 215. Disagreement also obtained about the origin of the American System, but there is much to support the claim of Adams that he and not Clay was its real author. See Samuel Flagg Bemis, *John Quincy Adams and the Union* (New York: Alfred A. Knopf, 1965), 68, 269; Charles Francis Adams (ed.), *Memoirs of John Quincy Adams*, VIII, 444 (December 27, 1831). Not until the administration of Andrew Jackson did the Second Bank of the United States become fully identified, in the eyes of both foes and friends, with the American System of policies.

[2]Turner, *Rise of the New West, 1819-1829* (New York: Harper and Brothers, 1906), 5-6; Livermore, *The Twilight of Federalism, passim*. Glyndon G. Van Deusen similarly dealt with the new alignments of 1828 in *The Jacksonian Era, 1828-1848* (New York: Harper and Brothers, 1959), 27.

[3]*Annals of Congress*, 14 Cong., 2 Sess., 854 (February 4, 1817). Further analysis of attitudes about time and space held by many Americans in the period can be found in Somkin, *Unquiet Eagle*, 55-130.

[4]Dangerfield, *The Awakening of American Nationalism*, 289, 299, *passim*.

[5]The phrase appeared in the letter Van Buren wrote to Thomas Ritchie, editor of the Richmond *Enquirer*, on January 13, 1827. Cited in Remini, *Martin Van Buren and the Making of the Democratic Party*, 130-133. Bemis likewise stressed the slavery element: *John Quincy Adams and the Union*, 147-48. For an explicit treatment of the tariff matter, see Remini, "Martin Van Buren and the Tariff of Abominations," *American Historical Review*, LXIII (July, 1958), 903-17.

[6]*Annals of Congress*, 18 Cong., 1 Sess., 1308 (January 30, 1824).

[7]Meyers, *The Jacksonian Persuasion, passim*; Peterson, *The Jefferson Image in the American Mind*, 69-87.

[8]Somkin, *Unquiet Eagle*. In this connection John Higham has challenged historians to look beyond the economic cleavage between haves and havenots to the different emphases Americans have placed on the communal and the individual elements in their freedom. "Beyond Consensus: The Historian as Moral Critic," *American Historical Review*, LXVII (April, 1962), 623.

[9]Inaugural Address, March 4, 1825, James D. Richardson (comp.), *A Compilation of the Messages and Papers of the Presidents* (20 vols., New York: Bureau of National Literature, 1897-1917), II, 860-61; Ruggiero, *The History of European Liberalism*, 347-69. Lee Benson has well noted this element of positive liberalism in *The Concept of Jacksonian Democracy: New York as a Test Case* (Princeton: Princeton University Press, 1961), 86-109.

[10]*Annals of Congress*, 14 Cong., 1 Sess., 839 (January 31, 1816); 14 Cong., 2 Sess., 854 (February 4, 1817); Annual Treasury Report, *Register of Debates in Congress*, 20 Cong., 1 Sess., Appendix, 2828 (December 8, 1827).

[11]*Annals of Congress*, 16 Cong., 1 Sess., 2041, 2040 (April 26, 1820). In a letter to Francis Brooke on August 28, 1823, Clay expressed a similar sentiment: "It has appeared to me, in the administration of the general Government, to be a just principle to inquire what great interests belong to each section of our country, and to promote those interests, as far as practicable, consistently with the Constitution, having always an eye to the welfare of the whole." Calvin Colton (ed.), *The Private Correspon-*

dence of Henry Clay (New York: A. S. Barnes, 1856), 82. Edward Stanwood made a useful distinction between the kind of "log rolling" which revolved around a principle of legislation and another kind which merely indulges a host of selfish interests. *American Tariff Controversies in the Nineteenth Century* (2 vols., Boston: Houghton Mifflin, 1903), I, 158.

[12]*Annals of Congress*, 15 Cong., 2 Sess., 116 (January 11, 1819); 16 Cong., 1 Sess., 2150 (April 29, 1820); Bemis, *John Quincy Adams and the Union*, 65; Inaugural Address, March 4, 1825, Richardson (comp.), *Messages and Papers*, II, 862. Further analysis of Adams' position can be found in Richard Hofstadter, *The Idea of a Party System: The Rise of Legitimate Opposition in the United States, 1780-1840* (Berkeley: University of California Press, 1969), 231-37.

[13]A good summary of Raymond's views appears in Joseph Dorfman, *The Economic Mind in American Civilization, 1606-1865* (5 vols., New York: Viking Press, 1946-1959), II, 566-74; Bemis, *John Quincy Adams and the Union*, 55-65.

[14]*Annals of Congress*, 18 Cong., 1 Sess., 1631, 1632 (February 24, 1824); 14 Cong., 2 Sess., 577 (January 17, 1817); First Annual Message, December 6, 1825, Richardson (comp.), *Messages and Papers*, II, 882; *Niles' Weekly Register*, XXIV (July 19, 1823), 308; XXVI (March 6, 1824), 2.

[15]*Annals of Congress*, 15 Cong., 1 Sess., 1178 (March 6, 1818); 1187 (March 9, 1818); 18 Cong., 1 Sess., 1016 (January 13, 1824).

[16]Seventh Annual Message, December 5, 1815, Richardson (comp.), *Messages and Papers*, II, 552; Eighth Annual Message, December 3, 1816, *ibid.*, 561; *Annals of Congress*, 14 Cong., 2 Sess., 851-55 (February 4, 1817).

[17]*Ibid.*, 16 Cong., 1 Sess., 1916-44 (April 21, 1820); 2049, 2034-52 (April 26, 1820). Background for the change in the goals of economic policy can be found in Norris W. Preyer, "Southern Support for the Tariff of 1816: A Reappraisal," *Journal of Southern History*, XXV (August, 1959), 306-22, and Stanwood, *American Tariff Controversies*, I, 160-99.

[18]*Annals of Congress*, 18 Cong., 1 Sess., 1630 (February 24, 1824); Everett, "British Opinions on the Protecting System," *North American Review*, XXX (January, 1830), 160-216; *Annals of*

Congress, 16 Cong., 1 Sess., 2040 (April 26, 1820); Annual Treasury Report, *Register of Debates*, 20 Cong., 1 Sess., Appendix, 2828 (December 8, 1827); *Annals of Congress*, 16 Cong., 1 Sess., 2147 (April 29, 1820).

[19]*Ibid.*, 18 Cong., 1 Sess., 1260 (January 28, 1824); Clay's speech on a Cumberland Road bill, January 17, 1825, *Niles' Weekly Register*, XXVII (February 5, 1825), 360. For a full analysis of the idea of the "sovereignty of the present generation" in Jefferson's thought, see Daniel J. Boorstin, *The Lost World of Thomas Jefferson* (New York: Henry Holt, 1948), 204-13.

[20]Bemis, *John Quincy Adams and the Union*, 78; Roy M. Robbins, *Our Landed Heritage: The Public Domain, 1776-1936* (Princeton: Princeton University Press, 1942), 32-38.

[21]Annual Treasury Report, *Register of Debates*, 20 Cong., 1 Sess., Appendix, 2832 (December 8, 1927); King cited in New York *Evening Post*, November 13, 1819; *Annals of Congress*, 18 Cong., 2 Sess., 42 (December 22, 1824). The present study is clearly indebted to the analysis of the twilight of mercantilism found in William Appleman Williams, *The Contours of American History* (Chicago: University of Chicago Press, 1966), 204-23. But it would seem that Williams overemphasized the imperative of expansion in the mercantile outlook. A close reading of the debates rather suggests that the corporate impulse to build up a national community through time was seen by many at the time as an alternative to rapid expansion. The distinction was a relative one, to be sure, but it helps in understanding more fully the thrust of the national debate.

[22]Quincy, "Maine Statehood," *North American Review*, III (September, 1816), 397-98; *Register of Debates*, 20 Cong., 1 Sess., 495 (March 25, 1828); *Annals of Congress*, 18 Cong., 1 Sess., 2080, 2079 (April 2, 1824).

[23]Sparks on education and land policies, *North American Review*, XIII (October, 1821), 310-42; *Niles' Weekly Register*, XXVI (March 6, 1824), 1; Rush Welter, *Popular Education and Democratic Thought* (New York: Columbia University Press, 1962), 23-41. In parallel fashion, Clifford S. Griffin has shown how many other reform efforts commencing at the time had a conservative purpose: "Religious Benevolence as Social Control, 1815-1860," *Mississippi*

Valley Historical Review, XLIV (December, 1957), 423-44; *Their Brothers' Keepers, passim.*

[24]*Niles' Weekly Register* VII (December 31, 1814), 280; Joseph Lancaster to Clay, December 22, 1819, *ibid.*, XVII (January 15, 1820), 323; Clay's speech on a Cumberland Road bill, January 17, 1825, *ibid.*, XXVII (February 5, 1825), 357-59; editorial from New York *Commercial Advertiser*, October 11, 1823, cited in *ibid.*, XXV (October 18, 1823), 103. A fuller analysis of this matter appears in Merle Curti, *The Roots of American Loyalty* (New York: Columbia University Press, 1946), 92-121, and Robert F. Berkhofer, Jr., "Space, Time, Culture and the New Frontier," *Agricultural History,* XXXVIII (January, 1964), 21-30.

[25]Everett on power in the states, *North American Review*, XXII (April, 1826), 374; *Annals of Congress*, 16 Cong., 1 Sess., 2044 (April 26, 1820).

[26]Annual Treasury Report, *Register of Debates*, 20 Cong., 1 Sess., Appendix, 2826, 2829 (December 8, 1827); Everett's views are well developed in Dorfman, *Economic Mind in American Civilization*, II, 593-97; Francis C. Gray, Phi Beta Kappa Address, *North American Review*, III (September, 1816), 303, 289-305.

[27]Address to the Harrisburg Convention, July 30, 1827, *Niles' Weekly Register*, XXXIII (October 13, 1827), 107; *Annals of Congress*, 18 Cong., 1 Sess., 1993-94 (March 31, 1824); Everett, "British Opinions on the Protecting System," *North American Review*, XXX (January, 1830), 208. Smith, *Virgin Land: The American West as Symbol and Myth* (Cambridge: Harvard University Press, 1950). Three works explore the way easterners sought to assimilate the primitive frontier to the progress of civilization: Arthur K. Moore, *The Frontier Mind: A Cultural Analysis of the Kentucky Frontiersman* (Lexington: University of Kentucky Press, 1957), 139-80; Rush Welter, "The Frontier West as Image of American Society: Conservative Attitudes before the Civil War," *Mississippi Valley Historical Review*, XLVI (March, 1960), 593-614; Marvin Fisher, "The 'Garden' and the 'Workshop': Some European Conceptions and Preconceptions of America, 1830-1860," *New England Quarterly*, XXXIV (September, 1961), 311-27.

[28]First Annual Message, December 6, 1825, Richardson

(comp.), *Messages and Papers*, II, 882; Adams, "Society and Civilization," *Whig Review*, II (July, 1845), 80-89. See also Charles A. and Mary R. Beard, *The American Spirit: A Study of the Idea of Civilization in the United States* (New York: Macmillan, 1942), 152-62; Bemis, *John Quincy Adams and the Union*, 55-70; Arthur A. Ekirch, Jr., *The Idea of Progress in America, 1815-1860* (New York: Columbia University Press, 1944), 73-75; Wendell Glick, "The Best Possible World of John Quincy Adams," *New England Quarterly*, XXXVII (March, 1964), 3-17.

[29]Jefferson to Edward Livingston, April 4, 1824, Washington (ed.), *The Writings of Thomas Jefferson*, VII, 343; Nashville *Banner*, October 17, 1826, cited in Charles Grier Sellers, *James K. Polk: Jacksonian, 1795-1843* (Princeton: Princeton University Press, 1957), 110; Remini, *Martin Van Buren*, 134; Charles M. Wiltse, *John C. Calhoun: Nationalist, 1782-1828* (Indianapolis: Bobbs-Merrill, 1944), 321.

[30]*Annals of Congress*, 1 Sess., 1202 (March 9, 1818); 18 Cong., 1 Sess., 1264 (January 29, 1824); Cooper's speech at Columbia, South Carolina, July 2, 1827, cited in *Niles' Weekly Register*, XXXIII (September 8, 1827), 32.

[31]*Register of Debates*, 20 Cong., 1 Sess., 794 (May 20, 1828); *Annals of Congress*, 14 Cong., 1 Sess., 845 (January 31, 1816); 16 Cong., 1 Sess., 1959 (April 24, 1820).

[32]*Ibid.*, 1961, 1956, 1952-63 (April 24, 1820); 18 Cong., 1 Sess., 2360 (April 15, 1824).

[33]*Ibid.*, 2403 (April 16, 1824); 1923 (March 26, 1824); 2014 (April 1, 1824).

[34]*Ibid.*, 2169 (April 5, 1824). The high priest of this kind of southern "primitivist" thought was John Taylor of Caroline. A good analysis of his outlook is given in Loren Baritz, *City on a Hill: A History of Ideas and Myths in America* (New York: John Wiley and Sons, 1964), 159-203.

[35]For Calhoun's attitudes about party see Hofstadter, *The Idea of a Party System*, 252-56; William W. Freehling, "Spoilsmen and Interest in the Thought and Career of John C. Calhoun," *Journal of American History*, LII (June, 1965), 25-42. The process of nullification, as Calhoun conceived of it, seemed very simple and

straightforward. In a convention called for the purpose, a sovereign state might declare null and void any federal law deemed to be unconstitutional. This action by a single state then bound the federal government to cease further efforts to enforce the measure anywhere in the nation. Only after specific authority had been granted by a new amendment could the federal government resume action in the matter. Good background on the idea of nullification appears in Freehling, *Prelude to Civil War*, 134-76; Louis Hartz, "South Carolina vs. the United States," Daniel Aaron (ed.), *Americans in Crisis* (New York: Alfred A. Knopf, 1952), 73-91.

[36]Remini, *Martin Van Buren*, 123-46; Hofstadter, *The Idea of a Party System*, 236-52; Peterson, *The Jefferson Image in the American Mind*, 20-29.

[37]The fullest account of the development of the new party outlook is given in Michael Wallace, "Changing Concepts of Party in the United States: New York, 1815-1828," *American Historical Review*, LXXXIV (December, 1968), 453-91.

[38]Clearly the position of Van Buren reflected the laissez faire outlook. Basic here was the belief that the interaction of freemen in the present would, without any essential government control or planning, lead to the good of a "natural social order." For an extended analysis of this position, see Yehoshua Arieli, *Individualism and Nationalism in American Ideology* (Baltimore: Penguin Books, 1966), 88-118.

[39]If the Union as the highest good seemed implicit in the idea of a two-party system, Richard H. Brown has well demonstrated the other side of the matter, namely, how the party system helped to preserve the Union by generating conflict along national rather than sectional lines. The contrast he has drawn between Van Buren and Calhoun in this regard is very illuminating. "The Missouri Crisis, Slavery, and the Politics of Jacksonianism," 55-72. Though it developed out of strongly sectional attitudes about presidential candidates, Richard P. McCormick also stressed how the new two-party system served to attenuate sectional differences and promote national consensus. *The Second American Party System: Party Formation in the Jacksonian Era* (Chapel Hill: University of North Carolina Press, 1966), 353, *passim*.

Chapter 4

[1]Second Inaugural Address, March 4, 1833, Richardson (comp.), *Messages and Papers*, III, 1122. Editorials in the Washington *Globe* on January 2 and 4, 1833, sought to answer the critics and demonstrate the unity of Jackson's views. The first part of this chapter, dealing with Jackson's actions as a compromiser, reproduces in a somewhat altered form an article by the present author, "Andrew Jackson: The Great Compromiser," *Tennessee Historical Quarterly*, XXVI (Spring, 1967), 64-78.

[2]Clay to Francis Brooke, December 1832, Colton (ed.), *Private Correspondence of Clay*, 345; Charles Francis Adams (ed.), *Memoirs of John Quincy Adams*, VIII, 510 (December 24, 1832); *Niles' Weekly Register*, LXIII (December 15, 1832), 249; William Cabell Bruce, *John Randolph of Roanoke* (2 vols., New York: G. P. Putnam's Sons, 1922), II, 25; William E. Dodd, "The Place of Nathaniel Macon in Southern History," *American Historical Review*, VII (July, 1902), 668; South Carolina editors cited in Chauncey Samuel Boucher, *The Nullification Controversy in South Carolina* (Chicago: University of Chicago Press, 1916), 249, 254; Van Buren to Jackson, December 27, 1832, Bassett (ed.), *Correspondence of Jackson*, IV, 507.

[3]Parton, *Life of Andrew Jackson* (3 vols., New York: Mason Brothers, 1861), III, 469, 481; Schouler, *History of the United States of America under the Constitution* (Revised Edition, 7 vols., New York: Dodd, Mead, 1894-1913), IV, 95; Von Holst, *The Constitutional and Political History of the United States* (8 vols., Chicago: Callagan, 1881-1892), I, 505; McMaster, *A History of the People of the United States from the Revolution to the Civil War* (8 vols., New York: D. Appleton, 1900-1937), VI, 173; Bowers, *The Party Battles of the Jackson Period* (Boston: Houghton Mifflin, 1922), 277; James, *Andrew Jackson: Portrait of a President* (Indianapolis: Bobbs-Merrill, 1937), 323; Abernethy, "Andrew Jackson and the Rise of Southwestern Democracy," *American Historical Review*, XXXIII (October, 1927), 76; Bassett, *The Life of Andrew Jackson* (New Edition, New York: Macmillan, 1925), 483, 583; Wiltse, *John C. Calhoun: Nullifier, 1829-1839* (Indianapolis: Bobbs-Merrill, 1949), 172. One old and one recent work provide notable exceptions, for both grasp the essential unity in Jackson's com-

promise efforts: Stanwood, *American Tariff Controversies in the Nineteenth Century*, I, 410; Freehling, *Prelude to Civil War*, 294.

⁴By the people, as Marvin Meyers has perceptively shown, Jackson meant "the great social residuum after alien elements have been removed." *The Jacksonian Persuasion*, 15. This illustrates again the essence of negative liberalism discussed in Chapter 1, that is, the assumption of original perfection and the recurring need to purge alien elements that creep in through time.

⁵Benton, *Thirty Years' View* (2 vols., New York: D. Appleton, 1854-1856), I, 297; *Daily National Intelligencer*, December 6, 1832; Washington *Globe*, December 11, 1830.

⁶Fourth Annual Message, December 4, 1832, Richardson (comp.), *Messages and Papers*, III, 1160-63, 1165.

⁷*Ibid.*, 1163-64.

⁸Publicly, Jackson outlined the policy in his first and second annual messages and in the veto of the Maysville Road bill. Privately, he expressed the ideas in rough drafts of his first and second inaugurals and in a long letter to John Overton on December 31, 1829, Bassett (ed.), *Correspondence of Jackson*, IV, 109.

⁹"The American System," Calhoun wrote to Christopher Van Deventer on May 25, 1831, "is not so odious here as the distribution scheme." J. Franklin Jameson (ed.), *Correspondence of John C. Calhoun, Annual Report* of the American Historical Association for 1899 (2 vols., Washington: Government Printing Office, 1900), II, 293. Hayne stated the matter just as emphatically in a letter to James H. Hammond on March 29, 1830, "Letters on the Nullification Movement in South Carolina, 1830-1834," *American Historical Review*, VI (July, 1901), 738.

¹⁰Jackson to L. H. Coleman, April 26, 1824, Bassett (ed.), *Correspondence of Jackson*, III, 249-50. A very balanced account of the tariff measure in 1832 can be found in Bemis, *John Quincy Adams and the Union*, 240-58.

¹¹James Hamilton, Jr., to Hammond, January 16, 1832; Hayne to Hammond, December 29, 1831, "Letters on the Nullification Movement in South Carolina, 1830-1834," 748-49; Calhoun to Armistead Burt, December 27, 1831, Jameson (ed.), *Correspondence of Calhoun*, II, 308; Jackson to John Coffee, July

17, 1832; Jackson to Amos Kendall, July 23, 1832, Bassett (ed.), *Correspondence of Jackson*, IV, 463; 465.

¹²Richard P. Longaker, "Was Jackson's Kitchen Cabinet a Cabinet?" *Mississippi Valley Historical Review*, XLIV (June, 1957), 103.

¹³Frederick L. Nussbaum, "The Compromise of 1833: A Study in Practical Politics," *South Atlantic Quarterly*, XI (October, 1912), 339-40; Frank W. Taussig, *The Tariff History of the United States* (7th Edition, New York: G. P. Putnam's Sons, 1923), 106-09; Robert W. July, *The Essential New Yorker: Gulian Crommelin Verplanck* (Durham: Duke University Press, 1951), 144-63; Jackson to Reverend Andrew J. Crawford, May 1, 1833, Bassett (ed.), *Correspondence of Jackson*, V, 72.

¹⁴Van Buren to Robert Patterson and others, February 25, 1833, *Niles' Weekly Register*, XLIV (March 16, 1833), 39; *Register of Debates*, 22 Cong., 2 Sess., 468 (February 12, 1833); Clay to Peter B. Porter, February 16, 1833, cited in Van Deusen, *Life of Clay*, 269; Abbott Lawrence to Clay, March 26, 1833, Colton (ed.), *Private Correspondence of Clay*, 358; Benton, *Thirty Years' View*, I, 316.

¹⁵Charles Francis Adams (ed.), *Memoirs of John Quincy Adams*, VIII, 522 (January 28, 1833); Wiltse, *John C. Calhoun: Nullifier*, 193; *National Intelligencer*, February 28, 1833. One student of the period has concluded most emphatically that Clay considered the distribution of the land revenues "an essential part of the adjustment." Frederick Jackson Turner, *The United States, 1830-1850: The Nation and Its Sections* (New York: Henry Holt, 1935), 420. See also Van Deusen, *The Jacksonian Era*, 79. *Register of Debates*, 22 Cong., 2 Sess., 221 (January 24, 1833).

¹⁶Jackson to Joel R. Poinsett, March 6, 1833, Bassett (ed.), *Correspondence of Jackson*, V, 28.

¹⁷Washington *Globe*, February 27, 1833, left no doubt at all that there would not have been a tariff without the Force Bill. Mercer to Edgar Snowden, March 4, 1833, *Niles' Weekly Register*, XLIV (March 9, 1833), 21. Freehling has well argued that Jackson stressed the great "symbolic importance" of the Force Bill, for it brought to the support of his position the full force of a congressional declaration. *Prelude to Civil War*, 285.

[18]John C. Fitzpatrick (ed.), *The Autobiography of Martin Van Buren, Annual Report* of the American Historical Association for 1918 (2 vols., Washington: Government Printing Office, 1920), II, 544; Jackson to Grundy, February 13, 1833, Bassett, *Life of Jackson*, 582.

[19]Van Buren to Jackson, December 27, 1832; Jackson to Van Buren, December 25, 1832, Bassett (ed.), *Correspondence of Jackson*, IV, 507, 506; Jackson to Grundy, February 13, 1833, Bassett, *Life of Jackson*, 582; Jackson to Reverend Hardy M. Cryer, February 20, 1833, Bassett (ed.), *Correspondence of Jackson*, V, 19. Representative James K. Polk of Tennessee illustrated the plight of many southern Jacksonians. While reluctantly voting for the Force Bill, he also supported an amendment by George McDuffie of South Carolina that it was an act "to subvert the sovereignty of the States of the Union. . . ." Sellers, *James K. Polk: Jacksonian*, 161.

[20]Jackson to James Hamilton, Jr., June 29, 1828, Bassett, *Life of Jackson*, 553; Jackson to Poinsett, October 26, 1830, Bassett (ed.), *Correspondence of Jackson*, IV, 191; Jackson Letter to Fourth-of-July Unionist Celebration in Charleston, June 14, 1831, *Niles' Weekly Register*, XL (July 16, 1831), 350-51.

[21]Jackson to Hayne, February 6, 1831, Bassett, *Life of Jackson*, 561; Parton, *Life of Jackson*, III, 466-67. His biographer has argued that Edward Livingston, after showing Jackson the implications of nullification, actually supplied the basic ideas of the Proclamation. William B. Hatcher, *Edward Livingston: Jeffersonian Republican and Jacksonian Democrat* (University: Louisiana State University Press, 1940), 382. The evidence above and the testimony of other scholars rather suggests that Jackson was his own man. See Bassett, *Life of Jackson*, 703; Longaker, "Was Jackson's Kitchen Cabinet a Cabinet?" 94-108; Special Message, January 16, 1833, Richardson (comp.), *Messages and Papers*, III, 1195.

[22]Jackson's Fragmentary Journal, November, 1832, Bassett, *Life of Jackson*, 564-65; Jackson to Poinsett, January 24, 1833, Bassett (ed.), *Correspondence of Jackson*, IV, 505; *Register of Debates*, 22 Cong., 2 Sess., 463 (February 12, 1833). Many historians have stressed the fact that the capitulation of the nullifiers on January 21, 1833, actually marked the passing of the nullification crisis: Nussbaum, "The Compromise of 1833: A Study in Practical

Politics," 338-39; Charles Sydnor, *The Development of Southern Sectionalism, 1819-1848* (Baton Rouge: Louisiana State University Press, 1948), 216.

[23]*Ibid.*, 216; Freehling, *Prelude to Civil War,* 295. Throughout his work Freehling stressed the moderating role of Calhoun among the nullifiers.

[24]Adams to William Ellis, March 15, 1833, Bemis, *John Quincy Adams and the Union*, 269; Calhoun to Thomas Holland and others, July 2, 1833, Jameson (ed.), *Correspondence of Calhoun*, II, 324-25; *Niles' Weekly Register*, LXIV (March 2, 1833), 1; Isaac Hill quoted in Claude Moore Fuess, *Daniel Webster* (2 vols., Boston: Little, Brown, 1930), II, 4. A very recent work deals fully with Webster's political flirtation with Jackson during the crisis: Sydney Nathans, *Daniel Webster and Jacksonian Democracy* (Baltimore: Johns Hopkins University Press, 1973), 48-73.

[25]Jackson to James Buchanan, March 21, 1833, John Bassett Moore (ed.), *The Works of James Buchanan* (12 vols., New York: Antiquarian Press, 1960), II, 328.

[26]Sellers, *James K. Polk: Jacksonian*, 135-67.

[27]*Register of Debates*, 22 Cong., 2 Sess., 1346 (January 24, 1833); Fourth Annual Message, December 4, 1832, Richardson (comp.), *Messages and Papers*, III, 1168-69; Eliade, *Cosmos and History*, *passim*.

[28]Niebuhr, "The Protestant Movement and Democracy in the United States," 20-71; a New York toastmaster at Tammany Hall, quoted in *Daily Albany Argus*, December 4, 1832; Fourth Annual Message, December 4, 1832, Richardson (comp.), *Messages and Papers*, III, 1162. Marvin Meyers has perceptively characterized Jackson's administration as a "dismantling operation." *The Jacksonian Persuasion*, 21.

[29]*Register of Debates*, 21 Cong., 1 Sess., 1144 (May 28, 1830); 1142 (May 28, 1830); Washington *Globe*, July 12, 1832; Richmond *Enquirer*, March 7, 1833.

[30]"Upon these two great maxims," according to the Richmond *Enquirer* on March 7, 1833, "hang almost all the law and the prophets." Fourth Annual Message, December 4, 1832, Richardson (comp.), *Messages and Papers*, III, 1165. Though Jefferson and many of his disciples believed the distinction between Whig

and Tory reposed in human nature, they yet yearned for a restoration of primal truth and harmony. Hofstadter, *The Idea of a Party System*, 74-121.

³¹Bank Veto Message, July 10, 1832; Maysville Road Veto Message, May 27, 1830, Richardson (comp.), *Messages and Papers*, III, 1153; 1052. In his analysis of George Bancroft's thought, David W. Noble has clearly shown this anti-institutional impulse and restoration theme in the Jacksonian outlook. *Historians Against History*, 18-36.

³²Kendall cited in Nagel, *One Nation Indivisible*, 113. Nagel dealt extensively with the development of the idea of Union from an "experiment" to an "absolute."

³³Jackson to Poinsett, November 7, 1832, Bassett (ed.), *Correspondence of Jackson*, IV, 486; Proclamation, December 10, 1832, Richardson (comp.), *Messages and Papers*, III, 1219. "Providence," to use the categories of John William Ward, here delimited the area in which human "will" could operate. *Andrew Jackson: Symbol for an Age*, 99-149.

³⁴Cambreleng to Van Buren, December 18, 1832, Bassett (ed.), *Correspondence of Jackson*, IV, 505n; Jackson to Van Buren, December 23, 1832, *ibid.*, 505.

³⁵Proclamation, December 10, 1832, Richardson (comp.), *Messages and Papers*, III, 1205, 1204, 1206; Jackson to Van Buren, December 25, 1832, Bassett (ed.), *Correspondence of Jackson*, IV, 506.

³⁶Jackson to John Coffee, December 14, 1832, *ibid.*, 499-500; Proclamation, December 10, 1832, Richardson (comp.), *Messages and Papers*, III, 1212.

³⁷Bank Veto Message, July 10, 1832, *ibid.*, 1153.

³⁸Jackson to Hayne, February 8, 1831, Bassett (ed.), *Correspondence of Jackson*, IV, 241; Arthur M. Schlesinger, Jr., *The Age of Jackson* (Boston: Little, Brown, 1945), 401-21.

³⁹Washington *Globe*, November 26, 1832; Cambreleng cited in John Arthur Garraty, *Silas Wright* (New York: Columbia University Press, 1949), 103; Wright to Azariah C. Flagg, February 19, 1833, *ibid.*, 102.

⁴⁰Van Buren's compromising spirit found full expression in the resolutions he authored for the New York state legislature.

Among other things they proclaimed "a determination to maintain the union at all hazards, and a willingness to make liberal concessions, nay sacrifices, for the preservation of peace and reciprocal good will among its members." Fitzpatrick (ed.), *Autobiography of Van Buren*, II, 552. Fuller treatment of his dealings during the crisis and his concept of party can be found in Joseph Hobson Harrison, Jr., "Martin Van Buren and His Southern Supporters," *Journal of Southern History*, XXII (November, 1956), 438-58; Hofstadter, *The Idea of a Party System*, 236-52.

[41]Wright's attitude about the Union, compromise, and the tariff was given in a speech before the Senate during the final crisis. *Register of Debates*, 22 Cong., 2 Sess., 806-07 (March 1, 1833). A tabular demonstration of the large but unsystematic appropriations under Jackson for internal improvements can be seen in John G. Van Deusen, *Economic Bases of Disunion in South Carolina* (New York: AMS Press, 1928), 128. Daniel J. Boorstin was surely wrong (*Genius of American Politics*) in claiming that the pragmatic outlook of American democracy did not itself constitute an ideology. If the analysis of the present study is valid, the democratic outlook represented a clear alternative to the concepts of liberty and Union involved in the American System and to those held by the nullifiers.

[42]Meyers, *The Jacksonian Persuasion*, 1-23; Edwin C. Rozwenc (ed.), *Ideology and Power in the Age of Jackson* (Garden City, N. Y.: Doubleday, 1964), *vii-xxi*; Rowland Berthoff, "The American Social Order: A Conservative Hypothesis," *American Historical Review*, LXV (April, 1960), 495-514. For an overview of Jacksonian historiography, including a good analysis of the entrepreneurial school of Bray Hammond, Richard Hofstadter, and others, see Charles Grier Sellers, "Andrew Jackson Versus the Historians," *Mississippi Valley Historical Review*, XLIV (March, 1958), 615-34.

[43]Jacksonians clearly recognized at the time that silence on the slavery issue constituted a fundamental condition of their consensus. "On the *Tariff*, the North & South are not irreconcileably [sic] divided," Michael Hoffman wrote to Azariah Flagg on February 19, 1833, "but on *Slavery* they are." Cited in Garraty, *Silas Wright*, 104. Jackson also saw how consensus would end if

Calhoun were "to blow up a storm on the subject of the slave question." Jackson to John Coffee, April 9, 1833, Bassett (ed.), *Correspondence of Jackson*, V, 56.

Chapter 5

¹"Introduction," *Democratic Review*, I (October, 1837), 7; "The Great Nation of Futurity," *ibid.*, VI (November, 1839), 427. See also Arieli, *Individualism and Nationalism in American Ideology*, 179-206.

²The sections of this chapter on the thought of Webster and Adams during the nullification controversy first appeared in an article by the present author, " 'Liberty and Union': An Analysis of Three Concepts Involved in the Nullification Controversy," *Journal of Southern History*, XXXIII (August, 1967), 331-55. Copyright 1967 by the Southern Historical Association. Reprinted by permission of the Managing Editor.

³*Register of Debates*, 21 Cong., 1 Sess., 38 (January 20, 1830); Public Dinner at New York, March 10, 1831, Webster, *Writings and Speeches*, II, 45; *Register of Debates*, 22 Cong., 2 Sess., 553-87 (February 16, 1833).

⁴First Settlement of New England, December 22, 1820, Webster, *Writings and Speeches*, I, 182; *Register of Debates*, 21 Cong., 1 Sess., 38 (January 20, 1830).

⁵*Ibid.*, 80 (January 27, 1830).

⁶*Ibid.*, 38, 69 (January 20, 27, 1830). Representative Rufus Choate likewise invoked a conservative stricture against the "original perfect freedom" which Jackson and others assumed in destroying the policy of protection. "You have put your hand to the plough," he protested, "and how can you turn back?" *Ibid.*, 22 Cong., 1 Sess., 3516 (June 13, 1832).

⁷*Ibid.*, 1240, 1222 (July 11, 1832).

⁸Public Dinner at New York, March 10, 1831, Webster, *Writings and Speeches*, II, 57; Reception at Buffalo, June, 1833, *ibid.*, 134.

⁹Richard N. Current, *Daniel Webster and the Rise of National Conservatism* (Boston: Little, Brown, 1955), 184-93. Clarence Mondale has, in a like vein, analyzed Webster's changing rhetoric

in "Daniel Webster and Technology," *American Quarterly*, XIV (Spring, 1962), 37-47.

[10]*Register of Debates*, 21 Cong., 1 Sess., 68 (January 27, 1830); Public Dinner at New York, March 10, 1831, Webster, *Writings and Speeches*, II, 46, 57-58. Webster's open attitude toward the West is dealt with in Peter J. Parish, "Daniel Webster, New England, and the West," *Journal of American History*, LIV (December, 1967), 524-49. For a fuller analysis of the balance of sectional interests and the importance of "national character" in Webster's concept of nationalism, see Robert F. Dalzell, Jr., *Daniel Webster and the Trial of American Nationalism, 1843-1852* (Boston: Houghton Mifflin, 1973).

[11]*Register of Debates*, 22 Cong., 2 Sess., 576, 554 (February 16, 1833). Webster exemplified here the English historical element that went into the composite national idea of freedom analyzed so well in Kohn, *American Nationalism*, 1-37.

[12]Andrew C. McLaughlin, "Social Compact and Constitutional Construction," *American Historical Review*, V (April, 1900), 470; Charles Warren, *The Making of the Constitution* (Boston: Little, Brown, 1937), 394-95; Charles E. Merriam, *A History of American Political Theories* (New York: Macmillan, 1924), 252-90.

[13]*Register of Debates*, 22 Cong., 2 Sess., 556 (February 16, 1833); William Sullivan to Webster, March 23, 1830, Webster, *Writings and Speeches*, XVII, 497.

[14]*Register of Debates*, 22 Cong., 2 Sess., 564 (February 16, 1833). This reflected a consensus among such legal nationalists as Nathan Dane, Joseph Story, and James Kent. See Elizabeth Kelly Bauer, *Commentaries on the Constitution, 1790-1860* (New York: Columbia University Press, 1952), 219-26.

[15]Dartmouth College Case, March 10, 1818, Webster, *Writings and Speeches*, X, 194-233; *Register of Debates*, 22 Cong., 2 Sess., 564 (February 16, 1833).

[16]*Ibid.*, 21 Cong., 1 Sess., 62 (January 27, 1830). Criticism of Webster's concept of the "executed contract" came even from John Quincy Adams, who otherwise shared the belief that the Union was founded by the people as a whole. Webster had "hung his cause upon a broken hinge," Adams noted, for "all constitutional government is a compact." Charles Francis Adams (ed.),

Memoirs of John Quincy Adams, VIII, 526 (February 16, 1833). For a contemporary critique of Webster's position see Alexander H. Everett, "The Union and the States," *North American Review*, XX-XVII (July, 1833), 190-249.

[17]*Register of Debates*, 22 Cong., 2 Sess., 571 (February 16, 1833). The preoccupation with order to be found in the "doctrine of institutions" is dealt with in Fredrickson, *The Inner Civil War*, 23-36.

[18]Report of the Committee on Manufactures, *Register of Debates*, 22 Cong., 2 Sess., Appendix, 45 (February 28, 1833); Report on Manufactures, *ibid.*, 1 Sess., Appendix, 85 (May 23, 1832). Works pertaining to Adams and the idea of progress have already been cited in Note 28 of Chapter 3.

[19]*Ibid.*, 2 Sess., Appendix, 46, 59 (February 28, 1833).

[20]*Ibid.*, 1 Sess., Appendix, 80 (May 23, 1832).

[21]*Ibid.*, 79-92 (May 23, 1832); Charles Francis Adams (ed.), *Memoirs of John Quincy Adams*, VIII, 229 (May 22, 1830).

[22]This is not to say, however, that Adams was indifferent to the integrity of the Union or the threat of the nullifiers. He voted without hesitation for the Force Bill in 1833, while his Fourth-of-July Address in Quincy two years earlier anticipated many of the constitutional arguments Jackson used in his Proclamation. Bemis, *John Quincy Adams and the Union*, 269, 233-36.

[23]*Register of Debates*, 22 Cong., 2 Sess., Appendix, 46, 49, 59 (February 28, 1833); Adams to Charles W. Upham, February 2, 1837, cited in Bemis, *John Quincy Adams and the Union*, 151.

[24]Charles Francis Adams (ed.), *Memoirs of John Quincy Adams*, VIII, 503 (December 5, 1832); Adams to Upham, February 2, 1837, Bemis, *John Quincy Adams and the Union*, 151.

[25]*Register of Debates*, 22 Cong., 2 Sess., Appendix, 53, 41-61 (February 28, 1833). This quote and the fuller analysis of the slave power came from his minority report of the Committee of Manufactures. He considered it at once the epitaph of the American System and a clarion call to awaken the people. Bemis, *John Quincy Adams and the Union*, 270-72; Charles Francis Adams (ed.), *Memoirs of John Quincy Adams*, VIII, 537 (March 12, 1833).

[26]*Register of Debates*, 22 Cong., 2 Sess., Appendix, 59 (February

28, 1833); Charles Francis Adams (ed.), *Memoirs of John Quincy Adams*, VIII, 433 (December 11, 1831); 519 (January 9, 1833). "The great difficulty," Justice Joseph Story had similarly discovered in 1831, "is to make the mass of the people see their true interests." Cited in Nagel, *One Nation Indivisible*, 51.

[27]Lynn L. Marshall has well demonstrated the undemocratic elements in the make-up of the Whig party in "The Strange Stillbirth of the Whig Party," *American Historical Review*, LXXII (January, 1967), 445-68. In contrast to the tendency of the consensus historians to stress the similarities between Whig and Democrat, Charles Grier Sellers has set forth their differences in "Who Were the Southern Whigs?" *ibid.*, LIX (January, 1954), 335-46. Though his purpose was somewhat different, Glyndon G. Van Deusen achieved much of the same effect in "Some Aspects of Whig Thought and Theory in the Jacksonian Period," *ibid.*, LXIII (January, 1958), 305-22.

[28]Jackson's phrase appeared in a letter to Aaron V. Brown, February 9, 1843, Bassett (ed.), *Correspondence of Jackson*, VI, 201. Though considerably altered from the original, the remainder of this chapter dealing with the debate over manifest destiny is drawn from an article by the present author, "The Concept of Time and the Political Dialogue in the United States, 1828-1848," *American Quarterly*, XIX (Winter, 1967), 619-44. Copyright 1967, Trustees of the University of Pennsylvania.

[29]*Democratic Review*, VI (November, 1839), 427. *Italics* added. *Congressional Globe*, 28 Cong., 2 Sess., Appendix, 178 (January 29, 1845).

[30]*Ibid.*, 138 (January 28, 1845). Albert K. Weinberg overstated the case when he argued that the ideals of democracy and expansionism did not become linked together until the 1840s and only then as a defensive effort to forestall the encroachments of Europe in North America. *Manifest Destiny: A Study of Nationalist Expansionism in American History* (Baltimore: Johns Hopkins Press, 1935), 109. The tendency toward a spatial, atemporal concept of freedom lodged in Jacksonian thought, it would rather seem, made expansionism one of its essential attributes. Frederick Merk discovered something of this in his analysis of the federative nature of the Union. *Manifest Destiny and Mission in American*

History, 24-60. The argument of the present study also gains support from Ward, *Andrew Jackson: Symbol for an Age*, 133-49. A good bibliographical essay can be found in Norman A. Graebner (ed.), *Manifest Destiny* (Indianapolis: Bobbs Merrill, 1968), *lxxiv-lxxxii*. The distinction Graebner made in another work, *Empire on the Pacific: A Study in American Continental Expansion* (New York: Ronald Press, 1955), between the goal of acquiring Pacific ports and of annexing new territory is a valid one, but it should not be pushed too far. The mission of regenerating benighted Asia by means of commerce on the Pacific was, in the minds of many at the time, an integral part of the "westward course of empire" which also included new territorial acquisitions.

³¹Meyers, *The Jacksonian Persuasion*, 15; *Congressional Globe*, 24 Cong., 1 Sess., Appendix, 340 (April 29, 1836); *Democratic Review*, I (October, 1837), 6; *Congressional Globe*, 29 Cong., 1 Sess., Appendix, 769 (July 1, 1846).

³²*Democratic Review*, XXI (October, 1847), 332; Greeley cited in *Whig Review*, IV (July, 1846), 30.

³³Fourth Annual Message, December 4, 1832, Richardson (comp.), *Messages and Papers*, II, 1164; *Congressional Globe*, 28 Cong., 2 Sess., Appendix, 178 (January 29, 1845).

³⁴*Ibid.*, 27 Cong., 3 Sess., Appendix, 154 (January 26, 1843); *Democratic Review*, XXI (November, 1847), 425. The dichotomy of "primitivism" and "civilization" first used extensively by Henry Nash Smith in *Virgin Land*, has been qualified in two later studies. Leo Marx developed the concept of "pastoralism" in *The Machine in the Garden: Technology and the Pastoral Ideal in America* (New York: Oxford University Press, 1964, 3-11); John William Ward, the idea of "cultivated nature" in *Andrew Jackson: Symbol for an Age*, 30-45.

³⁵Inaugural Address, March 4, 1845, Richardson (comp.), *Messages and Papers*, V, 2230. For a very penetrating analysis of this matter see William T. Hutchinson, "Unite to Divide, Divide to Unite: The Shaping of American Federalism," *Mississippi Valley Historical Review*, XLVI (June, 1959), 3-18. Background for the ideas and policies in Polk's "continental vision" can be found in

Charles Grier Sellers, *James K. Polk: Continentalist, 1843-1846* (Princeton: Princeton University Press, 1966), 213-66.

³⁶*Congressional Globe*, 29 Cong., 1 Sess., Appendix, 76 (January 5, 1846); 2 Sess., Appendix, 104 (January 15, 1847); *Democratic Review*, XVII (July, 1845), 5; *Congressional Globe*, 27 Cong., 3 Sess., Appendix, 111 (January 30, 1843). A very good analysis of the idea of "extended genesis" appears in Max Lerner, *America as a Civilization: Life and Thought in the United States Today* (New York: Simon and Schuster, 1957), 35-39. Nor did the experience of re-creation necessarily require the initial settlement of new territories by Americans. It could also be realized as the force of freedom served to regenerate neighboring areas settled or to draw them into the Union by its "gravitational pull." Weinberg, *Manifest Destiny*, 160-89, 224-51.

³⁷*Congressional Globe*, 28 Cong., 2 Sess., Appendix, 178 (January 29, 1845); Jackson to Francis P. Blair, May 11, 1844, Bassett (ed.), *Correspondence of Jackson*, VI, 286; *Congressional Globe*, 29 Cong., 1 Sess., Appendix, 278 (January 8, 1846); 427 (March 30, 1846).

³⁸*Ibid*., 639 (April 15, 1846); 45 (December 15, 1845); 28 Cong., 2 Sess., Appendix, 68 (January 6, 1845). In a speech on the Oregon question Senator Daniel Dickinson of New York used the terms, "monarchy and freedom," to define the ideology of conflict on the continent. *Ibid*., 29 Cong., 1 Sess., Appendix, 327 (February 24, 1846).

³⁹*Democratic Review*, VI (November, 1839), 427.

⁴⁰*Congressional Globe*, 29 Cong., 1 Sess., Appendix, 640 (April 15, 1846); 211 (January 10, 1846); *Democratic Review*, XVI (June, 1845), 532; *Congressional Globe*, 29 Cong., 1 Sess., Appendix, 276 (January 8, 1846); 430 (March 30, 1846).

⁴¹Fourth Annual Message, December 5, 1848, Richardson (comp.), *Messages and Papers*, VI, 2481-82; *Congressional Globe*, 29 Cong., 1 Sess., Appendix, 76 (January 5, 1846); Merle Curti, "Young America," *American Historical Review*, XXXII (October, 1926), 34-55.

⁴²Second Speech on the Sub-Treasury, March 12, 1838, Webster, *Writings and Speeches*, VIII, 237; *Whig Review*, IV (July, 1846),

30; *Congressional Globe*, 26 Cong., 2 Sess., Appendix, 78 (January 19, 1841); Annual Message to New York Legislature, January 7, 1840, George E. Baker (ed.), *The Works of William H. Seward* (5 vols., New York: Redfield, 1853-1884), II, 240, 241.

⁴³*Congressional Globe*, 28 Cong., 2 Sess., Appendix, 56 (January 4, 1845); *Whig Review*, VII (May, 1848), 440; Objects of the Mexican War, March 23, 1848, Webster, *Writings and Speeches*, X, 32; The Admission of Texas, December 22, 1845, *ibid.*, IX, 56.

⁴⁴River and Harbor Improvements, March 12, 1846, Winthrop, *Addresses and Speeches on Various Occasions* (4 vols., Boston: Little, Brown, 1852-1886), I, 500; Clay to James F. Babcock and others, December 17, 1844, Colton (ed.), *Private Correspondence of Clay*, 515; *Whig Review*, I (January, 1845), 3, 2; II (October, 1845), 447; IX (March, 1849), 225. Clay, like many other Whigs at the time, privately found much to commend in the Native American movement. Clay to John S. Littell, November 17, 1846, Colton (ed.), *Private Correspondence of Clay*, 536.

⁴⁵Mass Meeting of Whigs in Auburn, February 22, 1844, Baker (ed.), *Works of Seward*, III, 245; *Congressional Globe*, 29 Cong., 1 Sess., Appendix, 490 (March 13, 1846); *Whig Review*, VII (February, 1848), 149; III (June, 1846), 616.

⁴⁶*Democratic Review*, XVIII (January, 1846), 13; *Whig Review*, I (April, 1845), 423; *Congressional Globe*, 30 Cong., 1 Sess., Appendix, 217 (February 1, 1848); Henry C. Carey, *The Past, the Present, and the Future* (Philadelphia: Carey and Hart, 1848), 416.

⁴⁷"The Necessity of Education in a Republic," 1838, Mrs. Mary Mann (ed.), *Life and Works of Horace Mann* (5 vols., Boston: Walker, Fuller, 1865-1868), II, 150, 168; Address Before the Young Men's Lyceum of Springfield, Illinois, January 27, 1838, Basler (ed.), *Collected Works of Lincoln*, I, 114. Harry V. Jaffa provided a very stimulating analysis of this matter in *Crisis of the House Divided*, 183-232.

⁴⁸To the Whigs of Orleans, May 13, 1844, Baker (ed.), *Works of Seward*, III, 395; Annual Message to the New York legislature, January 1, 1839, *ibid.*, 205; Annual Message, January 7, 1840, *ibid.*, 242; *Congressional Globe*, 29 Cong., 1 Sess., Appendix, 1012, 1013 (June 30, 1846); 2 Sess., Appendix, 373 (February 13, 1847).

⁴⁹*Ibid.*, 29 Cong., 1 Sess., Appendix, 483 (March 12, 1846).

Chapter 6

¹*Congressional Globe*, 28 Cong., 2 Sess., Appendix, 347 (January 22, 1845). Joseph G. Rayback has demonstrated how rapidly the new contest over slavery expansion brought the old debate to an end. *Free Soil: The Election of 1848*.

²Again, the article by Richard H. Brown cited earlier is of great significance in this regard: "The Missouri Crisis, Slavery, and the Politics of Jacksonianism," 55-72. Merrill Peterson stressed this negative quality in the old Jeffersonian consensus. *The Jefferson Image in American History*, 76-79.

³The political background for the emergence of the issue of slavery expansion is treated fully in Chaplain W. Morrison, *Democratic Politics and Sectionalism: The Wilmot Proviso Controversy* (Chapel Hill: University of North Carolina Press, 1967). Two articles are especially helpful in the same way: Norman A. Graebner, "James K. Polk: A Study in Federal Patronage," *Mississippi Valley Historical Review*, XXXVIII (March, 1952), 613-32; Eric Foner, "The Wilmot Proviso Revisited," *Journal of American History*, LVI (September, 1969), 262-79.

⁴*Congressional Globe*, 29 Cong., 2 Sess., 377 (February 10, 1847). Merrill Peterson has shown that the Free Soilers were not on solid historical ground at this point. Jefferson had authored the Ordinance of 1784, but the one passed in 1787, while he was in France, was a fundamentally different measure. *The Jefferson Image in the American Mind*, 189-209. But many Free Soilers apparently believed that Jefferson was the author.

⁵*Congressional Globe*, 29 Cong., 2 Sess., 455 (February 19, 1847).

⁶*Ibid.*, 30 Cong., 1 Sess., Appendix, 88 (January 12, 1848); 2 Sess., Appendix, 155 (February 17, 1849); Cass letter to A. O. P. Nicholson, December 24, 1847, *Niles' Weekly Register*, LXXIII (January 8, 1848). Fuller background for the doctrine of popular sovereignty is given in Milo Milton Quaife, *The Doctrine of Non-Intervention with Slavery in the Territories* (Chicago: M. C. Chamberlain, 1910).

[7]The substance of the two preceding paragraphs leans heavily upon the brilliant work of Aileen S. Kraditor, *Means and Ends in American Abolitionism: Garrison and His Critics on Strategy and Tactics, 1834-1850* (New York: Random House, 1969). The distinction she drew between the higher-law radicalism of Garrison and the position of political antislavery with which the Free Soilers identified is especially crucial. In this context the dichotomy drawn by George M. Fredrickson in *The Inner Civil War*, 7-35, between the higher-law radicalism of Garrison and the conservative "doctrine of institutions" of a Webster is also helpful. The belief of the Free Soilers that the fathers had "instituted" the higher law placed them in the middle and enabled them to synthesize the opposing impulses to liberty and institutional order.

[8]Speech at a Whig Convention at Springfield, Massachusetts, September 29, 1847, Charles Sumner, *The Works of Charles Sumner* (15 vols., Boston: Lee and Shepard, 1870-1873), II, 59; Address of the Southern and Western Liberty Convention, Cincinnati, June 11, 12, 1845, Salmon P. Chase and Charles Dexter Cleveland, *Anti-Slavery Addresses of 1844 and 1845* (Philadelphia: J. A. Bancroft, 1867). Focus upon the slave power as the dialectical foil, and not upon slavery as such, involved an enormously significant point about the nature of individual freedom here reckoned by the Free Soilers to be the national idea. With notable exceptions, as recent studies suggest, equality for free white men was essentially at issue and not the equality of all men, black and white. Larry Gara, "Slavery and the Slave Power; A Crucial Distinction," *Civil War History*, XV (March, 1969), 5-18; Litwack, *North of Slavery, passim.*; Berwanger, *The Frontier Against Slavery, passim.*

[9]Speech to a Whig Convention in Springfield, Massachusetts, September 29, 1847, Sumner, *Works of Sumner*, II, 60. The process of affirmation by negation which H. Richard Niebuhr found at work in Protestant revivalism seems clearly to describe the rhythms of political antislavery. "The Protestant Movement and Democracy in the United States," 20-71. The impulse to secular reform also had religious roots, as shown in two important articles: David Brion Davis, "The Emergence of Immediatism in British and American Antislavery Thought," *Mississippi Valley Historical Review*, XLIX (September, 1962), 209-30; Anne C.

Loveland, "Evangelicalism and 'Immediate Emancipation' in American Antislavery Thought," *Journal of Southern History*, XXXII (May, 1966), 172-88.

[10]*Congressional Globe*, 30 Cong., 2 Sess., Appendix, 128 (February 17, 1849); Address of the Liberty Party to the Voters of Illinois, July 26, 1842, cited in Edward Magdol, *Owen Lovejoy: Abolitionist in Congress* (New Brunswick: Rutgers University Press, 1967), 61; Stanwood, *History of the Presidency*, 239; Address of the Southern and Western Liberty Convention, 75.

[11]Three works by David Brion Davis throw considerable light on the way many Americans by the middle of the nineteenth century viewed reality in terms of conspiracy and conflict: "Some Themes of Counter-Subversion: An Analysis of Anti-Masonic, Anti-Catholic, and Anti-Mormon Literature," *Mississippi Valley Historical Review*, XLVII (September, 1960), 205-24; "Some Ideological Functions of Prejudice in Ante-Bellum America," *American Quarterly*, XV (Summer, 1963), 115-25; *The Slave Power Conspiracy and the Paranoid Style* (Baton Rouge: Louisiana State University Press, 1969). These works lend support to the argument of the present study that the formulas of negative liberalism best expressed the outlook of democratic and slaveholding America. The idea of original perfection and of an essentially timeless freedom necessarily disposed most Americans to perceive and act upon reality in this way. The pattern Richard Hofstadter found among Populists and especially among right-wing "pseudo-conservatives" of the mid-twentieth century suggests that negative liberalism is even less adequate than before to deal with the complex and corporate dimensions of the common life. *The Age of Reform from Bryan to F.D.R.* (New York: Alfred A. Knopf, 1955), 60-93; *The Paranoid Style in American Politics and Other Essays* (New York: Alfred A. Knopf, 1966), 3-141.

[12]*Congressional Globe*, 28 Cong., 2 Sess., Appendix, 178 (January 29, 1845); 30 Cong., I Sess., Appendix, 133 (January 26, 1848); 1079 (August 3, 1848); Stanwood, *History of the Presidency*, 239.

[13]Kraditor, *Means and Ends in American Abolitionism, 185-217*.

[14]*Congressional Globe*, 29 Cong., 1 Sess., Appendix, 835 (February 10, 1846); 27 Cong., 3 Sess., Appendix, 78 (February 19,

1847); 30 Cong., 1 Sess., Appendix, 597 (May 5, 1848); 29 Cong.,
1 Sess., Appendix, 310 (February 16, 1846); 327 (February 25,
1846); 211 (January 10, 1846). This section of the chapter comparing Manifest Destiny and Free Soil represents an abridged
and considerably altered version of material dealt with in an
article by the present author: "Manifest Destiny and Free Soil:
The Triumph of Negative Liberalism in the 1840s," *Historian*,
XXXI (November, 1968), 36-56.

[15]*Congressional Globe*, 30 Cong., 1 Sess., Appendix, 923 (June
28, 1848); 1109 (August 7, 1848); 28 Cong., 2 Sess., Appendix,
121 (January 13, 1845). The phrases were used by Charles
Sumner in the Free Soil convention in Worcester, Massachusetts,
June 28, 1848. Cited in David Donald, *Charles Sumner and the
Coming of the Civil War* (New York: Alfred A. Knopf, 1960), 166.

[16]*Congressional Globe*, 30 Cong., 1 Sess., Appendix, 1080 (August 3, 1848); 958 (July 26, 1848).

[17]For an analysis of President Polk's claim and the idea of the
nation's natural right to all of Oregon, see Weinberg, *Manifest
Destiny*, 130-59.

[18]*Congressional Globe*, 28 Cong., 1 Sess., Appendix, 601 (June 3,
1844); 29 Cong., 1 Sess., Appendix, 839 (February 10, 11, 1846).

[19]First Annual Message, December 2, 1845, Richardson
(comp.), *Messages and Papers*, V, 2248. For an extended treatment
of this matter see Frederick Merk, *The Monroe Doctrine and American Expansionism, 1843-1849* (New York: Alfred A. Knopf, 1967);
Dexter Perkins, *The Monroe Doctrine, 1826-1867* (Baltimore:
Johns Hopkins Press, 1933), 62-125.

[20]*Congressional Globe*, 30 Cong., 1 Sess., Appendix, 614 (May 10,
1848).

[21]*Ibid.*, 2 Sess., Appendix, 236 (February 17, 1849); 28 Cong., 2
Sess., Appendix, 372 (January 25, 1845); 29 Cong., 2 Sess., Ap-
pendix, 284 (February 4, 1847); 169 (January 12, 1847); 30
Cong., 1 Sess., Appendix, 688 (May 31, 1848).

[22]*Ibid.*, 28 Cong., 1 Sess., Appendix, 623 (June 4, 1844); 29
Cong., 1 Sess., Appendix, 639 (April 15, 1846); 46 (December 15,
1845); 28 Cong., 1 Sess., Appendix, 245 (February 23, 1844).

[23]*Ibid.*, 239 (February 22, 1844); 29 Cong., 1 Sess., Appendix,

216 (February 6, 1846); 841 (February 10, 11, 1846); 429 (March 30, 1846).

²⁴*Ibid.*, 30 Cong., 1 Sess., Appendix, 1146 (July 22, 1848); 2 Sess., Appendix, 136 (February 17, 1849); 1 Sess., Appendix, 1197 (July 26, 1848); 688 (May 31, 1848).

²⁵*Ibid.*, 30 Cong., 2 Sess., Appendix, 101 (February 17, 1849); 1 Sess., Appendix, 1080 (August 3, 1848); Charles Francis Adams (ed.), *Memoirs of John Quincy Adams*, XI, 103 (March 3, 1842).

²⁶*Congressional Globe*, 31 Cong., 1 Sess., Appendix, 942 (July 24, 1850). Because of his interest in the contrast between the general welfare idea and that of laissez faire after the Civil War, Sidney Fine failed to place the latter in an adequate historical perspective. He was therefore compelled to admit that the laissez faire of the Gilded Age was not consistently applied, since tariffs, land grants, and other favors were being passed out. If the present analysis is valid, the laissez faire he spoke of was in fact the operation of broker-state individualism which had emerged during the sectional controversy over slavery. *Laissez Faire and the General Welfare State*. Vernon L. Parrington would rather seem to be on the right track when he discovered the "Great Barbecue" to be a blend of Whiggery and Jacksonian leveling. *The Beginnings of Critical Realism*, 17-26.

²⁷Roy M. Robbins, "Pre-Emption—A Frontier Triumph," *Mississippi Valley Historical Review*, XVIII (December, 1931), 331-50. John Quincy Adams bitterly condemned the selfish manufacturing interests of the East for selling out the American System. With the prospect of getting higher tariff duties passed, they turned against the "interest of the whole people" to be found in the wise management of the land revenues for improving the nation. Charles Francis Adams (ed.), *Memoirs of John Quincy Adams*, XI, 228 (August 4, 1842). Sydney Nathans did a good job in showing how Webster tailored his conservative instincts to the demands of democratic politics: *Daniel Webster and Jacksonian Democracy*, 130-47.

²⁸*Congressional Globe*, 30 Cong., 1 Sess., Appendix, 1041 (July 27, 1848); 29 Cong., 1 Sess., Appendix, 1066 (June 30, 1846).

²⁹*Ibid.*, 449 (February 27, 1846); 29 Cong., 1 Sess., 1183 (Au-

gust 3, 1846); Appendix, 881 (July 20, 1846); 28 Cong., 1 Sess., Appendix, 385 (April 30, 1844).

³⁰Milo Milton Quaife (ed.), *The Diary of James K. Polk During His Presidency, 1845-1849* (4 vols., Chicago: A. C. McClurg, 1910), II, 308; Fourth Annual Message, December 5, 1848, Richardson (comp.), *Messages and Papers*, VI, 2511; *Whig Review*, VIII (October, 1848), 340; *Congressional Globe*, 29 Cong., 1 Sess., Appendix, 487 (March 12, 1846). Evidence of party orthodoxy can also be found in Joel H. Silbey, *The Shrine of Party: Congressional Voting Behavior, 1841-1852* (Pittsburgh: University of Pittsburgh Press, 1967).

³¹Stanwood, *History of the Presidency*, 239. This is not to deny an affirmative side to the middle class outlook of the mid-nineteenth century. Eric Foner has well demonstrated this side of the Free-Soil ideology as it matured in the following decade. His insistence that the economic views of the new Republican party were not a mere reincarnation of Whiggery, as traditional accounts have supposed, also lends support to the present interpretation of the broker state. *Free Soil, Free Labor, Free Man*, 11-72. Some of the ideas about the broker state were first explored in an article by the present author, "The Broker State Concept of the Union in the 1840s: A Synthesis of Whig and Democratic Views," *Louisiana Studies*, VIII (Winter, 1969), 321-47.

³²LeMoyne to Birney, December 10, 1839; Errett to Birney, August 27, 1844, Dwight L. Dumond (ed.), *Letters of James Gillespie Birney, 1831-1857* (2 vols., New York: D. Appleton-Century, 1938), I, 511; II, 837.

³³LeMoyne to Birney, December 10, 1839; Leavitt to Birney, January 18, 1842, *ibid.*, I, 514; II, 660.

³⁴Liberty Party Address to the Citizens of the United States, May 12, 13, 1841, cited in Julian P. Bretz, "The Economic Background of the Liberty Party," *American Historical Review*, XXXIV (January, 1929), 258; Birney to Errett, August 5, 1844, Dumond (ed.), *Letters to Birney*, II, 831; *Congressional Globe*, 29 Cong., 2 Sess., Appendix, 404 (February 13, 1847).

³⁵Foster to Birney, December 7, 1845, Dumond (ed.), *Letters of Birney*, II, 982; Chase to George Reber, June 19, 1849, Edward G. Bourne (ed.), *Diary and Correspondence of Salmon P. Chase, Annual*

Report of the American Historical Association for 1902 (2 vols., Washington: Government Printing Office, 1903), II, 178; Foner, *Free Soil, Free Labor, Free Men*, 309.

³⁶Stanwood, *History of the Presidency*, 240; Address to the People of Massachusetts, September 12, 1849, Sumner, *Works of Sumner*, II, 288; Leavitt's speech cited in Schlesinger, *The Age of Jackson*, 466. In addition to Schlesinger's work, good background for the Free Soil party in 1848 can be found in: Morrison, *Democratic Politics and Sectionalism*; Rayback, *Free Soil: The Election of 1848*; Kinley J. Brauer, *Cotton and Conscience: Massachusetts Whig Politics and Southwestern Expansion, 1843-1848* (Lexington: University of Kentucky Press, 1967); Theodore Clark Smith, *The Liberty and Free Soil Parties in the Northwest* (New York: Longmans, Green, 1897).

³⁷Chase to Benjamin F. Butler, July 26, 1849, Bourne (ed.), *Diary and Correspondence of Chase*, II, 180, 181. By combining a policy of building "up" the country with another for spreading it "out," the Free Soil platform gave political expression to that blending of "civilization" and "primitivism" Henry Nash Smith found in the outlook of the nineteenth century (*Virgin Land*). This ideological confusion in the broker-state outlook, as seen in the perspective of the old debate about space and time, found a parallel in the sectionalized outlook of the South. Here, an assumption of southern "civilization" was that slavery, as a positive good, constituted the permanent basis for society, even within its present spatial limits. But it was linked to the "primitive" urgency for slavery to spread across space as the very condition of its existence. See Major L. Wilson, "The Controversy over Slavery Expansion and the Concept of the Safety Valve: Ideological Confusion in the 1850s," *Mississippi Quarterly*, XXIV (Spring, 1971), 135-53.

³⁸Foster to Birney, September 29, 1845; Foster to Birney, July 7, 1845, Dumond (ed.), *Letters of Birney*, II, 973; 951; *Congressional Globe*, 30 Cong., 1 Sess., Appendix, 380 (February 28, 1848). "The way was clear," Avery O. Craven noted in a critical vein, "for the creation of a new type of political organization, one which could carry all the high and noble purposes of the Liberty party, and yet which also could represent the material interests of the

sections now in conflict." *The Coming of the Civil War* (2nd Edition, Chicago: University of Chicago Press, 1957), 226.

³⁹Corwin cited in Norman A. Graebner, "Thomas Corwin and the Election of 1848: A Study in Conservative Politics," *Journal of Southern History*, XVII (May, 1951), 176; Speech at Worcester, Massachusetts, September 12, 1848, Basler (ed.), *Collected Works of Lincoln*, II, 3; Judge Nye cited in Bretz, "The Economic Background of the Liberty Party," 258-59.

⁴⁰Address of the Southern and Western Liberty Convention, June 11, 12, 1845, cited in Albert Bushnell Hart, *Salmon Portland Chase* (Boston: Houghton Mifflin, 1899), 60.

⁴¹*Congressional Globe*, 30 Cong., 2 Sess., Appendix, 100 (February 17, 1849); 1 Sess., Appendix, 393 (March 2, 1848). Two articles stress the "homestead" side of Greeley's outlook: John R. Commons, "Horace Greeley and the Working Class Origins of the Republican Party," *Political Science Quarterly*, XXIV (September, 1909), 468-88; Roy M. Robbins, "Horace Greeley: Land Reform and Unemployment, 1837-1862," *Agricultural History*, VII (January, 1933), 18-41. Two other works redress the balance by their emphasis upon the "tariff" side of Greeley's synthesis: Jeter Allen Isely, *Horace Greeley and the Republican Party, 1853-1861* (Princeton: Princeton University Press, 1947); Earle D. Ross, "Horace Greeley and the West," *Mississippi Valley Historical Review*, XX (June, 1933), 63-74. Jaffa, *Crisis of the House Divided*, argued for the position that the debate over slavery expansion was a reincarnation of the old Whig and Democratic debate.

⁴²It is very revealing, in this context, that the Federalists had attached far greater significance to the three-fifths clause than was given to it in the Free-Soil movement leading to the Civil War. Simpson, "The Political Significance of Slave Representation, 1787-1821," 315-42. The tone of the argument was also different. Federalists looked to its effects on corporate power at the center, while latter-day Free Soilers used a rhetoric which stressed the gross inequality it created among freemen. That an owner of five slaves in the South possessed the same power as four freemen in the North was an argument that recurred in the debates.

⁴³Speech in Congress on the Mexican War, February 22, 1847,

Winthrop, *Addresses and Speeches on Various Occasions*, I, 599; *Congressional Globe*, 30 Cong., 1 Sess., Appendix, 499 (April 11, 1848).

[44]*Ibid.*, 1047 (July 29, 1848); 30 Cong., 1 Sess., 1077 (August 12, 1848); 2 Sess., Appendix, 273 (February 24, 1849). Two articles place in historical perspective the relative novelty of the constitutional views which Duer and Webster here opposed: Bestor, "The American Civil War as a Constitutional Crisis," 327-52; Russel, "Constitutional Doctrines with Regard to Slavery in Territories," 466-86.

Chapter 7

[1]Allan Nevins, *Ordeal of the Union* (2 vols., New York: Charles Scribner's Sons, 1947), I, 23-26.

[2]By its decision in the case of *Prigg v. Pennsylvania* in 1842, the Supreme Court absolved state officials from responsibility to return fugitive slaves and declared it to be an exclusive function of the federal government. On this basis many northern states passed personal liberty laws, while the South raised the demand for a new fugitive slave law. Larry Gara, "The Fugitive Slave Law: A Double Paradox," *Civil War History*, X (September, 1964), 229.

[3]Calhoun to Hammond, December 7, 1849; Hammond to Calhoun, March 5, 1850, Jameson (ed.), *Correspondence of Calhoun*, II, 775; 1211; *Congressional Globe*, 31 Cong., 1 Sess., Appendix, 150 (February 13, 1850); 31 Cong., 1 Sess., 28 (December 13, 1849).

[4]*Ibid.*, Appendix, 1083 (August 9, 1850). Taylor's course is outlined in Nevins, *Ordeal of the Union*, I, 256-60, and Holman Hamilton, *Zachary Taylor: Soldier in the White House* (Indianapolis: Bobbs-Merrill, 1951), 254-69.

[5]*Congressional Globe*, 31 Cong., 1 Sess., Appendix, 614 (May 21, 1850); 1399 (July 19, 1850); Van Deusen, *Life of Clay*, 394-413; Nevins, *Ordeal of the Union*, I, 264-68; Holman Hamilton, *Prologue to Conflict: The Crisis and Compromise of 1850* (Lexington: University of Kentucky Press, 1964), 43-62.

[6]Older works generally tend to attribute greater credit to Clay,

Webster, and the Whigs for the Compromise of 1850, and the
work of Nevins still reflects this view. But in addition to the study
of Holman Hamilton cited above, two other studies make out a
convincing case for the greater contribution of Democrats: Frank
H. Hodder, "The Authorship of the Compromise of 1850,"
Mississippi Valley Historical Review, XXII (March, 1936), 525-36;
Russel, "What Was the Compromise of 1850?" 292-309.

   [7]*Congressional Globe*, 31 Cong., 1 Sess., Appendix, 451-55
(March 4, 1850). He did not specifically propose a dual executive,
as many historians have assumed, though this was one of the
things which some contemporaries deduced from his intention-
ally vague suggestions. Charles M. Wiltse, *John C. Calhoun: Sec-
tionalist, 1840-1850* (Indianapolis: Bobbs-Merrill, 1951), 465-69.
Calhoun held the view that slavery probably could not become
established in Mexico south of the areas already acquired. John
D. P. Fuller, "The Slavery Question and the Movement to Acquire Mexico," *Mississippi Valley Historical Review*, XXI (June,
1934), 31-48. The fuller context of the southern response is dealt
with in Major L. Wilson, "Ideological Fruits of Manifest Destiny:
The Geopolitics of Slavery Expansion in the Crisis of 1850,"
Journal of the Illinois State Historical Society, LXIII (Summer, 1970),
132-57. Permission to use given by editor.

   [8]*Congressional Globe*, 31 Cong., 1 Sess., Appendix, 1162, 1167
(August 6, 1850); 582 (May 15, 1850). Background for the way
manifest destiny was being sectionalized can be found in Merk,
Manifest Destiny and Mission in American History, 202-14.

   [9]*Congressional Globe*, 31 Cong., 1 Sess., Appendix, 258 (March 6,
1850); 737 (June 8, 1850); 445 (April 9, 1850); 1167 (August 6,
1850).

   [10]*Ibid.*, 202 (February 11, 1850); 31 Cong., 1 Sess., 29 (December 13, 1849).

   [11]Though he discussed it in other terms, Jesse T. Carpenter
likewise discovered how the crisis of 1850 evoked in fullest form
the argument for the national nature of slavery under the Constitution. *The South as a Conscious Minority, 1789-1861* (New York:
New York University Press, 1930), 127-70.

   [12]*Congressional Globe*, 31 Cong., 1 Sess., Appendix, 199 (February 27, 1850); 497 (April 23, 1850); 242 (March 5, 1850).

¹³*Ibid.*, 650 (May 27, 1850); 292 (March 12, 1850); 1385 (July 18, 1850).

¹⁴*Ibid.*, 293 (March 12, 1850); 151-52 (February 13, 1850); 544 (May 8, 1850).

¹⁵*Ibid.*, 382 (March 25, 1850); 748 (June 7, 1850); 53 (January 10, 1850); 189 (February 26, 1850).

¹⁶*Ibid.*, 395 (March 27, 1850); 772 (June 11, 1850); 706 (June 6, 1850); 668 (June 3, 1850); 1146 (August 15, 1850). In *Cavalier and Yankee: The Old South and American National Character* (New York: George Braziller, 1961), 240-78, William R. Taylor made a good analysis of the "spirit of '76" which developed in the nullification controversy and spread from South Carolina in the ensuing decades.

¹⁷*Congressional Globe*, 31 Cong., 1 Sess., Appendix, 835 (June 10, 1850); 344 (March 6, 1850); 1053 (August 9, 1850). Revisionist historians could find support from Gentry and Williams here in their claim that the argument over the issue of slavery expansion was essentially irrational and unreal. But Chaplain W. Morrison has well argued that, however objectively unreal it seems in retrospect, the people at the time took the issue to be very real. *Democratic Politics and Sectionalism*, 52-74. Because of the federal nature of the Union, Arthur Bestor has also shown that the debate over slavery within the nation necessarily had to take place with regard to the territories. "The American Civil War as a Constitutional Crisis," 327-52.

¹⁸*Congressional Globe*, 31 Cong., 1 Sess., Appendix, 389 (March 19, 1850); 580 (May 15, 1850); 1501 (August 2, 1850); 345 (March 6, 1850); 292 (March 18, 1850).

¹⁹Arthur Bestor, "State Sovereignty and Slavery: A Reinterpretation of Pro-slavery Constitutional Doctrines, 1846-1860," *Journal of the Illinois State Historical Society*, LIV (Summer, 1961), 119, *passim*.

²⁰Webster's famous Seventh-of-March speech, according to Robert C. Winthrop, "was *tremendously* Southern" as given in the Senate, but the balance was somewhat redressed in the printed version. Winthrop cited in Hamilton, *Prologue to Conflict*, 80-81. The part of this chapter covering the debate between Webster and the Free Soilers reproduces with some alterations an article

by the present author, "Of Time and the Union: Webster and His Critics in the Crisis of 1850," *Civil War History*, XIV (December, 1968), 293-306.

[21]Speech at Syracuse, May, 1851, Webster, *Writings and Speeches*, XIII, 419, 417; *Congressional Globe*, 31 Cong., 1 Sess., Appendix, 1268 (July 17, 1850); 274, 271 (March 7, 1850).

[22]*Ibid.*, 767 (June 10, 1850); 740 (June 7, 1850); 729 (June 4, 1850); 1301 (September 25, 1850); 304 (May 12, 1850).

[23]The Dignity and Importance of History, New York, February 23, 1852, Webster, *Writings and Speeches*, XIII, 466, 467; The Rhode Island Government, January 27, 1848, *ibid.*, XI, 220; *Congressional Globe*, 31 Cong., 1 Sess., Appendix, 271, 276, (March 7, 1850).

[24]*Ibid.*, 470 (March 26, 1850); 941 (July 24, 1850); 1065 (May 20, 1850); 759 (June 3, 1850); 567 (March 13, 1850). The Free-Soil adversaries of Webster here manifested something of that ahistorical and anti-institutional spirit which Stanley M. Elkins dealt with at length in *Slavery: A Problem in American Institutional and Intellectual Life*, 140-222.

[25]*Congressional Globe*, 31 Cong., 1 Sess., Appendix, 269 (March 7, 1850); 1268 (July 17, 1850); Speech at Syracuse, May, 1851, Webster, *Writings and Speeches*, XIII, 425-26, 420. Robert F. Dalzell, Jr., dealt especially well with the elements of pluralism in Webster's concept of the nation. *Daniel Webster and the Trial of American Nationalism*, 157-95.

[26]*Congressional Globe*, 31 Cong., 1 Sess., Appendix, 1267 (July 17, 1850); Reception at Buffalo, May 22, 1851, Webster, *Writings and Speeches*, IV, 244.

[27]*Congressional Globe*, 31 Cong., 1 Sess., Appendix, 269 (March 7, 1850); The Dignity and Importance of History, New York, February 23, 1852, Webster, *Writings and Speeches*, XIII, 495; *Congressional Globe*, 31 Cong., 1 Sess., Appendix, 1267 (July 17, 1850).

[28]*Ibid.*, 1268, 1270 (July 17, 1850).

[29]*Ibid.*, 1024 (July 2, 1850); 578 (May 14, 1850); 1302 (September 25, 1850). It will be the burden of Chapter 9 to show that Seward was not a Free Soiler in the sense of the term used in this

study. He did, however, serve as one important foil to Webster in the crisis of 1850.

[30]*Ibid.*, 691 (June 3, 1850); 1126 (August 12, 1850); 480 (March 27, 1850).

[31]*Ibid.*, 1278 (August 30, 1850); 511 (May 11, 1850); 230 (March 4, 1850); 1302 (September 25, 1850); 142 (February 20, 1850).

[32]Webster to Professor Stuart, April 30, 1850, Webster, *Writings and Speeches*, XVIII, 367; Speech at Capon Springs, Virginia, June 28, 1851, *ibid.*, 433; Speech to the Young Men of Albany, May 28, 1851, *ibid.*, IV, 282; *Congressional Globe*, 31 Cong., 1 Sess., Appendix, 269 (March 7, 1850). Webster's profound commitment to the Union as the central motive for his support of compromise is well noted in Herbert Darling Foster, "Webster's Seventh of March Speech and the Secession Movement, 1850" *American Historical Review*, XXVII (January, 1922), 245-70.

[33]"The Dignity and Importance of History," New York, February 23, 1852, Webster, *Writings and Speeches*, XIII, 493; Webster to B. F. Ayer, November 16, 1850, *ibid.*, XVI, 578; Reception at Buffalo, May 22, 1851, *ibid.*, IV, 258. What Webster especially objected to was the position of many Free Soilers that the constitutional provision for fugitive slaves provided no basis for federal legislation. Chase and others took it to be a compact between the states and in no sense a clear constitutional duty of the federal government.

[34]Secretary of State to Mr. Hulsemann, December 21, 1850, *ibid.*, XII, 165-78; Webster to George Ticknor, January 16, 1851, *ibid.*, XVI, 586.

[35]*Congressional Globe*, 31 Cong., 1 Sess., Appendix, 270-71 (March 7, 1850).

[36]Speech at Wall Street, September 28, 1840, Webster, *Writings and Speeches*, III, 79; Webster to Reverend Mr. Furness, February 15, 1850, *ibid.*, XVIII, 353. Webster's argument here reflected a conservative pattern of modern thought which goes back at least to David Hume. For an analysis of Hume's thought about the nature of man in time, see Sheldon S. Wolin, "Hume and Conser-

vatism," *American Political Science Review*, XLVIII (December, 1954), 999-1016.

[37]*Congressional Globe*, 31 Cong., 1 Sess., Appendix, 642 (May 27, 1850); 254 (March 11, 1850); 508 (April 19, 1850); 518 (April 23, 1850); 658 (June 4, 1850).

[38]Put in another way, past struggles for power have tended to generate intense passions and the need to identify with lofty and absolute ideals. Roy F. Nichols, *The Stakes of Power, 1845-1877* (New York: Hill and Wang, 1961), *ix-x*.

[39]*Congressional Globe*, 31 Cong., 1 Sess., Appendix, 1300 (September 25, 1850); 474 (March 26, 1850); 511 (April 19, 1850).

[40]*Ibid.*, 769 (June 10, 1850); 511 (May 3, 1850); 564 (May 13, 1850); 1301 (September 25, 1850).

[41]The urge of second and third generation Puritans to "own the covenant" of their fathers, as seen by Perry Miller, finds a clear parallel here in the Free Soilers. *The New England Mind: From Colony to Province* (Cambridge: Harvard University Press, 1953), 19-39.

[42]*Congressional Globe*, 31 Cong., 1 Sess., Appendix, 739 (June 7, 1850); 733 (June 4, 1850); 511 (April 19, 1850).

[43]*Ibid.*, 453 (April 10, 1850); 400 (March 27, 1850); 1124 (August 14, 1850); 1502 (August 2, 1850). A tabular summary of votes on the different compromise proposals is given in Hamilton, *Prologue to Conflict*, 191-200.

[44]*Congressional Globe*, 31 Cong., 1 Sess., Appendix, 614 (May 21, 1850); 116 (February 5, 1850); Clay to Daniel Ullman, February 2, 1850; February 15, 1850, Colton (ed.), *Private Correspondence of Clay*, 600-01.

[45]*Congressional Globe*, 31 Cong., 1 Sess., Appendix, 1413 (July 22, 1850).

[46]William O. Lynch, "Antislavery Tendencies in the Democratic Party in the Northwest, 1848-1850," *Mississippi Valley Historical Review*, XI (December, 1924), 319-31.

[47]*Congressional Globe*, 31 Cong., 1 Sess., Appendix, 99 (February 8, 1850); John H. McHenry to Hunter, February 21, 1850, Charles Henry Ambler (ed.), *Correspondence of Robert M. T. Hunter, 1826-1876, Annual Report* of the American Historical

Association for 1916 (2 vols., Washington: Government Printing Office, 1918), II, 105; Douglas to Charles H. Lamphier and George Walker, August 3, 1850, Robert W. Johannsen (ed.), *The Letters of Stephen A. Douglas* (Urbana: University of Illinois Press, 1961), 191-92.

[48]Hodder, "The Authorship of the Compromise of 1850," 530-32; Russel, "WhatWas the Compromise of 1850?" 304. Resolution of subsequent conflict between new territorial acts and old Mexican laws was to be made by the federal courts.

[49]*Congressional Globe*, 31 Cong., 1 Sess., Appendix, 370 (March 13, 1850).

[50]*Ibid.*, 320 (March 12, 1850); 840 (June 5, 1850); 59, 73 (June 21, 22, 1850); 371 (March 13, 1850).

[51]*Ibid.*, 368 (March 13, 1850). For a fuller background see Merle Curti, "Young America," *American Historical Review*, XXXII (October, 1926), 34-55.

[52]Penetrating comment upon this same matter can be found in Sidney E. Mead, "The American People: Their Space, Time, and Religion," *Journal of Religion*, XXXIV (October, 1954), 251, 244-55.

[53]*Congressional Globe*, 31 Cong., 1 Sess., Appendix, 840 (June 5, 1850); 424 (April 3, 1850); 1150 (August 5, 1850). Lewis Cass was among a distinct minority of Northerners in 1850 who embraced popular sovereignty *as a constitutional principle*. Russel, "Constitutional Doctrines with Regard to Slavery in Territories," 473-74.

[54]Foote to Calhoun, September 25, 1849, Jameson (ed.), *Correspondence of Calhoun*, II, 1205; Cobb to William Hope Hull, July 17, 1850, Ulrich B. Phillips (ed.), *The Correspondence of Robert Toombs, Alexander H. Stephens, and Howell Cobb, Annual Report* of the American Historical Association for 1911 (2 vols., Washington: Government Printing Office, 1913), II, 198. For an extended analysis of the ambiguities touched on here, see Quaife, *The Doctrine of Non-Intervention with Slavery in the Territories, passim*.

[55]The effects of the operation of the new fugitive slave law are treated rather fully in the article by Larry Gara already cited, "The Fugitive Slave Law: A Double Paradox," 229-40.

Chapter 8

[1]Robert R. Russel has shown how the Nebraska territory, by this first draft, enjoyed the same status New Mexico and Utah were given in the Compromise of 1850. By the terms of that compromise, the old Mexican laws against slavery presumably remained in force; yet they were made to coexist with the new and conflicting prescription of popular sovereignty. "The Issues in the Congressional Struggle over the Kansas-Nebraska Bill, 1854," *Journal of Southern History*, XXIX (May, 1963), 193.

[2]Russel noted that the phrase, "inoperative and void," had been carefully chosen, for it would grate less on the northern sensibilities than the starker term, "repeal." *Ibid.*, 199. For a less sympathetic account of the background and making of the bill, see Nevins, *Ordeal of the Union*, II, 78-100.

[3]Jaffa, *Crisis of the House Divided*, 63-103; Nevins, *Ordeal of the Union*, II, 108, 100-09; Roy F. Nichols, "The Kansas-Nebraska Act: A Century of Historiography," *Mississippi Valley Historical Review*, XLIII (September, 1956), 187-212.

[4]Avery O. Craven, *The Growth of Southern Nationalism, 1848-1861* (Baton Rouge: Louisiana State University Press, 1953), 184-205, demonstrates that the solidity of southern opinion developed in response to northern outrage over the Kansas-Nebraska bill. Within the framework of his Free-Soil interpretation of the event, Henry Wilson's conclusion about the effect of the Kansas-Nebraska bill seems very sound: "No single act of the Slave Power ever spread greater consternation, produced more lasting results upon the popular mind, or did so much to arouse the North and to convince the people of its desperate character." *History of the Rise and Fall of the Slave Power in America* (3 vols., Boston: J. R. Osgood, 1872-1877), II, 378.

[5]*Congressional Globe*, 33 Cong., 1 Sess., Appendix, 178 (February 11, 1854); 754 (May 20, 1854).

[6]*Ibid.*, 469 (April 5, 1854); 506 (February 27, 1854); 710 (May 10, 1854). For a fuller analysis of the conservative response see an article by the present author, "Of Time and the Union: Kansas-Nebraska and the Appeal from Prescription to Principle," *Midwest Quarterly*, X (Autumn, 1968), 73-87.

[7]*Congressional Globe*, 33 Cong., 1 Sess., Appendix, 337 (March 3, 1854). By the end of the decade Douglas provided an even more systematic statement of his "great principle." Robert W. Johannsen, "Stephen A. Douglas, 'Harper's Magazine,' and Popular Sovereignty," *Mississippi Valley Historical Review*, XLV (March, 1959), 606-31. See also Russel, "Constitutional Doctrines with Regard to Slavery in Territories," 473-74. In defense of the Douglas position by the end of the 1850s, Russel also noted that the Dred Scott decision only ruled against congressional action on slavery and did not, as Southerners assumed, rule out territorial action. The doctrine of popular sovereignty, in other words, had not had its day in court.

[8]*Congressional Globe*, 33 Cong., 1 Sess., Appendix, 352 (March 15, 1854); 310 (March 3, 1854); 256, 255 (February 28, 1854); 270 (February 20, 1854).

[9]*Ibid.*, 612 (April 27, 1854); 751 (May 18, 1854); 346 (February 23, 1854); 229 (February 24, 1854); Stanwood, *History of the Presidency*, 287-88.

[10]*Ibid.*, 291-94.

[11]For a general discussion see: Bury, *The Idea of Progress*, 68-69; Frankel, *The Faith of Reason*, 3-38; R. V. Sampson, *Progress in the Age of Reason: The Seventeenth Century to the Present Day* (Cambridge: Harvard University Press, 1956), 24-30; Lois Whitney, *Primitivism and the Idea of Progress in English Popular Literature of the Eighteenth Century* (Baltimore: Johns Hopkins Press, 1934), 1-10; Stow Persons, "The Cyclical Theory of History in Eighteenth Century America," *American Quarterly*, VI (Summer, 1954), 147-63. With some minor alterations the remainder of the present chapter first appeared as an article, "The Free Soil Concept of Progress and the Irrepressible Conflict," *ibid.*, XXII (Winter, 1970), 769-90. Copyright 1970, Trustees of the University of Pennsylvania.

[12]Boorstin, *The Genius of American Politics*, 20; Craven, *The Legend of the Founding Fathers*, v; Kohn, *American Nationalism*, 3-37.

[13]In an article cited earlier contrasting the American idea of progress with the revolutionary concept in Europe, Rush Welter summarized the matter as follows: "Progress, that is, would be a continuation of the present. To use the distinction already drawn,

it would have forward movement but not upward; it would be horizontal, not vertical." "The Idea of Progress in America: An Essay in Ideas and Methods," 404, 401-15.

[14]Ekirch, *The Idea of Progress in America*, does not deal with the idea of progress as it specifically pertained to the slavery controversy.

[15]Wilmot before the Republican National Convention on May 16, 1860, Charles Buxton Going, *David Wilmot, Free Soiler: A Biography of the Great Advocate of the Wilmot Proviso* (New York: D. Appleton, 1924), 529; *Congressional Globe*, 34 Cong., 1 Sess., Appendix, 108 (February 28, 1856); 294 (April 1, 1856); Speech at Peoria, October 16, 1854, Basler (ed.), *Collected Works of Lincoln*, II, 249, 276; *Congressional Globe*, 35 Cong., 1 Sess., Appendix, 331 (March 31, 1858).

[16]An Old Liberty Party man to George W. Julian, October 18, 1860, Joshua R. Giddings-George W. Julian Papers (Manuscript Division, Library of Congress, Washington); James R. Briggs to Lincoln, November 7, 1860, Robert Todd Lincoln Collection (Manuscript Division, Library of Congress).

[17]Herndon to Lyman Trumbull, December 21, 1860, Lyman Trumbull Papers (Manuscript Division, Library of Congress); Milton Sutliff to Fessenden, February 15, 1861, William Pitt Fessenden Papers (Manuscript Division, Library of Congress); Jonathan Ward to Wade, January 12, 1861, Benjamin F. Wade Papers (Manuscript Division, Library of Congress).

[18]Eliade, *Cosmos and History*, 75. The pattern also exhibits the dynamics of Protestant revivalism. But the experience of an "eternal return" and of "revival" have much in common and, as indicated in Chapter 1, points to different facets of the same reality. Eliade's concept is used in the present chapter because it serves to underline with special clarity the certainty of confrontation in the thought of those who identified with the national idea of original perfection.

[19]Three important works cover this matter: Miller, *The New England Mind: From Colony to Province*; Bernard Bailyn, *The Ideological Origins of the American Revolution* (Cambridge: Belknap Press of the Harvard University Press, 1967); Meyers, *The Jacksonian Persuasion*.

[20]Rowland Berthoff, "The American Social Order: A Conservative Hypothesis," *American Historical Review*, LXV (April, 1960), 500. Though critical of the process, Avery O. Craven has clearly noted the deranging forces in northern life by mid-century and how the dialectical presence of the slaveholder provided a new sense of unity and meaning. "The 1840s and the Democratic Process," *Journal of Southern History*, XVI (May, 1950), 165; *The Coming of the Civil War*, 117-50. Eric Foner has somewhat redressed the balance by his stress upon the positive and affirmative side to the Free-Soil ideology: *Free Soil, Free Labor, Free Men*, 11-39.

[21]Arthur P. Dudden has analyzed, in this connection, how the "overt" optimism of Americans about the future has been accompanied by a "covert" anxiety which disposed them to look to the past. "Nostalgia and the American," 515-31. See also Somkin, *Unquiet Eagle, passim.*

[22]For a fuller treatment of reform as a "cultural purge" see Clifton E. Hart, "The Minor Premise in American Thought" (Unpublished Ph.D. dissertation, State University of Iowa, 1962), 62-64, *passim.*

[23]*Congressional Globe*, 34 Cong., 1 Sess., Appendix, 108 (February 28, 1856); 31 Cong., 1 Sess., Appendix, 469 (March 26, 1850); 33 Cong., 1 Sess., Appendix, 266 (February 24, 1854); 34 Cong., 1 Sess., Appendix, 1160 (August 4, 1858).

[24]Stanwood, *A History of the Presidency*, 291; Fragment on the Constitution and the Union, *c.* January, 1861, Basler (ed.), *Collected Works of Lincoln*, IV, 169; *Congressional Globe*, 34 Cong., 1 Sess., Appendix, 906 (July 23, 1856).

[25]*Ibid.*, 33 Cong., 1 Sess., Appendix, 350 (February 23, 1854); John L. Thomas, *The Liberator: William Lloyd Garrison, A Biography* (Boston: Little, Brown, 1963).

[26]*Congressional Globe*, 33 Cong., 1 Sess., Appendix, 269 (February 24, 1854); 34 Cong., 1 Sess., 1075-76 (August 2, 1856).

[27]*Ibid.*, 35 Cong., 1 Sess., Appendix, 897 (February 26, 1858). For an extended presentation of this mode of argument see the "Freedom National" speech given by Sumner in the Senate on August 26, 1852.

[28]*Ibid.*, 31 Cong., 1 Sess., Appendix, 472 (March 26, 1850). See

also Salmon P. Chase, *Reclamation of Fugitives From Service: An Argument for the Defendant . . . in the Case of Wharton Jones v. John Van Zandt* (Cincinnati: R. P. Donogh, 1847).

²⁹*Congressional Globe*, 34 Cong., 1 Sess., Appendix, 300 (April 1, 1856); Speech at New Haven, March 6, 1860, Basler (ed.), *Collected Works of Lincoln*, IV, 22. In a remarkably parallel fashion, evangelical religious leaders in the North by the end of the 1850s had come to reject all Biblical sanctions for slavery and to reinterpret the Bible as an antislavery document. Timothy L. Smith argued with a good deal of plausibility that these evangelical churches thereupon comprised one of the greatest forces behind Lincoln and the triumphant Free-Soil movement. *Revivalism and Social Reform: American Protestantism on the Eve of the Civil War* (New York: Harper and Row, 1965), 178-224.

³⁰*Congressional Globe*, 35 Cong., 1 Sess., 1284 (March 23, 1858); "Justice" to Senator Wade, December 24, 1860, Wade Papers; *Congressional Globe*, 34 Cong., 1 Sess., Appendix, 530 (May 19, 1856); 35 Cong., 1 Sess., Appendix, 151 (March 19, 1858).

³¹*Ibid.*, 35 Cong., 1 Sess., 859 (February 24, 1858).

³²*Ibid.*, 33 Cong., 1 Sess., Appendix, 139 (February 3, 1854). Eric Foner rightly attributed to Chase considerable credit for working out the Free-Soil position. *Free Soil, Free Labor, Free Men*, 73-102.

³³Appeal of the Independent Democrats in Congress to the People of the United States, January 19, 1854, *Congressional Globe*, 33 Cong., 1 Sess., 281 (January 30, 1854).

³⁴*Ibid.*, Appendix, 262 (February 24, 1854); 499 (April 1, 1854); 764 (May 25, 1854).

³⁵Speech at Peoria, October 16, 1854, Basler (ed.), *Collected Works of Lincoln*, II, 276, 275, 274, 266.

³⁶*Ibid.*, 255; *Congressional Globe*, 34 Cong., 1 Sess., Appendix, 84 (February 12, 1856).

³⁷*Ibid.*, 366-78 (April 3, 1856); 848-51 (July 9, 1856); 35 Cong., 1 Sess., 1256 (March 22, 1858).

³⁸*Ibid.*, 894 (February 26, 1858); 617 (February 8, 1858).

³⁹*Ibid.*, 36 Cong., 1 Sess., Appendix, 103 (January 3, 1860). By establishing the right of slavery to receive recognition and protec-

tion in all national territories, the Dred Scott decision fulfilled the *goal* of John C. Calhoun. But Doolittle was wrong in assuming that the decision also vindicated the precise line of Calhoun's constitutional thought about "slavery national." Whereas the South Carolinian argued from the premises of state sovereignty, Edwin S. Corwin has shown that Chief Justice Roger B. Taney proceeded on the "strongly nationalistic" grounds of John Marshall. "The Dred Scott Decision, in the Light of Contemporary Legal Doctrines," 60-61.

[40]Speech at Springfield, June 16, 1858, Basler (ed.), *Collected Works of Lincoln*, II, 462, 461-69. While most historians have not taken Lincoln's conspiracy theory very seriously, Harry V. Jaffa presented a strong argument of a legal sort in behalf of Lincoln. *Crisis of the House Divided*, 275-93. Further background and analysis of the House Divided speech is given in Fehrenbacher, *Prelude to Greatness*, 70-95.

[41]Julian to Reverend Higginson, October 24, 1857, Giddings-Julian Papers; *Congressional Globe*, 31 Cong., 1 Sess., Appendix, 1301 (September 25, 1850).

[42]The first quote is from a speech by Representative Edward Wade of Ohio,*ibid*., 34 Cong., 1 Sess., Appendix, 1078 (August 2, 1856); 35 Cong., 1 Sess., 1384 (March 26, 1858).

[43]*Ibid*., 34 Cong., 1 Sess., Appendix, 1219 (August 6, 1856); Speech at Chicago, December 10, 1856, Basler (ed.), *Collected Works of Lincoln*, II, 383; *Congressional Globe*, 33 Cong., 1 Sess., Appendix, 140 (February 3, 1854).

[44]Chase to William H. Seward, January, 1861, Salmon P. Chase Papers (Manuscript Division, Library of Congress).

[45]Address to the People of Massachusetts, September 12, 1849, Sumner, *Works of Sumner*, II, 287.

[46]*Baltimore Democracy and Independent Democracy: Letter of S. P. Chase to A. P. Edgerton* (Cincinnati: n.p., 1853), 5-12.

[47]Speech at New Haven, March 6, 1860, Basler (ed.), *Collected Works of Lincoln*, IV, 17-18.

[48]Speech at Chicago, July 10, 1858, *ibid*., II, 492. Italics added.

[49]Speech at Chicago, March 1, 1859, *ibid*., III, 369. Arthur E. Bestor, "Patent Office Models of the Good Society: Some Rela-

tionships Between Social Reform and Westward Expansion," *American Historical Review*, LVIII (April, 1953), 521, 505-26. A good sampling of opinion about the crucial influence of the West upon the whole Union can be found in Rush Welter, "The Frontier West as Image of American Society: Conservative Attitudes Before the Civil War," 593-614.

⁵⁰*Congressional Globe*, 31 Cong., 1 Sess., Appendix, 943 (July 24, 1850); First Debate with Stephen A. Douglas at Ottawa, August 21, 1858, Basler (ed.), *Collected Works of Lincoln*, III, 18; Speech at Chicago, March 1, 1859, *ibid.*, 370.

⁵¹Lincoln to James N. Brown, October 18, 1858, *ibid.*, 328; *Congressional Globe* 33 Cong., 1 Sess., Appendix, 262 (February 24, 1854).

⁵²*Ibid.*, 310 (May 3, 1854); 34 Cong., 1 Sess., Appendix, 274 (March 27, 1856); 1166 (August 4, 1856).

⁵³"Settlement in a new, unknown, uncultivated country," Eliade also noted, "is equivalent to an act of creation." *Cosmos and History*, 10. In other terms, the outlook of the Free Soilers here manifested in a sectionalized form the experience of what Max Lerner has called "extended genesis." *America as a Civilization*, 35-39.

⁵⁴Speech at Peoria, October 16, 1854, Basler (ed.), *Collected Works of Lincoln*, II, 276. This part of the argument of the present chapter is greatly indebted to the work of Harry V. Jaffa. Of Lincoln's whole outlook he has concluded: "Thus we see that, for the republic to live, the act of creation or founding must be repeated." *Crisis of the House Divided*, 224, 183-232. But one of his supporting arguments, namely, that the "new birth" of freedom actually transcended Jefferson's views in the Declaration of Independence (308-46), is in need of qualification. The stress Lincoln and other Free Soilers placed on the morally substantial nature of individual freedom, in contrast to the procedural right of freedom for local communities from central control, did not go beyond Jefferson. It served, rather, to polarize the two elements of individual and federative freedom which had heretofore existed in a state of tension within the Jeffersonian heritage. In other words, a sundered Jefferson made for civil strife. Peterson, *The Jefferson Image in the American Mind*, 189-209.

⁵⁵Stephens quoted in Edmund Wilson, "The Union as Religious Mysticism," *Eight Essays* (Garden City: Doubleday, 1954), 197.

⁵⁶Address at Cooper Institute, New York, February 27, 1860, Basler (ed.), *Collected Works of Lincoln*, III, 550.

⁵⁷The eighth resolution of the platform contained the Free-Soil credo. It held that "the normal condition" of the national territories was freedom, that "our republican fathers" had provided for this in the due-process clause of the fifth amendment, and that, as a consequence, neither Congress nor a territorial legislature could give legal existence to slavery. Stanwood, *History of the Presidency*, 293.

⁵⁸While differing about the relative chances for compromise, two leading works on the secession crisis agree that the Crittenden plan held out the best hope for saving the Union by peaceful means: Potter, *Lincoln and His Party in the Secession Crisis*; Kenneth Stampp, *And the War Came: The North and the Secession Crisis, 1860-1861* (Baton Rouge: Louisiana State University Press, 1950).

⁵⁹Lincoln to Lyman Trumbull, December 10, 1860; to John D. Defrees, December 18, 1860; to Stephens, December 22, 1860, Basler (ed.), *Collected Works of Lincoln*, IV, 149-50; 155; 160.

⁶⁰Jaffa, *Crisis of the House Divided*, 143; Allan Nevins, *The Emergence of Lincoln* (2 vols., New York: Charles Scribner's Sons, 1950), I, 392; Moore, *The Missouri Controversy*, 292.

⁶¹Two articles clearly distinguish the older constitutional interpretation from the new positions of the Free Soilers and the slavery expansionists: Bestor, "The American Civil War as a Constitutional Crisis," 327-52; Russel, "Constitutional Doctrines with Regard to Slavery in Territories," 466-86.

Chapter 9

¹Bancroft, *Life of Seward*, I, 263; II, 87-89; Rhodes, *History of the United States from the Compromise of 1850 to the End of the Roosevelt Administration* (9 vols., New York: Macmillan, 1928), II, 303. With some minor changes the material in this chapter on Seward

reproduces an article by the present author, "The Repressible Conflict: Seward's Concept of Progress and the Free-Soil Movement," *Journal of Southern History*, XXXVII (November, 1971), 533-56. Copyright 1971 by the Southern Historical Association. Reprinted by permission of the Managing Editor.

²Among those who have supposed Seward to be basically radical are Emerson D. Fite, *The Presidential Campaign of 1860* (New York: Macmillan, 1911); Arthur C. Cole, *The Irrepressible Conflict, 1850-1865* (New York: Macmillan, 1934); Reinhard H. Luthin, *The First Lincoln Campaign* (Cambridge: Harvard University Press, 1944); Wayne R. Merrick, "A Study of William Henry Seward, Reformer" (Unpublished D.D.S. dissertation, Syracuse University, 1956). Nevins, *The Emergence of Lincoln*, II, 300. Bancroft and Rhodes would hold with Nevins on this point.

³Glyndon G. Van Deusen, *William Henry Seward* (New York: Oxford University Press, 1967), 198-210, is a notable exception. Van Deusen here provides an excellent summary of Seward's thought about "the higher destiny" of the nation as it complements his views on slavery expansion. Part of the burden of the present chapter is to bring his analysis of Seward's vision more explicitly to bear upon the senator's dealings with slavery expansion at critical points in the 1850s. Walter G. Sharrow, "William Henry Seward: A Study in Nineteenth Century Politics and Nationalism" (Unpublished Ph.D. dissertation, University of Rochester, 1965), does a good deal of this sort of thing for the very end of the decade.

⁴*Congressional Globe*, 31 Cong., 1 Sess., Appendix, 1023 (July 2, 1850); 262 (March 11, 1850).

⁵Bury, *The Idea of Progress*, 2; *Congressional Globe*, 31 Cong., 1 Sess., Appendix, 265 (March 11, 1850).

⁶"The True Greatness of Our Country," Baltimore, December 22, 1848, Baker (ed.), *Works of Seward*, III, 15; *Congressional Globe*, 31 Cong., 1 Sess., Appendix, 1024 (July 2, 1850); 263 (March 11, 1850).

⁷Speech at Whig Mass Meeting, Yates County, New York, October 29, 1844, Baker (ed.), *Works of Seward*, III, 270. Central in the speech proclaiming the "irrepressible conflict" was the idea that conflict had ripened with the progress of the nationalizing

tendencies in the life of the country. "The Irrepressible Conflict," Rochester, October 26, 1858, *ibid.*, IV, 289-302. While the phrase itself was new and doubtless calculated to have a political effect, the idea can be found throughout his writings and speeches in the two decades before the Civil War. Frederick W. Seward, *Seward in Washington; As Senator and Secretary of State. A Memoir of His Life with Selections from His Letters, 1846-1861* (New York: Derby and Miller, 1891), 352.

[8]Chase thus wrote to Charles Sumner: "You mistake when you say, 'Seward is with us'." Chase to Sumner, April 13, 1850, Bourne (ed.), *Diary and Correspondence of Chase*, II, 207. In a subsequent letter about Seward, Chase also noted: "He is too much of a politician for me." December 14, 1850, *ibid.*, 224.

[9]*Congressional Globe*, 31 Cong., 1 Sess., Appendix, 271-74 (March 7, 1850).

[10]See Van Deusen, *Seward*, 587*n*. The motive would apparently have been the political one of pinning the unpopular measure on the Democrats.

[11]*Congressional Globe*, 33 Cong., 1 Sess., Appendix, 769 (May 25, 1854). Letters from Henry Raymond of New York and Senator Edward Everett of Massachusetts remarked the contrast between Seward's optimism and their own sense of gloom. Raymond to Seward, May 30, 1854; Everett to Seward, June 16, 1854, William Henry Seward Papers (Rush Rhees Library, University of Rochester, Rochester, New York). "I had no idea," Raymond said, "such a rainbow could be hung out on such a cloud."

[12]*Congressional Globe* 35 Cong., 1 Sess., 943-45 (March 3, 1858). Horace Andrews, Jr., "Kansas Crusade: Eli Thayer and the New England Emigrant Aid Society," *New England Quarterly*, XXXV (December, 1962), 497-514. The reaction of the two correspondents here quoted to Seward's remarks about popular sovereignty are very revealing. Gilly Pittman, avowedly an "extreme southerner," professed to discover "that you are not so complete a *devil* as they would have you be." Chase, to the contrary, "regretted the apparent countenance you give to the idea that the Douglas doctrine of popular sovereignty will do . . . for the present." Pittman to Seward, March 6, 1858; Chase to Seward, March 6, 1858, Seward Papers. To Senator John Hale of

New Hampshire, equally critical of his course on a closely related matter, Seward replied: "Sir, I regard this battle as fought; it is over." *Congressional Globe*, 35 Cong., 1 Sess., 521 (February 2, 1858).

¹³*Ibid.*, Appendix, 140 (March 18, 1858).

¹⁴The Election of 1848, Cleveland, Ohio, October 26, 1848, Baker (ed.), *Works of Seward*, III, 292-93.

¹⁵*Congressional Globe*, 32 Cong., 1 Sess., 1635-36 (June 30, 1852); 35 Cong., 1 Sess., 944 (March 3, 1858). The fullest statement of Seward's ideas about national progress can be found in a speech given at the dedication of Capital University in Columbus, Ohio, September 14, 1853. William H. Seward, *The Destiny of America* (Albany: Weed, Parsons, 1853).

¹⁶*Congressional Globe*, 33 Cong., 1 Sess., 1566 (December 21, 1858); 32 Cong., 2 Sess., Appendix, 127 (January 26, 1853). For a discussion of the idea of gravitational pull see Weinberg, *Manifest Destiny*, 190-251.

¹⁷*Congressional Globe*, 31 Cong., 1 Sess., Appendix, 262 (March 11, 1850). It was no accident that many letters of praise poured in from California. Seward, *Seward at Washington*, 128. Reactions of an opposite sort also came in from those who believed Seward's concern for California made him faithless to freedom. Fears of its political effect were also voiced in letters from Abijah Fitch, March 16, 1850, and Thurlow Weed, March 17, 1850, Seward Papers.

¹⁸*Congressional Globe*, 32 Cong., 1 Sess., 1975 (July 29, 1852). A good discussion of the Pacific orientation in Seward's outlook can be found in: Frederic Bancroft, "Seward's Ideas of Territorial Expansion," *North American Review*, CLXVII (July, 1898), 79-89; Tyler Dennett, "Seward's Far Eastern Policy," *American Historical Review*, XXVIII (October, 1922), 45-62; Charles Vevier, "American Continentalism: An Idea of Expansion, 1845-1910," *ibid.*, LXV (January, 1960), 330-32; Walter G. Sharrow, "William Henry Seward and the Basis for American Empire, 1850-1860," *Pacific Historical Quarterly*, XXXVI (August, 1967), 325-42.

¹⁹*Congressional Globe*, 31 Cong., 1 Sess., Appendix, 262 (March 11, 1850). For the domestic emphasis which one Free Soiler placed on the national mission, see James A. Rawley, "The

Nationalism of Abraham Lincoln," *Civil War History*, IX (September, 1963), 285. "The world mission of America was to be an example," he said of Lincoln, "and little more."

[20]*Congressional Globe*, 32 Cong., 2 Sess., Appendix, 146 (February 8, 1853); 1 Sess., 1202 (April 27, 1852); 31 Cong., 1 Sess., 851 (April 29, 1850); 32 Cong., 2 Sess., Appendix, 127 (January 26, 1853).

[21]Seward to Edward A. Stansbury, September 2, 1844, cited in Van Deusen, *Seward*, 103. The same balanced outlook can be found in his speech to a strong antislavery audience in the Western Reserve of Ohio during the campaign of 1848. The Election of 1848, Baker (ed.), "Minnesota as Seen by Travellers: Campaigning with Seward in 1860," *Minnesota History*, VIII (June, 1927), 153; speech at Lawrence, Kansas, September 26, 1860, William H. Seward, *The National Divergence and Return* (Albany: Weed, Parsons, 1860), 52-53.

[23]Annual Message to the New York State Legislature, January 7, 1840, Baker (ed.), *Works of Seward*, II, 240-41.

[24]The Election of 1848, *ibid.*, III, 291; speech on John Quincy Adams at Albany, April 6, 1848, *ibid.*, II, 99. The term, "doctrine of institutions," was used by Henry W. Bellows, a conservative Unitarian minister, in his Divinity Address at Harvard in 1859. Cited in Fredrickson, *The Inner Civil War*, 27.

[25]"The Pilgrims and Liberty," December, 1855, Baker (ed.), *Works of Seward*, IV, 181. It should be stressed here that Seward actually had the Puritans and not the "come outer" Pilgrim separatists in mind. On the matter of fugitive slaves, however, Seward was vulnerable to the charge of anti-institutional radicalism. Van Deusen, *Seward*, 65-67.

[26]Address to the Chatauqua Convention at Auburn, March 31, 1846, Baker (ed.), *Works of Seward*, III, 409; William H. Seward, *The Elements of Empire* (New York: C. Shepard, 1844), 11; *Congressional Globe*, 36 Cong., 1 Sess., 944 (March 3, 1858).

[27]*Ibid.*, 31 Cong., 1 Sess., Appendix, 269 (March 11, 1850). Retrospectively, Seward had this to say about Webster's course in 1850: "While he was for 'Liberty and Union,' he was for Union more than Liberty." Seward to Theodore Parker, January, 1853, Seward, *Seward at Washington*, 198. Don E. Fehrenbacher is wrong

in claiming that Lincoln was the first statesman to link the idea of indissoluble Union to that of irrepressible conflict. *Prelude to Greatness,* 86. The link between the two constituted a basic premise in Seward's outlook in the two decades before the bcivil War.

28*Congressional Globe,* 33 Cong., 1 Sess., Appendix, 155 (February 17, 1854); 31 Cong., 1 Sess., Appendix, 1024 (July 2, 1850).

29*Ibid.,* 1642 (September 11, 1850).

30Some of Seward's choicest sarcasm was heaped upon the premise of moral neutrality avowed by Douglas and other champions of popular sovereignty. "Popular sovereignty offered the indulgence of a taste of the fruit of the tree of the knowledge of evil as well as of good," he noted in 1858, "a more perfect freedom." Elsewhere he scorned the "wretched sophistry" of extending to a territorial people the "ruinous privilege" of choosing the evil of slavery. *Ibid.,* 35 Cong., 1 Sess., 940 (May 3, 1858); 34 Cong., 1 Sess., Appendix, 791 (July 2, 1856).

31Seward to James Watson Webb, February 1, 1849, Baker (ed.), *Works of Seward,* III, 415; Seward to Theodore Parker, June 23, 1854, Seward Papers; Seward to Parker, December, 1855, Seward, *Seward in Washington,* 262. A very good argument for the view, which Seward seemed here to assume, that the task of shaping public opinion can be regarded as "institutional" is in Robert D. Marcus, "Wendell Phillips and American Institutions," *Journal of American History,* LVI (June, 1969), 41-58.

32Seward, *Elements of Empire,* 39.

33The Election of 1848, Baker (ed.), *Works of Seward,* III, 301; Seward, *Elements of Empire,* 22.

34Seward to Salmon P. Chase, Samuel Lewis, and others, May 26, 1845, Baker (ed.), *Works of Seward,* III, 441; Seward, *Seward at Washington,* 452; The Election of 1848, Baker (ed.), *Works of Seward,* III, 293.

35*Congressional Globe,* 34 Cong., 1 Sess., Appendix, 1076 (August 2, 1856); 36 Cong., 1 Sess., 914 (February 29, 1860).

36This is not to say that Lincoln was above "politics." In *Prelude to Greatness,* 78-83, Fehrenbacher well demonstrates the political advantages—indeed necessities—involved for Lincoln in the Free-Soil cause in Illinois. But Fehrenbacher also shows the con-

sistent way in which Lincoln dealt with the morality of the issue
and how it contrasted with the lesser moral fervor of Seward.
Allan Nevins likewise called attention to this contrast in *Emergence
of Lincoln*, II, 183-88. See also Ronald Dean Rietveld, "The Moral
Issue of Slavery in American Politics, 1854-1860," (Unpublished
Ph.D. dissertation, University of Illinois, 1967).

[37]Jaffa, *Crisis of the House Divided*, 41-180.

[38]*Congressional Globe*, 35 Cong., 1 Sess., 618 (February 8, 1858).

[39]Annual Message to the New York State Legislature, January
1, 1839, Baker (ed.), *Works of Seward*, II, 205; *Congressional Globe*,
35 Cong., 2 Sess., 159 (December 21, 1858).

[40]*Ibid.*, 34 Cong., 1 Sess., Appendix, 404 (April 9, 1856).

[41]In a letter to the editor of the New York *Independent* on
February 23, 1861, Seward explicitly states why he had opposed
compromise in 1850 and favored it during the secession crisis:
"Twelve years ago, freedom was in danger, and the Union was
not. I spoke then so singly for freedom that short-sighted men
inferred that I was disloyal to the Union. . . . Today, practically
freedom is not in danger, and Union is. With the loss of Union, all
would be lost." Seward, *Seward at Washington*, 507.

[42]Seward made no effort to repudiate an editorial by Weed in
the Albany *Evening Journal* on December 17, 1860, calling for the
resumption of the line of 36°30', even though he had taken pains
to reject a similar editorial that had appeared on November 30.
What made his silence on the second editorial most significant
was the fact that it came on the very eve of Weed's trip to Springfield to sound out the attitude of the President-elect on the
prospects for compromise. The personal testimony of others in
Washington at the time also suggests that Seward would have
supported the Crittenden plan if Lincoln had given the word. For
a full discussion see Bancroft, *Life of Seward*, II, 30-37; Rhodes,
History of the United States, III, 45-51; Potter, *Lincoln and His Party
in the Secession Crisis*, 183-84; Kirwan, *John J. Crittenden: The Struggle for the Union*, 379-84; Sharrow, "William Henry Seward,"
312-24.

[43]*Congressional Globe*, 36 Cong., 2 Sess., 343-44 (January 12,
1861).

[44]With regard to this policy of voluntary reconstruction, Ken-

neth Stampp has well noted in Seward's outlook "a failure to understand that in the South Unionism meant one thing, in the North another." *And the War Came*, 20. See also Martin B. Duberman, *Charles Francis Adams, 1851-1886* (Boston: Houghton Mifflin, 1961), 224-26.

[45]Bancroft, *Life of Seward*, II, 132-34.

[46]Though he conceived of the matter in different terms of mercantilism and laissez faire, William Appleman Williams has also stressed the difference between Seward and Lincoln. *The Contours of American History*, 285-319.

[47]Nevins, "A Major Result of the Civil War," *Civil War History*, V (September, 1959), 237-50; Nevins, *The War for the Union: War Becomes Revolution, 1862-1863* (New York: Charles Scribner's Sons, 1960), 456-511; Nagel, *One Nation Indivisible*, 104; Fredrickson, *The Inner Civil War*, 23-35; Peterson, *The Jefferson Image in the American Mind*, 209-26.

[48]Potter, "The Historian's Use of Nationalism and Vice Versa," *American Historical Review*, LXVII (July, 1962), 924-50.

Index

Adams, John Quincy: and corporate freedom, 5; on Missouri controversy, 23, 36, 48: and American System, 50, 54, 56-57, 61, 104; on progress, 65-66, 102-103; on nullification, 74; and tariff compromise, 84, 104-106; on slave power, 105-107; on democracy, 107; and civil war, 135
Allen, William, 129, 131, 134
Allison, Joseph, 186
American System: and corporate freedom, 4, 49; interpretations of, 50-53; as democratic foil, 53, 72, 85; policies of, 59-61; and economic self-sufficiency, 59-60; and Panic of 1819, 60-61; and social order, 62-63; and progress, 64-65; planter opposition to, 67-71; plain republican opposition to, 71-72; and manifest destiny, 95
Ashmun, George, 172
Atchison, David R., 133
Austin, Archibald, 67
Averett, Thomas H., 157

Badger, George F., 157, 159, 172
Baldwin, Henry, 59
Barbour, James, 43
Barbour, Philip P.: on Missouri controversy, 30, 31; on American System, 69; on

nullification, 86-87
Barry, William, 183
Barton, David, 62
Bell, John, 217
Bennett, Henry, 169
Benton, Thomas Hart, 76, 80, 129
Berrien, John M., 154
Bidlack, Benjamin A., 137
Bingham, Kinsley S., 130, 161, 171
Birney, James G.: and Liberty party, 139, 140
Blair, Francis P., 194
Bocock, Thomas S., 157
Booth, Thomas, 169
Bridges, Samuel A., 182
Brinkerhoff, Jacob: and Wilmot Proviso, 122, 130
Broker state: definition of, 14-15, 135-36; negative emphasis of, in Jacksonian Democracy, 87-88; and Free Soil, 136-43; Whig contributions to, 136-37; contributions of Jacksonian Democracy to, 137-38. See also Log rolling
Brown, Albert G., 183
Buchanan, James: and Lecompton Constitution, 18, 198
Burges, Tristam, 65
Burrill, James, 25, 27
Butler, Thomas B., 161

Cabell, Edward C., 155
Caldwell, George A., 156

301

and Free Soil, 127-35. *See also*
Geopolitics; Slavery diffusion
Sergeant, John, 25, 26, 29
Severance, Luther, 117, 132
Seward, William H.: on liberty and
Union, 3; statecraft of, during
1850s, 20-21; and irrepressible
conflict, 21, 211; and corporate
freedom, 115, 222-27; on
manifest destiny, 116-18; on
moral equivalent of war, 118,
229-31; on broker state, 145; in
crisis of 1850, 165, 215-16, 219;
interpretations of, 212-13; and
concept of progress, 214-15;
and repeal of 36°30', 216-17;
acclaims popular sovereignty,
217, 225; on progress of empire,
217-19; economic policies of,
220-21; on higher law, 225; on
Union as absolute, 224, 227;
comparisons of, with Douglas
and Lincoln, 227-31; and
Crittenden Compromise, 231;
ideas on peaceable reunion,
232; and proposal for foreign
war, 233; and repressible
conflict, 233-34
Shaw, Lemuel, 25
Silvester, Peter H., 163
Slavery diffusion: as safety valve
for South, 33-35, 153-54, 158;
and theory of Malthus, 34, 158,
193; constitutional
interpretations of, 146-47, 209.
See also Geopolitics; Safety valve
Slavery national: defined, 16, 155;
and Dred Scott decision, 16,
183, 199; formulated by
Calhoun, 123; in crisis of 1850,
155-57; rela- tion of, to popular
sovereignty, 156; criticism of, by
southerners, 158-59
Slave power: Adams on, 105-107;
in Free-Soil view, 126-28; and
evils of time, 144; Republican
views of, 193-94

Smith, Truman, 145, 181
Smith, William, 43
Southern Jeffersonians: in
Missouri controversy, 29-35,
41-46
Sparks, Jared, 62
Spooner, Lysander: and Liberty
League, 128
Stanly, Edward, 158
Stephens, Alexander: in crisis of
1850, 150, 154; on Lin- coln, 206
Stevens, Thaddeus: in crisis of
1850, 161, 166, 170
Stevenson, Andrew, 67
Stewart, Andrew, 60, 118
Stokes, Montfort, 45
Stowe, Harriet Beecher: and *Uncle
Tom's Cabin,* 177
Sumner, Charles: on slave power,
126; on original perfection,
190-91; on degeneration, 194,
197; on regeneration, 127,
201-202, 205

Tallmadge, James, Jr., 22, 38
Tallmadge Amendment, 22
Tariff of Abominations: contra
American System, 50, 72
Taylor, John (of Caroline), 32, 42
Taylor, John (New York), 40
Taylor, Zachary: in crisis of 1850,
150
Teleological development: and
American System, 54-55;
opposition to, 67, 71-72
Thompson, John R., 183
Three-fifths provision on slav-
ery: and geopolitics, 29, 126,
145; Republican interpreta-
tions of, 191-92, 194
Tocqueville, Alexis de: and
democratic statesmanship, 234
Toombs, Robert: on crisis of 1850,
150, 155; on slavery national,
183, 191
Trafton, Mark, 201
Tucker, George, 34